little <u>me</u>
My autobiography

Matt Lucas is an award-winning comedian, actor and writer.

He started his comedy career in the early nineties, working with Vic Reeves and Bob Mortimer on *The Smell of Reeves and Mortimer* and *Shooting Stars*, where he played giant baby George Dawes, but discovered major success with co-star David Walliams in *Little Britain* and *Come Fly With Me*, for which they won three BAFTAs, three NTAs and two International Emmy Awards.

Matt received much praise for his work on stage in *Les Misérables* and has since gone on to feature in many successful films and TV shows, including *Alice in Wonderland*, *Bridesmaids*, *Paddington*, *A Midsummer Night's Dream* and now *Doctor Who*.

little me

My autobiography

MATT LUCAS

CANONGATE

This paperback edition published in Great
Britain in 2018 by Canongate Books

First published in Great Britain in 2017 and in the USA and Canada in
2018 by Canongate Books Ltd, 14 High Street, Edinburgh EH1 1TE

Distributed in the USA by Publishers Group West
and in Canada by Publishers Group Canada

canongate.co.uk

1

British Library Cataloguing-in-Publication Data
A catalogue record for this book is available on
request from the British Library

ISBN 978 1 78689 250 8

Typeset by Biblichor Ltd, Edinburgh

Printed and bound in Great Britain by Clays Ltd, St Ives plc.

FSC
www.fsc.org

MIX
Paper from
responsible sources
FSC® C018072

Contents

Preface   1

A – Accrington Stanley   3
B – Baldy!   13
C – Chumley   25
D – Doing the Circuit   43
E – Eating   57
F – Frankie and Jimmy   77
G – Gay   89
H – Haberdashers' Aske's Boys' School   119
I – Idiot   141
J – Jewish   147
K – Kevin   154
L – Little Rumblings   155
M – Middle of the Book   172
N – Nearest and Dearest   179
O – Oh Look, it's Thingy   189
P – Prosopagnosia   205
Q – Queen (and other Teenage Pursuits)   207
R – Really Big Britain   217
S – Southend, Sydney and Sunset Boulevard   229
T – The TARDIS   245
U – Upstage   255
V – Various Other Things I've Been In   267
W – What are the Scores, George Dawes?   281
X – Xenophobia   304
Y – Yankee Doodle   305
Z – Zzzzzzzz   309

Acknowledgements   311
Image Credits   313
Index   315

This book is dedicated to Emily,
the kindest, most patient person in the world.

Preface

Hello. How are you? You been up to much?

And that's the first line of my book. Now I know a lot of people write books and the opening line is something all clever like 'I walked along the moors, leaves crunching beneath my feet, the dying sun retreating from view', but the publishers said I have to write the truth, and I don't think 'I was sat on the sofa, polishing off a Chambourcy Hippopotamousse in front of *Lovejoy*' is particularly suspenseful so I've decided to open with 'Hello', and then, even if you don't care for anything that comes after that, at least you'll say I was well mannered.

Secondly, this is, I guess, a sort-of autobiography, but, as you will have gathered, it isn't quite chronological. I have no attention span left. I give up halfway through reading a text message. This is my attempt to keep things zipping along. Life may begin at babyhood (I just checked and I'm slightly disappointed to learn that word already exists) but my thoughts and memories are dotted about. The alphabetical approach is actually an attempt to corral them somehow.

Tonally it's probably a bit all over the place, because that's me. Half my life has been spent with people complaining that I'm too serious, that – in the words of my late father – I 'think too much'. The rest of the time people tell me to stop mucking about.

Also, everything in this book is – as far as I know – true. But not everything is in this book. I know things that would ruin people's careers. I certainly know things that would finish mine. I'm not looking to burn bridges. You might have to read between the lines here and there. In Ethel Merman's autobiography there is a chapter entitled 'My Marriage To Ernest Borgnine' which just has one empty page. I'm not going to go that far, but there's no scorched-earth policy in this book. I'd like to keep working if I can. I'm only forty-three. If I spill ALL the beans, then no one will trust me, no one will hire me and I'll have no option but to go into the *Celebrity Big Brother* house. I'm far too crotchety in the mornings for that. It's not going to happen.

And finally, in this book, amongst many other things, I refer on occasion to Kevin McGee, the man I loved and lost, a kind, warm, beautiful being who didn't have the armour for this world. I have always been reticent to talk publicly about our relationship and the events that followed it. Grief for me has been profound and unrelenting, but also private. I have a moral discomfort with using his suffering to sell a book, to elicit public sympathy and money. We also had an agreement during our separation not to discuss what happened. He kept to it and so have I. So I'll talk about how I have tried to find a way forward after his death, but I won't be going into rich detail about our relationship, his illness or suicide. The other truth is that there is so much about him that I don't know and never will.

I'll tell you what I can about my life, but much of it, frankly, has been about learning to live without the answers.

Right, let's get on with it.

Edinburgh
Fringe
Festival, 1987

A – Accrington Stanley

I didn't often break into a run but on that spring morning in 1986 my pudgy twelve-year-old self jumped off the coach, hurtled along the path, took a left at the Art building, down the PE corridor, past the room full of state-of-the-art BBC Micro Model B computers, up the Chemistry corridor and into the house block.

There were already a few other boys waiting eagerly for the arrival of Barry Edwards, my lanky, mop-haired form master and proud writer of *Columbus!*, a new musical (score by Mr Hepworth) to be performed by the Junior School at Haberdashers' that summer.

I'd already pondered the impending bittersweetness of appearing – no – *starring* in the show while my father languished in Spring Hill open prison, unable to witness in person what would surely be the beginning of my prodigious rise to fame and glory.

Edwards appeared, pinning the cast list to the noticeboard, before swiftly exiting. We clustered around it. Being one of the shorter boys, I had to wait a moment to get a peek. At the top it said that Oliver White – from the year above – was to play the title role. I cast my eyes down the list and noted the names of a couple of friends, delighted that we would be performing together.

I scanned quickly to the bottom and started again – thoroughly, this time – from the top. After all, there were a lot of names on there – at least thirty, I would say.

Mine, however, was nowhere to be found.

My initial surprise quickly gave way to disappointment, but even that gave way pretty quickly to self-flagellation, something I'd been given to a fair deal of late. What on earth had I been thinking? Little me, the tubby boy with no hair, at the bottom of every class – what right did I have to suppose that I might be any part of this?

At morning break-time I went to my locker, reached into the brown pencil case full of coins and took out a couple. I had been appointed class charity monitor at the beginning of the year and I collected a donation from the less forgetful boys each Friday morning, during registration. Lately I had been given to pinching a coin or two to spend at the tuck shop, cramming my fat face full of jam dough-nuts and Lion bars.

I sat with my friend Andrew Bloch, who had also been waiting for the list to be posted, and who had evidently shone brighter at his audition than I had in mine. His glee at being cast was being kept in check so as not to make me feel any worse. There weren't many boys like that at this school.

We sucked determinedly on our rock-hard Jawbreakers (gobstop-pers, three for 10p, with chewing gum in the middle, if you ever actually made it that far) as the ramifications of the morning's key event became clear. Throughout my disastrous first year at Haberdashers' Aske's Boys' School I had consoled myself with the thought that my impending bril-liance in the Junior School musical would put everything else into context. Sure, I had failed academically across the board – a wobbly cast-off on the otherwise perfect production line of future Oxbridge graduates – but once everyone finally came to appreciate where my skills *really* lay, I, Lord Olivier elect, would be hailed by staff and pupils alike, my academic shortfalls a mere footnote. 'He struggles with Physics, *yes*,' they would say, 'but his Hedda Gabler was sublime. Leave him be.'

Life returned to normality. I spent my days sat in class, utterly befuddled by an overload of information – the Treaty of Rapallo, lowest common multiples and oxbow lakes – and my nights in front of the television, watching *Albion Market* and *Highway* – anything – when I should have been doing my homework.

And then suddenly, one day, a couple of weeks into rehearsals, a rumour went around. One of the boys had pulled out of the show and Barry Edwards was to hold further auditions for his replacement one lunch break. I checked the drama noticeboard and sure enough there was another opportunity to be in the show. This was it. This was the moment. Like Peggy Sawyer in *42nd Street* (which I had seen that year at the Theatre Royal, Drury Lane), I was to save the day. Four of us put our names down and took it in turns to deliver the same speech. But then came the final insult: Edwards decided not to cast any of us, not even Russell Donoff.

On the coach home from school I sat with Andrew, prising from him updates on how rehearsals were going. My envy had given way to awe. I accepted my place under the table, happy to feast on the scraps.

A couple of weeks before *Columbus!* was to be staged, it was announced at Assembly that ushers would be required. I eagerly signed up for all three nights, herding a parade of old toffs and proud parents to their seats.

As despondent as I felt on the sidelines, it was exciting to watch my friends onstage and hear them sing. Whenever I encountered one of the stars of the show over the coming weeks, I would compliment them. I informed Benjamin Cahn that he had a lovely singing voice. I praised James Kaye for his exquisite comic timing. I even said well done to the identical Salter twins, who I had decided were only in the show because there was a magic trick in which the same person exited stage right and immediately reappeared stage left. I guess you could say I was a *Columbus!* groupie. I drank it all in, learning all the tunes and humming them to myself in my bedroom for weeks afterwards, imagining how I would have played each part.

Fast forward ten months. The architect of my doom Barry Edwards had moved to Highgate School. A new teacher, the sweet, softly spoken Ian Rossotti, was to direct this year's musical which, it was announced during one Junior Assembly, was to be (*drumroll please*) . . . *The Roman Invasion of Ramsbottom*.

What? What on earth was that?

The Roman Invasion of *who*?

Couldn't we do *Oliver!*? I was really hoping we could do *Oliver!* and then I could play the Artful Dodger. Or *Starlight Express*? We could do it in the round in the dining hall. Hell, I know we're a boys' school, but couldn't we even do *Annie*? I'll play Sandy the dog, I don't mind. Anything but *The Roman Invasion of Ramsbottom*, whatever that is.

The Roman Invasion of Ramsbottom was, it turned out, a daft comic romp that had been written a few years earlier for the National Youth Music Theatre, about the regulars of a Lancashire pub and how they successfully thwarted an attempt by the Romans to build a motorway through it.

This time the auditions took place on a Sunday afternoon in the school drama room. Mr Rossotti was joined by an intriguing figure, a warm, garrulous dandy with a head of wild, wavy curls and lashings of presence. I instantly adored him, for this was no mere English teacher. This was *a man of the theatre*.

He took us through our paces, getting us all to sing 'Consider Yourself' from *Oliver!* pounding away at the piano, bellowing directions. He invested in us, sought to get the best out of all of us. Some of the boys visibly withdrew from this attention, but not me. Hell, no. I was going for it.

For I had decided, given that we were singing songs from *Oliver!*, that this must surely be the great Lionel Bart himself.

I was wrong. I later found out it was actually Jeremy James Taylor, the co-writer of *The Roman Invasion of Ramsbottom* (which I will just call *Ramsbottom* from now on because I clipped my nails earlier with rather too much gusto, my index finger is a little tender and it *pains* me to type).

Sometimes you just know. You just know. And this time I just knew. I didn't run to the house corridor. I didn't need to. I sauntered over to the noticeboard, where a group of boys were studying the cast list.

And there in black and white . . .

ACCRINGTON STANLEY – MATTHEW LUCAS

I didn't know who Accrington Stanley was and it didn't matter. Details weren't important. I had been cast in the Haberdashers' Aske's Junior School play. I was in *The Roman Invasion of Ramsbottom*. (Yes, I know I said I was going to abbreviate it from now on, but honestly I felt at that moment it was important to really sell it, do you know what I mean?)

I turned to Andrew, triumphant. His expression told a different story. He hadn't got a part. I offered what words of consolation I could muster. He started to cry and wandered off. Unsure whether to be happy or sad, I decided in that moment it was okay to be both.

Rehearsals took up a lot of time. I was told by Mr Wilson, the Junior School Head, that I was not to let the academic side of things slide just because I was in the play. Actually, my confidence at a high, I started to do a little better in class. I made more friends. I had even joined Weight Watchers shortly after my bar mitzvah and was losing weight. Everything seemed to be coming together.

Accrington Stanley wasn't the lead, but he was the star comic character, a boisterous, hearty Northerner. I had Brian Glover in mind when I played him. He didn't appear in the first half at all, but in the second act, set in the pub, he had plenty of jokes to crack.

He also had a solo number. Eek. I was terrified at the prospect of singing solo. During music lessons in the first year I had sung very badly on purpose, on the advice of my street-smart older brother Howard (at the same school), who had warned me that any boy with any *semblance* of being able to sing in tune would be coerced into the school choir, which often rehearsed on Saturdays, which meant one less lie-in and missing the Arsenal match. Bugger that.

So I had avoided the choir but in the process had convinced myself that I couldn't sing. Now I'm no Alfie Boe or even Alfie Moon, but I can hold a tune. I just didn't know that then.

The musical director of the show was Mr Barker, a kind, diligent teacher who would call me Matthew during rehearsals and Lucas again during lessons. A few weeks earlier I had set my friend Jake Moore the challenge of looking at Mr Barker and thinking of a potato without laughing. He had failed in his endeavours, as had all of my classmates. Now I too was so distracted during these one-on-one rehearsals with him that I found my face creasing at regular intervals. To make matters worse, Mr Barker had decided that I should sing the song in falsetto, which was perhaps his revenge.

I bottled it. Blamed it on my voice breaking. Michael Bourne sang it instead. Beautifully.

I loved rehearsals even more than I had enjoyed drama lessons at school. There was a purpose, an end result – the world's eyes would finally see the glory of the coming of the Matthew.

And then, one Sunday afternoon, as we rehearsed in the main hall, we were each handed a photocopied letter, explaining that the National Youth Music Theatre – of which Jeremy James Taylor was in charge – was taking a production of *The Roman Invasion of Ramsbottom* (again, it just felt right, sorry) to the Edinburgh Festival that summer. According to the letter there was a chance that one or two kids from our cast might be invited to take part.

Well now, this was something else. Suddenly the school play became a sideshow. I had my eyes on a bigger prize. From that point on I could think of little else. Even though I had never heard of the National Youth Music Theatre before, it sounded VERY IMPORTANT INDEED.

'Hi, Jeremy', I would say, in as casual a voice as possible, 'um, hey, just kinda checking in about that Glasgow . . . Edinburgh thing you guys might want me to do. I'm kinda interested, but you know summer's coming soon and we're thinking of booking a family holiday so I just thought I'd throw that out there, you know. Because I'd really hate for your people to come to me and then it's too late.'

We were not thinking of booking a family holiday. The last family holiday we'd been on was five years earlier, when my parents were still together.

One afternoon, a week before the school production was to open, I dropped JJT my customary hint. He had been waiting for it. He led me out of the main hall and into one of the music rooms. I sat next to him at the piano as he played those familiar opening chords to 'Consider Yourself' and sang my bestest singing.

'Jolly good. You'd better come to Edinburgh then, old chap.'

I gasped.

But first, the small business of the school production.

I paced backstage, listening intently to the first act, and then waited onstage behind the curtain during the interval.

The band started to play. The curtains opened and I was born.

And now I would like to take this opportunity to apologise whole-heartedly to anyone else who may or may not have been in the show with me, because I didn't see you. I saw only my glorious reflection in your eyes. And I didn't hear you. I heard only my voice and the audience's laughter. I trod on lines, jokes, feet and bits of the set. I stood where I fancied. I gurned and grimaced and improvised and ignored pretty much everything we had so studiously rehearsed – and just had the time of my life. It was selfish and innocent and wonderful, and again I'm sorry. It was the only time in those first two years at that school that I felt good enough to be there. And the audience played their part perfectly, indulging me at every turn.

As we came offstage, I was blissfully unaware I had done anything wrong. In the changing room, packing my bag to go home, JJT quietly took me aside.

'Well done, Matthew. Well done. Very good indeed. Wonderful. Can I give you a note, love? You're going eighty-five miles an hour and you really only need to go seventy-five.'

A kind, smart note. But not one I was able to hear or understand, because I was now a star. Move over, Judy Garland.

There were two more performances. Ego swollen and voice a little tired from so much onstage shouting, I actually tried to convince an older boy who was looking after the technical gear to give me my own radio mic.

'I'm only allowed to give them to the people who have solo songs,' said poor beleaguered Shaun, whose father happened to be Alvin Stardust.

I considered this grossly unfair. I was, after all, the money. But my diva demands fell on deaf ears.

My family was full of praise. My mum, in particular, was thrilled for me, gushing to all and sundry about her marvellous son in the way only a Jewish mother can. We call it *kvelling*. I joined in too, instructing my friend Mark Weston, who went to Highgate School, to let Barry Edwards know how fantastic I was. In my mind Edwards would be lying in bed at night, kicking himself. 'Damn! Damn! The one that got away!'

Other pupils were now stopping *me* in the corridors and saying nice things. I oozed charm in return, getting whatever I could out of it – usually a Nerd, some Scampi Fries or a bite of someone's rock-hard Wham bar.

As the term ended, school was but a distraction. My focus now was on my career. Next stop: the Edinburgh Festival, to rehearse and perform the show all over again, this time as part of the National Youth Music Theatre.

The cast (including four of us from the Haberdashers' production) convened at King's Cross station one Sunday in July 1987 and caught the train together up to Edinburgh.

Arriving at Heriot-Watt University, where we were all going to be living, I set my bags down and went into the common room, where the casts of two other NYMT shows had already assembled. My jaw dropped as I caught a glimpse of an impossibly handsome bequiffed blond boy in a designer black suit, arguing with one of the staff. I instantly recognised him as one of the kids from a TV show I watched on Channel 4 called *The Pocket Money Programme*. He looked like a movie star – and he became one. It was Jude Law.

Clang! Sorry for the name-drop! There'll be a few along the way. Keep a tally if you like.

Over the next couple of weeks we set about rehearsing *Ramsbottom* (we got there!). Many of the cast members were four or five years older than me and had also appeared in a version of the show at their school in south London. There was some consternation amongst them that I had taken the place of the boy who played Accrington Stanley in their production, and I sometimes overheard grumblings of 'how Tom had done it better'.

I made some friends – well, some of the younger cast members tolerated me – but I didn't make it easy for myself. Part of the problem was that I was a Habs boy. I'll tell you more about the school later on in the book, but put it like this – when you assemble all the new boys on the first day of school in a grand old hall and tell them that they are 'the cream' of the country, well, you're not exactly putting Humility on the school syllabus.

Up to this point I had struggled to impress in any department. Now that I was finally making a name for myself, I had become insufferable. Back at school it may have been the order of the day to crow about your achievements, but in the outside world people saw us for the entitled little shits we were. And while I had shone in the school production, I was certainly no better than anyone else in the NYMT. But I thought I was and it put a few noses out of joint.

I had trouble sleeping in the chatty, overpopulated science classroom-turned-dormitory and became tired during rehearsals. As I had done in the school production, I started to lose my voice. I remember feeling ill and mumbling during a run-through and some of the cast asking me to put in a bit more effort.

In fairness I was just a thirteen-year-old, away from home, going through puberty, and my home life had been rocky. At times I would be holding court, boring the others with the same old stories, but equally I could be moody and sullen, especially after a performance. As a counter to my arrogance, I was never convinced that I had done a good enough job onstage, and I would chastise myself endlessly. To this day I rarely watch things I have been in, because I am almost always mortified by the results.

There were happy times too. Although I was a nuisance, I could always find someone to while away the hours with, listening to Rick Astley on the radio (number one at the time with 'Never Gonna Give You Up'), swapping jokes and dance steps.

I loved performing and definitely grew from the experience but offstage I was a polarising figure, still working out how to be part of something, instead of the focus of it. On the last night we were each given a poster advertising the show and we all signed each other's. One boy simply wrote 'fuck off' on mine, in very small letters.

B – Baldy!

One of my earliest memories is of being three and a half years old at nursery, watching the other little boys and girls skip out of the classroom and noting how the folds in the backs of their legs were unblemished. My own legs, like my arms and neck, were already riddled with scratches. I had been told repeatedly not to scratch – but if I didn't scratch then there was nothing to do but wheeze. And, oh, how I wheezed. Dr David said I had eczema and asthma and hay fever and gave me some special cream and a blue-and-white Ventolin inhaler, which I was to use every morning and every night and in between if necessary.

When the summer came, my eyes got red and puffy and I sneezed and coughed even more. In the winter I caught every cold going. From a young age I felt at odds with my body. This blotchy, dumpy vessel betrayed my boisterous, carefree spirit. I wanted to run, jump, climb – and I did – but within seconds I was bent double at the kerb, gasping for air.

And yet I remained funny cheeky Matthew. Inquisitive, outgoing, playful, I had many friends, who I entertained with songs and jokes and silly voices aplenty. Even on the sidelines, while the others played football, I would pretend to be a TV commentator. My asthma and eczema were an inconvenience but they didn't define me.

However, an event would soon occur that would shape my childhood.

In 1978, when I was four, Mum and Dad took my older brother Howard and me to Portugal on a family holiday. Our grandmothers – both widowed – joined us.

I was struck with wonder at the otherness of everything and was easily distracted. I was always lagging a few steps behind, and my poor parents were constantly having to remind me not to wander off on my own.

One day, while we were walking along the street, I got separated from my family. I looked up and they were nowhere to be seen. I cast my eyes up and down and across the road. There were several people around and from a distance quite a lot of them looked like my mum and dad.

Eventually, I spotted them, on the other side, waving anxiously at me. I stepped off the kerb, into the road, and was knocked down by a car.

A small crowd gathered. My distraught father ran over, picked me up off the ground, swore at the driver, kicked the car and carried me off.

At school I recounted the story to friends and teachers. I enjoyed the drama of it. My father, coming to my rescue. Me, the survivor.

Two years later, in 1980, aged six, I woke up one morning to find several hairs on my pillow. The next day the same thing happened, only this time there were a lot more. By the end of the summer all of my hair had fallen out.

I wasn't initially all that concerned. At four my hair had been blond and curly, but at five it was a big brown pudding bowl and I loathed it. Why couldn't I have nice short hair like the other boys? I hated having it cut, because it made my neck and back all itchy. Worse, when Mum washed it in the bath I always got soap in my eyes.

In the changing room at Aylward First and Middle School – a ten-minute walk from our home in the north-west London suburb of Stanmore – I could do nothing but laugh as I easily pulled out the last two or three remaining strands in front of my friends. It didn't feel real.

But it was.

The doctors – and we saw an endless stream of them – concluded that it must have been a delayed response to the shock of being knocked down by the car in Portugal two years earlier.

And so I was the first six-year-old in my class to learn the word 'alopecia'.

Suddenly everything and anything else that I was at that age was eclipsed by the fact that I was the little boy in the town with absolutely no hair. And that is how it was, from the age of six for the remainder of my youth. Right up until I became famous, my lack of hair was considered the most – perhaps even the only – notable thing about me.

I was never allowed to forget for one moment that I was bald. If I went swimming or to the cinema or got the bus or went to a shop or simply walked down the street, adults and children stared at me.

'You got no hair,' said the younger kids, pointing.

Others who had previously called me Matthew now yelled 'Baldy!' as I passed by.

Or 'Skinhead' or 'Slaphead' – but mainly 'Baldy'.

Apart from my parents' friend Melvyn, who used to call me 'Curly', though I never got it.

My baldness was a source of amusement, sympathy and revulsion for everyone.

Some people chose to inform me that I had something called leukaemia. 'You're dying,' said one of the older girls in lunch break one day, matter-of-factly, as she tossed an apple core, missing the bin.

I pondered if maybe she was right, that perhaps there was something that my parents had thought not to tell me. I accepted I might be dying and I hoped that I had been a good enough boy to go to heaven.

Initially it was speculated – almost assured – that this was temporary, that my hair would grow back almost as quickly as it had fallen out.

And it did. A year after it disappeared, it started to return, thinner than before, yes, but this was definitely progress.

Then it fell out again.

The search for a cure began in earnest. I was taken out of school here and there and we'd traipse down to central London on the Tube to meet various specialists. Everyone had an opinion; no one had a solution.

Mum and Dad always did their best to turn the trips into some kind of treat. I'd be taken to tea in a department store or allowed to look around Hamleys. When we went to Great Ormond Street Children's Hospital, we would pop in afterwards to Alan Alan's Magic Spot nearby and I'd choose a Paul Daniels magic trick to take home.

I was prodded and poked and gazed at with curiosity, but with few conventional medicinal treatments available to us, we started to go down the homeopathic route. A Nigerian family had moved into our road and my brother had become friendly with one of their kids, Azubike (or 'A-Zed' for short). His father, having been a doctor in their homeland, was sure he could help and administered some small white pills, which did nothing. Then we bought a few bottles of an elixir made from seaweed, which arrived in the post, and which my dad would rub vigorously into my scalp every evening. After a few weeks we gave up – he had developed a nasty rash on his hands and my hair was still nowhere to be seen.

On Saturday mornings I started to see a friendly acupuncturist. My dad would sit with me while the acupuncturist stuck needles into me, but that didn't seem to do anything either. I don't know anybody who enjoys having needles stuck into them and I was quite relieved when we stopped going.

I thought little of it at the time, until I was at a party twenty years later, speaking with the wife of another comedian, who was also an acupuncturist. I asked her how business was going and if she had any male clients or just treated women. She explained she worked with both men and women.

'But it's so intimate,' I said. 'Don't you get embarrassed when you work with the men?'

She looked at me, puzzled. 'All therapy has a degree of intimacy, but why would I feel embarrassed?'

'Well,' I replied, 'I mean, there you are, sticking needles in someone's genitalia. That *must* be weird.'

'Um, that's . . . not part of acupuncture,' she said.

'No, no, of course it's not. No. Ha.' I changed the subject as swiftly as I could.

Now, I suspect that's perhaps not what you were expecting to read. I mean, it's clearly alarming. Feel free to swear out loud, if you like.

I've tried to process this a little over the years and I've come to the conclusion that I simply don't know whether the therapist was behaving inappropriately or whether he was genuinely trying to find areas on my body that could stimulate hair growth. Like I say in the Preface, life is sometimes about living without the answers.

What I will say is that I don't carry any baggage from the experience with the acupuncturist. I know a comedy producer who once told me that he went to a boys' only public school and had a swimming teacher who would make all the boys stand in a line in the showers with their legs wide open while he slid through them on the ground.

I asked him if he was traumatised by the incident.

'No,' he said, 'I just thought it was a bit odd.'

Well, that's what I think of the acupuncture. It was *a bit odd*. Shall we move on?

In 1981, I was seven years old. And – apart from that brief period when the hair grew back – I had been bald for a year. It became clear – to me, at least – that nothing had worked because nothing was going to work. My dad said he thought 'the roots might be dead by now'. And that was that.

I put my efforts into building a collection of caps, which I would proudly show to anyone who came to the house. Whenever a friend or relative went on holiday they were encouraged to bring me back a cap, as a souvenir. At school, other kids would pull my cap off and run away. Sometimes the wind would blow it off – but that didn't stop me collecting as many as I could find. I had a box full of them.

Nowadays if you lose your hair as a child – as a boy, at least – you might not care as much. That's not to diminish the devastation that childhood (or even adulthood) alopecia can wreak on the individual, but there are lots of bald people you can look up to.

There's the Mitchell brothers in *EastEnders*. You wouldn't mess with them, especially Phil. He's properly hard and you can tell this because he speaks really quietly. In drama, the quieter you are, the harder you are. This makes Phil Mitchell a British Don Corleone, and he doesn't even need to put grapes in his cheeks either. Sorry, Marlon.

You've got Vin Diesel, who is in those *Fast & Furious* films, and probably lots of other films with explosions in them, but I've never actually seen young Vincent in anything, so I'm not the one to ask. But anyway – him.

Bruce Willis.

And Demi Moore too, come to think of it (*G.I. Jane*).

The Rock. Who isn't actually a real rock. Although real rocks don't tend to have hair either, so he is aptly named.

Gail Porter.

Me.

Dara O'Briaiaian.

Ian Wright Wright Wright.

And Homer Simpson (virtually).

There will be more. Go and look on Wikipedia. But don't forget to come back and read the rest of this book. I tend to get trapped in a Wiki hole when I go there. I was reading about a disaster in a colliery for an hour yesterday.

Anyway, back when I was lickle, there were FOUR BALD PEOPLE.

Kojak, the TV detective. I've never seen the show. I was too young to watch it. But I know he was bald and he had a lollipop. People used to call me Kojak all the time and say 'Who loves ya, baby?'

Yul Brynner from *The King and I*.

The bald guy in *The Benny Hill Show* (whose head Benny used to pat and who was the reason for people constantly patting mine).

And Duncan Goodhew, who was a swimmer.

You'd see Duncan on telly all the time. If he wasn't actually competing in an event, he was being interviewed on *Saturday Superstore*, or appearing in an advert, or sticking his head through a hole on *Game for a Laugh* while a blindfolded contestant felt it and had to identify what it was, with hilarious consequences.

Duncan Goodhew was wonderful. And, encouraged by my parents, I wrote him a letter and sent a photo of my little bald self.

It wasn't long before a handwritten reply from Duncan himself arrived on the doormat. 'Hi Matt! You look *great* in your photo!' he told me. Also in the envelope were some badges. My favourite was a bright blue one, with a drawing of Duncan's grinning face and the caption 'Bald Is Beautiful'. I wore it every day.

Whenever my friend Duncan was on TV, someone would ask him how he lost his hair. He had been climbing a tree, he said, and fell out of it. The shock had made his hair fall out. I used to joke that it was my head he landed on, and that's how I'd lost mine.

Duncan would talk about how he believed not having hair actually helped him when competing, because it meant he had less resistance in the water.

Duncan was a winner.

I've never met you, but I love you, Duncan Goodhew. You taught me that being bald was something you could actually use to your advantage. Thank you.

Being bald has helped me in my career. Would I have had my big break as a baby in *Shooting Stars* if I had had a full head of hair? My baldness has made me distinctive, yet also allowed me to transform myself. Stick a wig on and I'm someone else. Swap the wig and I'm now another person. Perfect.

My childhood was tough, yes. No one wants to feel eternally self-conscious, constantly stared at, teased, mocked and bullied. But also it's important to get things into perspective.

When I was seven it was announced that a new 'handicapped' boy called Michael would be joining our class. Miss Robbins told me that I was to look after him.

Michael had – has – cerebral palsy. Tottering in with a winning smile on his first day, none of us found it easy to understand what he was saying. But in time, we learned his patterns and rhythms, knew to wait patiently because it took him longer to speak.

Michael was smart, funny, sweet and never complained about anything. He found writing a challenge so he did his work on a special computer. Michael was a marvel.

Maybe a generation or two earlier he would have gone to a special school, or not even gone to school at all, but I'm so glad he came to ours.

The truth is, it put things into perspective. Having no hair was unfortunate, but spending time with someone who had to face significantly greater challenges showed me that if nothing stopped him living his life to the full, why should my situation set me back?

I should point out that, when we were seventeen, Michael took me out for a spin in his specially adapted shiny red car. I've failed my test twice and still can't drive.

Meanwhile my ever-growing cap collection was coming in useful. My oldest friend Jeremy can scarcely recount the number of times he got into trouble at school for something we both did, while I bowed my head, smirk hidden beneath the huge brim of my cap. Before long, tears of laughter would be rolling down my face. If you were taller than me, you'd never know.

My favourite piece of headwear was different from the others, a small-peaked sailor's hat that my grandmother had bought for me. I fell in love with it after watching *Ghostbusters* in the cinema (twice in one week) as it resembled the one worn by the giant Stay Puft Marshmallow Man. I wore it for months and months, until it became filthy. Then one day, spurred on by my brother, I wrote 'STAY PUFT' on the front in thick black marker pen, which was great until it rained and the hat was ruined.

Though we would fight like cat and dog at home, my brother Howard was the first to stand up for me if anyone gave me any aggravation. Sure, he'd badger me mercilessly about my steadily increasing weight, but he never ever teased me about having no hair.

Quite the opposite. He loved my bald head so much that one day, as he sat in the back of the car, with me in front of him, and our mum outside chatting to a friend, Howard offered to draw a Pac-Man on my head. I thought it a terrific idea. First, I would have a Pac-Man on my head and who didn't like Pac-Man? And second, I knew he would get into trouble.

Howard whipped out one of the marker pens he habitually stole from school (for graffiti purposes) and started to draw. On Mum's return I gave a beautiful performance.

'Waaaah! Look what he's done *now*!'

Mum was furious with him. I was delighted. What I hadn't bargained for was that the Pac-Man wouldn't come off. Howard was instructed to scrub until my head was clean, but the traces were still visible three weeks later.

Joking around with my brother was one thing, but my baldness could also attract a more mean-spirited attention. Around the age of twelve or thirteen, I was deemed old enough to go out with a friend, rather than with a parent, so Jeremy and I would often get the bus to Copthall swimming pool or Harrow Leisure Centre.

I remember one time we were upstairs on a double-decker when we were joined by a couple of rough boys who seemed younger than us and were keen to stamp their authority. Without provocation, they pushed us around and took great pleasure in repeatedly slapping my head. I was petrified. This wasn't the usual teasing – there was something ungovernable about them. I doubt they even went to school.

I encountered them a few times in my youth. Once, one of them spotted me in Edgware when I was out with my mum and walked behind us in the street, kicking me in the rear at regular intervals. I didn't say a word.

On another occasion I was sat in the front passenger seat of the car, with my mum driving, when we stopped at some traffic lights. I was minding my own business when a biker in black leather pulled up next to us and repeatedly shouted 'Baldy' in a mocking voice. My mum and I sat in silence. When the lights changed to amber, I watched him zoom off laughing in the distance. I hoped he might crash.

The truth is, there was always some kind of incident whenever I went out – a confrontation, name-calling, sniggering. The dark side of young people, the lack of empathy, might feel like a new phenomenon, thanks to the camera-phone videos you see online of kids humiliating each other. It isn't new. Kids are inherently cruel. Kindness doesn't come for a while – not naturally, at least.

While children could be cruel, the younger ones were just confused. It didn't make sense to them. I understand why a three- or four-year-old would simply point at a bald kid. When I was that age my brother and I used to tease our father and tell him he wore a wig. It seemed such a fantastical notion to me, because of course he didn't. We were just having fun.

But then, one Sunday morning when I was maybe ten, as I was getting ready to go to Hebrew classes, Dad beckoned me into the bathroom. He shut the door and told me that he had actually lost his hair at thirteen years old and that he wore a toupee.

He then proceeded to slowly and carefully peel it back, until it came all the way off. He had hair round the back and sides, but otherwise, like me, he was bald, I was gobsmacked. He made me promise *not to tell a soul* and I swore blindly that I definitely wouldn't and then went straight to Hebrew classes and told EVERYONE.

'You'll never guess what! My dad . . . wears . . . a WIG!'

'Yeah, I know,' said Darren Swabel, rolling his eyes. 'It's pretty obvious.'

And then I remembered one evening a few months earlier, when he had come home and Mum had looked at him, unimpressed.

'I'm not sure about that at all,' she said.

Dad had been defensive. 'I think it looks nice.'

I have to admit his hair did look pretty different that day, kind of flatter, darker and shinier. A bit like a Brillo Pad or a small, flat hat.

It was a different time, I guess. In those days, not having hair was seen as socially unacceptable. People actually thought that it was preferable to wear a squirrel on their head than be bald.

So I guess I shouldn't have been entirely surprised when my parents suggested to me that I might want to wear a wig at secondary school. Certainly I didn't question it.

At this moment, as I type away, I do question it. I *really* question it.

What the hell was everyone thinking?

It was 1985, a full five years after my hair had fallen out. Five years. I had already done my best to somehow assimilate my baldness into my personality, if that makes sense. I had figured out jokey responses to the same old questions if I was in a good mood and withering retorts if I wasn't. I had mastered the art of staring back fearlessly at people when I caught them sneaking a look at me. I had figured out, in my own way, how to live with being bald.

This was survival, turning a disadvantage into something I could own – but in my heart I still wanted to be just like everyone else. Maybe the wig could do that for me.

I was assessed again by a doctor and then told that, yes, I could have a wig on the National Health Service, so off I went with my mum and grandma to a wig store in central London, where the offending item was waiting for me.

I don't know if they make wigs for children nowadays, but they certainly didn't in 1985. A large brown human-hair wig – intended for a woman – was placed on my little head and cut down to size. Unsurprisingly, it was still far too big for me, but Mum and Grandma and the lady in the wig shop all said it looked marvellous and so we left the shop with the wig in a bag.

Back at home I put it on and looked at myself in the mirror. I didn't like it, but I also didn't really feel – having come this far – that I could or should just give up on it. The fact that I didn't have any eyebrows made the giant hairpiece look even more unconvincing, but I don't think it occurred to anybody to teach me how to draw them in.

For a few days I wore the wig around the house to get used to it. The lining scratched my head so my lovely Aunty Denny kindly sewed a handkerchief into it.

And then one morning I tottered up the road to the primary school where I had been going every day for six years – but now with a colossal bloody wig on my head and even more self-conscious than I had been without it.

Head down, I walked across the playground. Suddenly, without saying a word, one of the tough boys in the year above me ran past, whipped it off and threw it on the ground. I picked it up in tears and hurried off to seek the comfort of a teacher.

I persisted with the wig for a few more days, but summer was approaching and it was just too hot and uncomfortable. I would slip it on and take it off as if it were a hat. Before long I was passing it round the class, letting everyone have a go.

Matt 1 Wig 0.

Poor Wiggy. It was only trying to help. Instead it found itself unceremoniously tossed into a cupboard, where it stayed until I could find a better use for it.

Years later, well into adulthood, I was speaking to a doctor who asked me how I had lost my hair. I told him the story about being knocked down by the car and how it had been assumed that it was the shock that had made it fall out two years later. It was a story I had recounted so many times that it was gospel to me now. I no longer questioned it.

But he did.

He asked me if I had asthma, eczema, hay fever or allergies. I said yes, funnily enough, the lot – chronically.

He said that my hair loss was most likely the consequence of my having an over-active immune system, one that was constantly fighting, even when it had nothing specific to beat. No one could say exactly what had made it 'reject' the hair but it wasn't necessarily anything as dramatic as being knocked down by a car.

I asked him what the significance of having this over-active immune system was and how it was likely to affect me.

'Um, well, you'll probably never get cancer, actually.'

For a brief moment I felt like a superhero. Then he added, 'But there's about fifty-five other things that might well get you, I'm afraid.'

I took a deep breath. 'So it's a shorter life?'

He shrugged. 'You could get hit by a bus tomorrow.'

'Wouldn't be the end of the world,' I replied. 'Maybe the shock would make my hair grow back.'

C – Chumley

The bespectacled, frizzy-haired Chigwell housewife stood in front of us, recounting her life story. She talked about school, her first job, how she met her husband. It was all going swimmingly.

'And then I was raped.'

We gasped.

'Well, no, I wasn't, but I wish I had been.'

Another gasp.

She continued her loose, improvised monologue for another minute or two, but we were now too shocked to laugh. As she came to an end, we applauded uncertainly, then turned as one to Ivor, who was running this stand-up comedy class.

'Thank you, Pamela. Um, very good. Yes.'

Not much seemed to faze Ivor, but it took him a moment to work out how to respond.

'Some nice observations there. If I had any criticism, I would say that, while there are no taboos in comedy *as such*, the "rape" line did take us all a bit by surprise. I felt that perhaps we found it hard to laugh again after that.'

We nodded our heads in agreement.

Summer 1992. Like some of my friends, I had opted to take a year out after my A levels. Unlike my friends, however, many of whom were travelling around the world, I had decided to launch myself on the London stand-up comedy circuit.

My teenage passion for performing had continued unabated. The year after my Edinburgh Festival experience, I'd bagged a background role in a West End play. Two years after that, at sixteen, I joined the National Youth Theatre – which mainly did Shakespeare and more serious stuff than the NYMT.

In the National Youth Theatre I had met a funny guy called David Williams, who was a few years older than me. (I'll tell you more about that later, of course.) David and his friend Jason Bradbury were doing 'open spots' on the comedy circuit – unpaid five-minute slots for aspiring acts – and I'd follow them around. Sometimes they went down a storm; other times you could almost see the tumbleweed – but I thought they were hilarious and I dreamed of being a stand-up comic too.

Ivor Dembina's stand-up comedy course was incredibly helpful. Not only did we get to write and test out routines on each other, building them up week by week, but Ivor also taught us how the alternative comedy circuit worked: no sexist, racist or homophobic material, don't go over your time, don't nick anyone's gags and don't badmouth other acts because you don't know who's friendly with who.

The only sticking point was that I had an idea for a character that I wanted to try out, but Ivor wouldn't let me. His reasoning was that we should be ourselves onstage. I was happy to do that on the course, but I knew that, as soon as I was playing the circuit itself, I would appear in character.

There were a few character comedians on the circuit and they were always my favourites to watch. As much as I enjoyed the observational comics, I had no desire at all to be one. I didn't want to walk out and do gags about being bald and I didn't have a girlfriend to talk about. I wanted to perform – to show off – but I wanted to do it in the guise of someone else.

And I had a character in mind – well, not really a character, more just a silly voice at that stage. Throughout my childhood I would both entertain and ultimately rile my mum and brother by doing silly voices. I'd often fixate on one and then get consumed by it for weeks. For a time I couldn't stop being Jack Wild in *Oliver!* After I returned from the Edinburgh Festival I was Miss Jean Brodie.

'Okay, that's enough now!' Mum would say, her patience wearing thin once again, especially if I was supposed to be studying for my bar mitzvah or mowing the lawn.

I had been a massive fan of Harry Enfield and had loved a spoof *South Bank Show* documentary he'd made, called *Norbert Smith – A Life*. Enfield played the subject – formerly the defining young actor of his generation, rather like Lord Olivier, and now a sweet, befuddled old man.

There were various interviewees in the film – characters who had supposedly worked with Sir Norbert and who shared their recollections. One of them – played by Moray Watson – was called Sir Donald Stuffy, seemingly a nod to a couple of other famous theatrical Donalds: Sinden and Wolfit. During his scenes he told long-winded anecdotes and appropriated the names of other actors. For instance, Dame Anna Neagle became 'Dame Anna Neagly Weagly' and Rex Harrison was 'Rexipoo Harrison'. He was the ultimate 'luvvie actor' and even though he only appeared onscreen for a minute or two, my brother Howard and I thought he was the funniest thing in the show.

I'd impersonate all the characters in the programme, but whenever I did Sir Donald Stuffy's voice it seemed to amuse Howard the most. I did it so often that it wasn't long before I stopped quoting lines from the programme and started using him as a vessel for my own jokes instead.

Gradually I built up a biography for the character – shows he'd been in, his friends, his agent, where he lived, until it felt like my own. Howard proposed the name Sir Bernard Chumley, which stuck.

If Ivor wasn't too sure about me appearing in character – at least, on his course – my mother had greater concerns. If I was going to be taking a break from full-time education and still living at home, I'd need to be contributing towards my upkeep. I couldn't argue with that and I knew it would probably be a long time before I'd be getting paid to perform, so I started to look for a day job.

Previously, while doing my A levels, I'd added to my pocket money by working as a babysitter. I didn't get much work – most parents told me that they would rather have a girl minding their children – but after I placed an advert in the synagogue magazine, one couple, Clive and Michelle Pollard, contacted me and I started looking after their kids on a Saturday evening.

Clive manufactured and imported football merchandise – like those mini-kits you see in car windows – and had the contract to sell his wares at Wembley Stadium and in various football club shops. He had also just won the contract to run the shop at Chelsea Football Club. I was Arsenal through and through, but, keen to fund my stand-up career, give my mum some money and aware that jobs were hard to come by in the recession-hit Britain of 1992, I asked Clive for a job.

'We're looking for an assistant manager,' he said.

'Yeah, I can do that.'

'You're only eighteen.'

'Well, I'm old enough to be trusted with your kids,' I replied. He said it was a good enough answer to get me a job, and so it was agreed that I would help set up the shop and work there during my year off.

The job kept me busy through the day, and during the evenings I set about launching my comedy career in earnest.

I began by writing a dreadful routine at the desk in my bedroom. The set took the form of a long, rambling theatrical anecdote about events at a party Sir Bernard had attended. He name-dropped frequently – but often got the names a bit wrong – Bruce Wallace, Mel Gibbons – and invariably I would use the name-drop simply as an excuse to do an impression of a particular celebrity – Jimmy Savile, Jim Bowen. I had no idea what I was doing and, in truth, my desire to perform and be acclaimed for it outweighed any particular comedic message I wanted to deliver.

My meteoric rise was carefully planned. I would do my first open spot at the Punchlines in West Hampstead on Saturday, 3 October 1992. I would perform the following evening at the club for open spots that Ivor had recommended – the VD Clinic (which promoter Kevin Anderson said stood for Val Doonican). And then on the Thursday night I would crush it at London's premier venue, the Comedy Store. In less than a week I would be a star. Job done.

What confidence. What delusion. But then I was only eighteen years old.

Actually I ended up having an unofficial first gig a few weeks earlier, somewhat spontaneously. David Williams and his friend Jason were performing at the Comedy Café in Rivington Street. On a Wednesday night the club traditionally featured a bunch of open spots. The first to arrive and put their names down on the list would get a slot. I had gone along with my friend Jeremy to watch David and Jason perform and, on learning that there was a space on the bill, couldn't resist putting my name down, so eager was I to get on the stage – and also to impress David and Jason.

I was one of the last to go up. I didn't have my costume. I had written my act down a few weeks before, but hadn't actually learned it yet (not that it would have made much difference, devoid as it was of any actual jokes). I busked it, as they say. And it didn't go down well.

Sir Bernard's tale about the events at his showbiz soirée ended with his arse exploding and faeces landing on the faces of various celebrities . . .

'There was shit on the ceiling, caca on the carpet, dump on the dining table, poo on the porcelain . . . I didn't know where to look. And I turned to Felicity Ken-dell and I said "Felicity, you've grown a moustache" but she hadn't – a bit of poo had deflected off the ceiling and landed on her upper lip!'

In my set I had contrived a reason for this arse explosion that involved Sir Bernard having been born in India and therefore being caught in some sort of 'Anglo-Asian curry zone'. I know it doesn't make any sense. I'm sure it didn't then, either. But as soon as I mentioned about coming from India, some of the audience started shouting 'Racist!' I was taken aback. I hadn't done an Indian accent or made any further comment, but the table of young men had had enough. I wasn't quite booed off, but everyone in the room could hear the reaction. I hurried through to the end of the set and got off.

Jeremy and I left the venue quickly, my heart racing as I sat on the Tube back to Edgware station, trying to process what had happened. It was clear that I would have to make some big changes to my set before my first 'official' gig.

A few weeks later I turned up at the Punchlines club for my proper debut. I knew the place well, having been a regular punter there for a year or two. Despite being underage, I would flash my fake ID and make half a pint last the night as I watched some of Britain's finest up-and-coming comedians take the stage.

I certainly hadn't been shy in letting people know about the big event and much of the audience was made up of friends (and their friends and their friends etc.).

When it was my turn to appear, the compère gave me a warm introduction. I had a pre-recorded intro on tape, which featured some speeded-up music that I had found in my parents' record collection, and me introducing myself in a bad Northern accent – 'Live from Barry Island . . .'

Why would a theatrical raconteur be in Barry Island and why was a Northern voice introducing him? And why was I pretending to be a theatrical raconteur? I barely even knew what one was. I'm sure the audience had no idea, either. It made little sense.

It also wasn't that funny.

But I *needed* to be onstage. Despite the confidence I'd got from those Youth Theatre appearances, I was still desperately unhappy, scared, freaked out by the events of my youth, by my paleness, baldness, fatness, gayness, *otherness*. Like many before me, and countless others since, I was convinced that becoming successful and achieving public recognition was the only way my sad story could end happily.

I was happy to use anything and everything I had in my pursuit. Sir Bernard was bald, though for much of the routine he proudly sported the wig that I had thrown in the cupboard a few years earlier.

The wig might have come out of the closet. I hadn't – yet. But Sir Bernard was *so* gay that I partly hoped it wouldn't occur to anyone that I wasn't. He would do my coming out for me, I hoped. I wouldn't have to say the words or live the life. I could hide in plain sight, at turns celebrating and mocking homosexuality, playing to both gay people and those who found gayness absurd, dancing nimbly backwards and forwards either side of the line.

Now people would laugh with me, not at me. I would control it.

The compère – Dave Thompson, later to find fame as Tinky Winky in *Teletubbies* – introduced me. The audience hollered loudly at my entrance and I sprinted on. I hadn't considered how long the introductory music was (i.e. far too long) and, eager to fill the time, spontaneously broke into a wild dance, which drew laughter. Ever the fat, sedentary asthmatic, by the time the music came to an end I was breathless.

That night I wheezed and panted my way through my muddled little routine. Each lame joke was greeted with a supportive cheer from those who knew me, rather than a laugh. Those who didn't know me would doubtless have been utterly bemused.

At the end of my act there were wild cheers. I took the applause – a little embarrassed, because I knew, despite the response, that it hadn't worked on a comedic level. Dave came back onstage and the audience continued to applaud. He generously waited there and acknowledged the reception I was getting.

And what did I do? Well, because I am a bloody idiot, I stood behind him, signalled in his direction and did the 'Wanker' hand-sign.

Why did I do that?

I can only think that I was just trying to generate another laugh. I was eighteen years old and unprepared for – and giddied by – the audience's applause. However, not only was my response unprofessional, it was also completely unwarranted, but that didn't occur to me in the moment.

I got another laugh and went off.

Downstairs, in the backstage area, sweating, waiting to get my breath back, I accepted the congratulations of the other comics, but I knew that this hadn't been a real victory. Half the crowd was already on my side. I'd shown balls – yes – but not much else.

The next act went onstage and then Dave appeared in the waiting area. He summoned me over and calmly asked me why I had called him a wanker onstage in front of the audience.

I gulped. I had no idea he'd seen the gesture. I stammered an apology. He told me, his anger coming to the surface, how I'd made a huge mistake, that comedians must never ever undermine each other like that onstage, that he had given me a great introduction and encouraged the audience to applaud me afterwards, that it was an incredibly selfish thing to do, that he was furious and that there was no place on the circuit for that kind of behaviour. If he told other people what had just happened, he said, I would never get booked *anywhere*.

What had I done? That was it. It was all over. My name would now be mud. People who hadn't seen my act yet – who hadn't heard of me – would know me by this story and this story alone.

He was apoplectic, but of course totally justified in his anger. I continued to apologise profusely. I told him I was completely out of my depth, that it was my first gig, that I'd been flustered and surprised by the audience's response. Unsure of what to do, I had made a grave error. I was genuinely contrite. I felt awful to have put us both in that position, had learned an important lesson and would never do anything like that again. He accepted my apology and we shook hands.

Outside I was met by friends and acquaintances and praise was poured on me, but I was very shaken up and just wanted to go home.

The following night, I arrived for the next gig –at the VD Clinic, a dedicated open-spot show which took place every Sunday evening in the downstairs bar of the White Horse pub in Belsize Park.

I walked in and my face dropped. There in front of me was Dave Thompson, the compère from the night before. By chance he was hosting this gig too. Sheepishly I went and said hello and he was a complete gentleman, making no reference at all to the previous night's incident. Onstage I was already calmer, wiser, more focused. The audience had been primed for an evening of new acts and it felt like a more natural environment for me. To my surprise, the set went down well. Afterwards Dave congratulated me. I thanked him and apologised again and again until he told me I could stop. Over the next few years I often found myself on the bill with him and we always laughed about our first meeting.

So my third gig was a success – or rather, I had got away with it – but the following morning I phoned Don Ward at the Comedy Store and told him I was going to pull out of the gig that week. Don admonished me for letting him down, but also said he respected the fact that I was saving us both from embarrassment. We agreed that I'd call him again when I had a bit more experience under my belt.

And so I focused on playing the smaller clubs. I would use that stage time to get good, I decided, and then approach the more established venues.

The act was thin, but I would listen to the audience and take out stuff that didn't work. And when all else failed, there was one thing that guaranteed a laugh . . . halfway through my set I would pretend to sneeze and then yank the wig off my head and use it as a tissue, before replacing it, all skew-whiff. Other times I would simply scratch my head, moving the wig in the process, and then continue talking without making any reference to it. I was eighteen years old and looked a lot younger – the audience was not expecting this to happen. They would half-gasp, half-roar. Sometimes they'd even applaud. At Churchill's in Southend, one man in the crowd was drinking his beer when I moved the wig and was so shocked he bit straight into his pint glass. As he left the club for the hospital with blood streaming down his face, still laughing, he told the manager to get me offstage. He said I was a health hazard.

At one of my early gigs I moved the wig but didn't get the laugh I was hoping for. One of the other acts pointed out afterwards that it was perhaps because I had walked in without the wig and put it on in view of some of the audience, while waiting at the bar. From that moment on, I always made sure to 'wig up' before I arrived at the venue. Often I would run into a neighbouring pub, into the toilet and ignore the raised eyebrows of the other occupants as I placed 'Kimberly' (David Williams had said I should give it a name) on my head.

On 8 November 1992, five weeks after that Punchlines show, I wigged up outside the Tube station, then arrived, as I now did every Sunday, at the White Horse to do a short set at the VD Clinic. You had to walk into the main room in the pub in order to get downstairs and, as usual, I arrived far too early, sat down and ordered my customary Diet Coke.

My jaw hit the floor when I saw, at the next table, my idol Bob Mortimer.

Was there a more brilliant, more vibrant, more original and just plain funnier act in British comedy in the early nineties than Reeves and Mortimer?

Let me answer that for you.

No.

In fact, no one came close.

Jim Moir, aka Vic Reeves, had been around for a while. I had seen him occasionally on Jonathan Ross's TV programmes and he and Bob Mortimer had developed a bizarre spoof variety show called *Vic Reeves Big Night Out*, which had transferred from the Goldsmith's Tavern to Channel 4, where it ran for two series on Friday nights.

As a teenager in Stanmore who wasn't quite allowed out yet on a Friday night, I had watched the first episode with expectations that weren't met. In fact, I was mystified. Reeves kept promising things that were going to come up later in the show that simply didn't. And there were no celebrity guests. I couldn't work it out at all. By the end of the episode I was so irritated that I pompously called up Channel 4 and told them that I didn't get it.

I tuned in again the following week, but only because I was convinced that I was watching something *historically* bad, something that would almost certainly be removed from air before the series could run in its entirety. This time I recognised the return of some of the weird non-jokes from the week before, understood that none of the so-called celebrity guests would actually be appearing, that instead Vic and Bob and their pals would be playing everyone. By the end of the series I was not just a convert, I was a fully fledged apostle.

In the White Horse pub that November night in 1992, I rushed over to Bob Mortimer, who had left his small group of friends and was on his way to the toilet.

'HiBobiamahugefaniamalsoacomedianlikeyouareyoucomingtothe-showtonight?'

And it turned out he was. He said his friend Dorian was compèring.

Dorian Crook was (and still is) a man from another age. The late fifties, I would say. The clothes he wore, the car he drove – even the jokes he told – could have come straight out of a Terry Thomas film. By day he was an air traffic controller, by night he was an aspiring comedian. He had been at art school with Vic Reeves and subsequently had become embroiled in Vic and Bob's antics, making brief appearances in their stage shows and joining them on tour. Now he was branching out on his own. His set – a parade of puns, one-liners and Christmas cracker-style jokes – was entirely original and of his own creation, but was so traditional in its tone and subject matter that it gave the impression of having been excavated from the distant past. Some audiences – hungry for something more biting and fashionable – resisted Dorian's charms, but those audiences who had had their fill of knob gags and hectoring political invective, and who were willing to go along for the ride, laughed uproariously throughout. There was something joyous and liberating about watching Dorian. As with Vic and Bob, it was a bit like he wasn't supposed to be there, like he had somehow wandered in and managed to get onstage. He was *cheeky*.

Downstairs the gig began. I lurked nervously at the back of the room, until it was my turn to perform. With the great Bob Mortimer in attendance, I decided to give it *everything*.

In the five weeks since my first 'official' gig at the Punchlines, I had added a dynamic new aspect to Sir Bernard's persona. I'd been heckled a few times – often before the act had got going – and, terrified and without any decent put-downs, had started to respond by screaming back at hecklers in a rough Cockney accent . . .

'I will cut your fucking face! Do you want some? DO YOU FUCKING WANT SOME?'

And then I would turn straight back into the elderly posh old man again, as if nothing had happened. The audience – initially startled – would burst into hysterics.

Eager to utilise *anything* that got a laugh, I had started to incorporate Chumley's outbursts into the set, regardless of whether anyone was heckling or not. The anecdote would be routinely punctuated with these horrendous, incongruous streams of abuse, often aimed at anyone who was returning from the bar or simply just someone who happened to be sitting in the front row.

As I performed, I noticed Bob Mortimer making his way down to the front. I certainly didn't scream at him. I idolised him. However, I did allow myself to glance in his direction once or twice and I saw that he was laughing heartily.

After the show I was in the pub upstairs, wondering if and how I could talk to Bob again. I needn't have wondered. He came over to me and, making no reference to our brief interaction before the show (maybe he had forgotten – after all, I had been wearing the wig), he introduced himself.

'Hello, my name's Bob. I work at a production company called Channel X. I really enjoyed your act. I wondered if you have an agent or a phone number I can pass on?'

Did I fly home that night? I might well have done. I might have soared up into the sky, circled a star and then floated back down over London, towards the suburbs. Did I sleep a wink? Did I even need to? History had been made. I had not only met Bob Mortimer – JESUS

CHRIST, I JUST MET BOB MORTIMER – but *he had asked for my phone number.*

I cannot emphasise enough what a pivotal moment this was for me – in my life, let alone my career. I adored Vic and Bob. To me they were gods. They were Lennon and McCartney. And I was to become their drummer.

Sorry, I couldn't resist.

I still pinch myself.

It was to be a few months before I heard from Bob, but with the confidence that grew from this chance meeting, nothing was going to stop me. Storm or die, paid or unpaid, I got as many gigs in my diary as possible. I didn't care what or where they were. I pushed and pushed myself, performing every night, twice a night if I could.

And . . . I got better. A lot better. And I decided it was time to call Don Ward again and get that open spot at the Comedy Store back in the diary.

The Comedy Store had played host to every great British alternative comic and you saw their photos lining the walls as you descended the stairs. Paul Merton (then Paul Martin), Jo Brand, Rik Mayall and Adrian Edmondson, French and Saunders, even Robin Williams had turned up on a few occasions to try stuff out.

I was never going to get a paid booking there, I was too new for that – so it was more a rite of passage. I just *had* to do a gig there, at least once.

I did it. And it actually didn't go too badly.

I did shit myself that morning, though – literally – while serving a customer in the shop.

Ah yes, the shop.

I was leading a double life. By night I was a caped crusader, swooping down through the windows of comedy clubs, reducing audiences to hysterics – or goading them into abuse – before disappearing off into the night. And by day I sold pencil cases, rosettes, scarves, ashtrays – anything, as long as it was emblazoned with Chelsea FC.

Chelsea Sportsland, it was called – a name that never sounded anything other than ridiculous, and which irritated and alienated the largely working-class English fan-base, who still ate dodgy burgers and pissed in each other's pockets at half-time. Chelsea Sportsland reflected the creeping Americanisation of British culture. Saturday nights on ITV were dominated by a new US format – *Gladiators*; rockers banged heads to the grisly nasal screeching of Axl Rose. London even had its own gridiron team – The Monarchs.

When Sky paid what was then an astronomical £304 million over five seasons for the rights to broadcast games from the brand new Premier League, they featured cheerleaders at half-time. Football fans were unimpressed, and Chelsea supporters were not too happy either about the vision that Chelsea Football Club and Clive Pollard had for a new football shopping experience. Alongside the Chelsea kits, footballs, posters and T-shirts were a load of baseball jackets.

'What the fuck is this shit?' asked one of the more articulate fans as he squinted at an obscenely priced and completely pointless Chelsea baseball shirt.

This was pre-Abramovich Chelsea. This was pre-Matthew Harding Chelsea, even. This was the Ken Bates era, when you stood on the Shed for a few quid, screamed at Nigel Spackman for missing a sitter and called Graeme Le Saux a poof because he read *The Guardian*.

Tony, the shop manager, was a Watford fan. Vince, who also worked there, supported Leeds, and I was, of course, a Gooner, but on a match day we'd all have to sport Chelsea tops – not the blue one, thank God, but their brand new third kit – white with vertical thin red stripes. Beneath it, in an act of defiance, I would wear my Arsenal top, but that would show through, so I'd have to wear a white T-shirt between the two layers. I was roasting!

Before and after the match, the shop would be mobbed. Despite supporting a rival team, I used to hope Chelsea would win purely because it would put the customers in a better mood.

The customers generally seemed to be made up of two different types. There was your rough'n'ready Chelsea diehard, who knew everything about the club and, not unreasonably, assumed I did too. I was often engaged in long, misty-eyed conversations about Peter Osgood and

Bobby Tambling, during which I would bluff my way through, pretending I knew who the hell they were.

One of the techniques I employed was to use an all-purpose word of my own invention that would hopefully buy me time or, if I was particularly successful, end the discussion completely.

'Oh yeah,' I would say, 'only one word for that: morditorial.'

Few people want to admit they don't know what a word means, so I used to get away with that one frequently – and still do, sometimes. Feel free to use it yourself, by all means, though I would request that you don't ascribe an actual meaning to it, because then it will simply be just like every other word.

#KeepMorditorialMeaningless.

The other type of customer we would play host to was your posh Kensington High Street-type chappie, clearly unfamiliar with the game but keen, as a local, to 'get stuck in, you know'. I'd lay it on thick with these guys, insisting that real fans bought the whole kit, and the jumpers, T-shirts, cufflinks and ties. I found you could sell them anything.

There was also a third type of customer in the shop – well, just this one guy, really – who was very friendly and had a giant spider tattoo on his face and a large thick swastika on his forehead. He was so nice and funny that I decided he surely must have had the tattoos done when he was young and incredibly stupid. He was a different person now. One day a Motown song came on the radio and I started humming along.

'We don't sing that stuff, mate,' he said. I changed the station.

I toiled in Chelsea Sportsland by day and toured the comedy clubs by night. On that morning in the winter of 1992, now a seasoned pro with a full two months of stand-up experience under my belt, I woke up in a cold sweat. I was calling my own bluff. *I was actually going to play the Comedy Store.*

As usual I grabbed two scalding strawberry Pop-Tarts (another recent American import) fresh from the toaster, wrapped them in silver foil, got in Vince's freezing-cold clapped-out Citroën and gave him two shiny pound coins to pay for petrol. He drove us to the shop – which took the best part of an hour. On the way, as ever, we raged about the villainous Tory government – Major, Portillo, Lilley and Co. We shared the hope that one day Labour would displace them and knew that when they did Britain would run perfectly again.

Our manager Tony had gone to the toilet. I had been left in charge of the shop, as Vince hadn't been working with us for very long. We had some customers in and I was climbing a shelf to bring down a selection of jumpers when I felt a fart brewing.

I had recently perfected – or so I thought – an ingenious method of concealing a blow-off in company. Not necessarily the scent of it – the severity of which was inevitably dependent on whatever mélange of backstreet junk food I had polished off the night before – but the *sound* of it.

It had occurred to me that if I could manufacture a strident enough cough to coincide with the expulsion of said gas, then those present would be none the wiser. Sure, they might pause at a later moment to enjoy the aroma of a nearby gardenia or peony and in the process inadvertently inhale and subsequently gag at the tang of Tuesday's Birds Eye Potato Waffle by way of the large intestine, but – crucially – at the moment of auditory impact they would be none the wiser as to the creator of the offending pop.

With two more customers appearing in the shop, the opportunity to further develop my groundbreaking theory of fartivity came upon me and, as I had been prone to do, I exercised my fine powers of coordination with focus and determination.

Reader, I am proud to inform you that fart and cough were fused quite exquisitely. Certainly there was not even the slightest turn of head or wrinkle of nose from any of the assembled personages.

I am less pleased to tell you that, because I had ejected perhaps too enthusiastically, a voluminous quantity of *merde* shot out of my anus and into my underpants. Indeed, I fear a pellet or two may even have made its way down the trouser leg and onto the floor.

A butt-clenched stagger to the door followed, as I excused myself, leaving a helpless Vince stranded on the shop floor with several eager customers, confusion and betrayal in his eyes. Where was I going? How could I forsake him? Had I forgotten he didn't know how to properly operate the till yet?

With Tony occupying our shop's only lavatory (he was later to return in fury at my absence), I somehow managed to totter to the travel agents next door: another Chelsea franchise, where you could book a trip to watch the team play abroad, though it was many more years before they would actually qualify for a European tournament.

I smiled weakly and asked for the key.

Catching it nimbly, I headed inside. There was nothing I could do but commence the industrial-sized clean-up job. Of course, had there been any toilet paper in there it might have been a little easier. Suffice to say I had a relatively decent reception at the Comedy Store that night, and if you looked closely enough you would have been able to see that I wasn't wearing any socks.

D – Doing the Circuit

It had been a few months and I hadn't heard anything from Bob Mortimer, so I thought I'd be proactive. Taking my trusty dictaphone into my bedroom, I shut the door, shouted downstairs to my mum *not to come in*, recorded my stand-up set on an audio tape, stuck it in an envelope and posted it off to him, with an accompanying letter explaining that I was enjoying gigging on the comedy circuit but that at the end of my year off I was going to go to university.

Not long afterwards, in a questionnaire in *Smash Hits* magazine, Bob named Sir Bernard as his favourite new act of the year. I was chuffed to bits and also delighted because I could use this as a quote on my publicity material.

Meanwhile I was ever-present on the circuit, going to clubs most nights, even when I wasn't performing. I made as many contacts, took down as many phone numbers as I could, and learned the names of every promoter at every club.

Back home I'd ring them up. Some warmed to me and welcomed me, others sighed wearily at the sound of my voice. My act was polarising, extreme, strange – but I made sure to tell *everyone* that Bob Mortimer had seen it and taken my number. I had also done a gig with Harry Hill, who – alongside Mark Thomas – was at that time the king of the circuit. Harry very kindly gave me the numbers of a few key promoters and said I could use his name as a reference.

It was a truth universally acknowledged that the most terrifying club to play was Up the Creek in Greenwich. Veterans told stories about its predecessor – The Tunnel Club – which had been closed down after bottles and glasses had been hurled at the acts.

Up the Creek had a similarly fearsome reputation. Both clubs were run by Malcolm Hardee, a deadpan comic – one of the older acts on the circuit – who wore thick bottle-rim glasses that made him look a bit like Eric Morecambe.

Hardee had an unusual way of introducing acts – particularly new ones that he hadn't seen before. 'Might be good, might be shit.'

And lots of very good people were shit at his club, as it happened, because it was often such a nightmare to play. The audience at Up the Creek didn't like observational comedians very much, even if they were headliners everywhere else. The weirder, quirkier acts had a better reception, but even then the crowd might bray and boo and hound the turns without mercy.

I had heard the horror stories and resolved to avoid the place, but one Friday evening I found myself on the bill elsewhere with Malcolm. He took a shine to my onstage antics and invited me to play his club that Sunday.

I turned up and realised this was no ordinary club. It was far grander in scale. The acts waited stoically like condemned men in a room upstairs where the wall was covered in a huge mural depicting the Last Supper, but with various comics taking the place of the Apostles and Malcolm himself in the middle as Jesus.

I received Malcolm's trademark non-committal introduction and went onto the stage. The audience could immediately sense my fear and it wasn't long before I was heckled. I gave as good as I got and won the audience over. From that moment on they laughed at everything and I finished my set on such a triumphant note that Malcolm slipped me a £20 note, even though I was an open spot. He also said he wanted to book me for two full sets.

'I haven't got twenty minutes yet,' I told him.

'Just do fifteen, then.'

The first set took place the day after my nineteenth birthday. I gathered a few friends and we headed across London on the train (from north-west to south-east) for the show. I had none of the luck of my previous visit, and lasted seven terrifying minutes before I was drowned out by the boos.

We were all shell-shocked, but my friends tried to cheer me up on the long journey home. 'You just made eighty quid in seven minutes. That's probably more than Paul McCartney,' said Jeremy. A couple of days later I rang up Malcolm and, before I could say anything, he said, 'I know why you're calling. You want to cancel the other gig. Well, you can't.'

I did the other gig and this time I didn't even manage five minutes before I was relieved of my duties. One crazed audience member was so incensed by my attempts to entertain that he grabbed me by the collar as I came offstage, screaming, 'You come back here again and I'll fucking finish you!' into my ear.

I played Up the Creek a few more times after that, but always had an absolute stinker, even though I was headlining regularly elsewhere. Malcolm wanted to carry on booking me regardless, but it was too disheartening. Despite the decent money, getting booed off isn't good for your confidence or your reputation. Everyone knew that Up the Creek was a law unto itself and that even the best of them could get destroyed there, but even so, every time you got booed off anywhere, other comics would witness it and talk about it amongst themselves.

Somehow I got away with it, though. I guess I was a bit of an anomaly on the circuit. There weren't many people who would 'die' as often as I did and yet still get booked, but promoters seemed to like what I was doing, and would accept that I was a risk worth taking.

If it went well, it tended to go really well. If it didn't, it was a disaster. There was no in between. People truly loved it or hated me. The act had developed – out went the dodgy impressions and in came some actual gags. It was no longer an echo of anything anyone else was doing. As I became more experienced, I grew bolder and braver onstage, interacting with the audience and improvising more.

I still had some disastrous shows, though. At St George's Medical School in Tooting the students had destroyed everyone on the bill before I came on. I went onstage already angry on behalf of my colleagues and it wasn't long before I too was the recipient of abuse. In my case someone threw a bottle and – in a rare and uncharacteristic moment of skill – I returned it on the volley, punting it over the heads of the front few rows. 'Come on then!' I screamed. Not wise. More bottles followed and I scarpered to the dressing room, where I had to be locked in for an hour for my own safety.

Some months later, I was performing at the intimate Aztec Club in Crystal Palace. I was more confident by then, but again alarmed as every act was falling prey to a huge, very drunk Irish guy, who was bellowing insults across the small room and ruining the evening. Even the compère was helpless.

I knew I was doomed to the same treatment, but I decided to meet the challenge head-on. I went onstage, dispensed with my material and instead focused my act solely on the man, hurling insults at him, belittling him, even impersonating him. The atmosphere changed. The tyrant was humiliated! The relief in the room was palpable. Now surely this bully had been silenced once and for all. Maybe he would even leave.

I came offstage to wild applause and the next act went on. I packed my wig and jacket into my bag, paused for a moment and leaned against the wall near the bar, smugly basking in a jubilant glow.

The floored giant came over and calmly spoke to me . . . 'Very funny, that. Good stuff. I like what you did.'

'Um, thank you,' I said, a little surprised.

'And now I'm gonna take you outside and beat the bollocks off of ya.'

I looked up to him and gulped. His eyes burned into mine. The moment seemed to last forever.

'Nah, I'm only playin' wit' ya.'

I exhaled loudly. The relief probably would have been visible from the moon.

He paused, studied me and then spoke again. 'Nah, you're gonna get a bruising. Pick up your bag. I'll meet you outside.'

A low whine from yours truly, then . . .

'I'm just mucking about. You're fine.' He patted me on the head.

Pause.

'Nah, screw it. Do you think you can talk to me like that in front of these people? In front of my lady? Fetch your coat.'

Imagine a nineteen-year-old arse quivering and then times it by ten.

'I'm messing. I'd never do that.'

'Ha. G-g-good.'

'Nah, this is my local. No one comes here and talks to me like that. Funny man, yeah? I'm gonna teach you a lesson. Come with me. Now!'

This went on and on, back and forth. He was going to beat me to a pulp. Of course he wasn't. He was going to smash my head into a lamp-post – no, he was just joking. He was going to punch my lights out. Only kidding.

One of the bar staff witnessed this exchange from a few feet away. He came and stood between us, and then whispered in my ear that it might be a good time to leave, and that he and a couple of others would walk me to the station. I didn't hesitate to accept his offer. I assume Goliath watched as I picked up my bag and coat and we slunk out of the bar, but I didn't look back so I'll never know.

Remember in the first chapter when I was name-dropping? Well, here is one of my proudest ever clangs. In 2008 David Walliams and I had the honour and pleasure of spending a little time with Robin Williams in LA. I told him this tale one night when a group of us were at dinner, swapping war stories, and he fell in love with it. Later I heard that he'd started doing an impression of my impression of the Irish guy in his act.

Does it get any clangier than that? Unlikely.

Except it just did, because Billy Crystal was at that dinner too.

Clang!

Clang!

Clang!

Clang!

Clang!

Sometimes when I played outside London, accommodation was provided as part of the deal. This sounded good on the face of it, but it usually meant a dodgy B&B, a flea-ridden bed in a cupboard in a university hall of residence, or a room in someone's mate's house, rather than a hotel.

I had a tough gig at a student union in Newton Abbot, where I was supporting the magnificent Jenny Eclair. Afterwards we were dispatched to the austere home of Mrs Dalton, a thin-lipped old lady who had been widowed just a couple of months before.

I couldn't get to sleep because it was freezing cold in my room – and also she had cats which set off my allergies and gave me a pretty severe asthma attack. Stupidly I had forgotten to bring my medicine with me and in the early hours, sleepless, wheezing and shivering as the window frames rattled in the wind, I quietly took myself downstairs to the kitchen.

An irritated Mrs Dalton, woken by the noise, followed, and kindly made me a cup of tea. We chatted for a little while and then I went back up to bed. A couple of hours later, still sleepless and now genuinely struggling to breathe, I returned downstairs. Mrs Dalton reappeared too. Close to tears, I told her that I might need to call an ambulance. Mrs Dalton had had enough of this strange man wandering around her house. She calmly told me that if I called an ambulance, she would call the police. I went back to my room, sat on the bed gasping for air, and waited for the sun to rise. Eventually Jenny surfaced, fresh from a lovely night's sleep, and we shared a taxi to the station. I told her about my night.

'Oh, you should have woken me,' she said. 'I get asthma sometimes. You could have used my inhaler.'

There were happier experiences. My favourite batch of out-of-town gigs was a mini-tour of the south-west – Exeter, Yeovil, Falmouth, Bridport and Torquay – booked and compèred by a lovely guy called Bentley, who worked away on the oil rigs for several months of the year and then returned to spend time with his family and run comedy shows. Everyone on the circuit was happy to do Bentley's gigs, even though they didn't pay a king's ransom, because he was such a generous host, cooking for us and driving us around.

When one of the other comics offered me a joint before the show one night, I declined because I didn't know how it would affect my act. Some comics could knock it back but I never had more than half a pint before I went on, and certainly didn't smoke pot ahead of a gig, though I often indulged afterwards. Bentley told me I should have a toke – it might inspire me. I warned him that I had no idea what would happen and he said he didn't mind and I should just enjoy the experience.

I had a few puffs, but to my surprise it was really strong stuff. I went onstage, started my set and the audience was laughing. I then got completely paranoid that they were doing so for the wrong reasons. I became convinced that I hadn't done my flies up properly, and kept stopping to adjust them, which the crowd thought was part of the act. I went down so well they gave me an encore. I promptly went back onstage and was so disorientated I repeated my entire set word-for-word, prompting more hysteria from the audience and more confusion from me as to what they were finding funny.

In the early nineties London had a burgeoning Jewish comedy circuit, where some established acts – Ivor Dembina, Mark Maier, Peter Moss, Dave Schneider, Ian Stone – would perform modified sets or even create new ones.

It was at one of these that I met the late Leelo Ross. A large, friendly Northerner, Leelo's quickfire set was jammed full of great gags. It was a pleasure to watch her and a pain to follow her.

Some years later I found myself by chance sitting opposite Leelo on a bus to Muswell Hill. She told me she had given up comedy and become a clairvoyant. We got off at the next stop and popped into a nearby café, where she read my tea leaves. She told me that I had Italian ancestry, came from a family of sailors and that she could see my late grandmother standing in front of us, hairs coming out of her chin, holding a tray of cheap cakes. I thought it was high time she returned to making people laugh and shortly afterwards David and I cast her as Tanya in the 'Fat Fighters' sketches in *Little Britain*. She did a great job, giving a very natural, sensitive performance and bearing Marjorie's ceaseless barbs with grace.

The audiences at the Jewish comedy nights were older than at most comedy clubs. They drank a lot less alcohol and didn't particularly want to see sweary comedy. And it was at one such event in Palmers Green that my poor mother saw my act for the first time.

I was on the bill with my school friend Ashley Blaker. Ashley had been in the year below me at Haberdashers' and we'd shared an interest in comedy and football. He used to do stand-up shows for charity at lunch break and hundreds would attend. Now, like me, he was starting to play the clubs, though his studies kept him from really making a fist of it.

Ashley had at least thought to come up with a few Jewish jokes for his set. There was nothing remotely Jewish about mine. As Sir Bernard cursed and screamed, my set – effective in the loud, smoky, combative atmosphere of a grotty pub backroom – played to total silence. My red-faced mum – who had been dubious enough when her son suddenly announced 'I'm going to be a comedian' – had brought a couple of friends and was understandably mortified by the whole thing. Is this what I had taken a year off for? As she drove us both home that night neither of us said much. Ashley too had generated more grumbles than laughs. He'd curtailed his set, telling the audience, 'I know I've died tonight. If anyone's interested, the shiva's at my parents'.' (If you're Jewish, that's a cracking joke, by the way.)

Autumn 1993. After a year on the circuit, having graduated from open spots to half-spots and now full twenty-minute paid spots in some of the smaller venues, and with agents starting to take an interest too, I put my stand-up career on hold and went off to Bristol University to study Theatre, Film and Television.

Within a few days of arriving there, I received a letter from Bob Mortimer. He said that there was going to be a new late-night ITV series called *Comedy Club* featuring stand-up comics and he thought I should audition for the producer, who he knew.

I phoned the Comedy Café and asked them if I could come down and do a short set. Bob and his girlfriend (now wife) Lisa came along, bringing the producer with them. Afterwards the producer said she'd love me to appear in the series. I was understandably thrilled. I was even more delighted to discover that I was going to be paid £600 – more than ten times what I'd normally get for a gig.

Comedy Club was taped on a Friday night at the Paris Studios in London. Backstage I sat waiting with Caroline Aherne, who I had seen on TV and been on the bill with a couple of times. She was doing her Sister Mary Immaculate character. I couldn't help but notice how beautiful she was up close.

Some of the other acts could barely hide their surprise at my presence. They were all bill-toppers, seasoned pros, whereas I was not fully established throughout the London comedy scene. Many of them had seen me die a death, but there I was, on the same show and the same money as them. Despite my nerves, my set went down well, generating laughs in all the right places.

A few months later the show aired on TV. I was horrified – not only at my pale, sweating, tubby form onscreen, but also by the fact that my set had been trimmed down in the edit so much that almost all of the set-ups had been removed, so that while I appeared to get plenty of laughs, nothing made any sense. Worse, the large microphone obscured the lower half of my face. I had hoped that this appearance might help me get more club bookings, but many of the promoters I contacted told me that they had seen me on TV and didn't think I was ready yet. It had done more harm than good!

Nonetheless I dug my heels in and continued to gig, and over the coming months I received more interest from TV producers. However, as much as I wanted to work in television I became anxious at the thought of having to surrender control to editors and producers. I was also concerned that I would be using up my best material on TV and would then have to drop it from my live act, as audiences would already be familiar with it. I wasn't yet confident enough, prolific enough or funny enough to churn out dozens of new gags for each TV show – nor was I established enough to have writers working for me – so I became judicious with my TV appearances, preferring Sir Bernard to appear in conversation, rather than give away the most valuable jokes from my stand-up act.

My favourite TV appearance as Chumley was on *Barrymore*. Michael Barrymore was one of my heroes. While Vic and Bob were innovators on BBC Two, Barrymore was truly anarchic on primetime ITV. These days he's remembered less for his work and more for events in his life, but at his peak he was in a league of his own. I was almost sleepless with excitement at the prospect of appearing on the sofa with him. He was perhaps the biggest comic in the country at the time, but he was generous and encouraging, both onscreen and off. Our chat finished with a duet – the Lee Dorsey hit 'Working In The Coalmine'. I was allowed to choose the song and it amused me to pick the most random one I could think of.

Though I had intended to gig a lot less while at university, I found it hard to resist the lure of the spotlight. There were a couple of comedy clubs in Bristol which I would play, and I'd head off most weekends either to London or some far-flung corner of Britain to perform.

The best place to improve, though, was at the Edinburgh Fringe Festival, not least because it was customary to take only one or two nights off. By gigging almost every night for a month, you could really sharpen and hone your act.

I went up four years in a row, the first time with Vic and Bob's pal Dorian Crook in 1994, and the next three years with my funny friend David Williams – now Walliams, as there was already a David Williams in the actors' union. As well as stand-up, the shows featured daft songs and we were joined by my university course mate Tim Atack on the keyboard.

It was during the Edinburgh Festival in 1995 that I had one of my most memorable gigs – and not for the right reasons . . .

Reeves and Mortimer had come to town, to headline a show at the Edinburgh Playhouse, which Mark Lamarr was hosting and which would also feature Harry Hill, Sean Lock and Charlie Chuck.

The gig was due to start at about 11 p.m. and the plan was for me to go on first and do ten minutes, and then dash off to the

Assembly Rooms for my hour-long midnight show with David and Tim as usual.

However, on arriving at the Playhouse, I saw that the street was full of people waiting to get in. The ballet that was on before us was seriously over-running, so I went over to the Assembly Rooms, did my regular midnight show with David and Tim and then returned to the Playhouse, where the gig had finally begun.

I popped my head around the back of the auditorium. The audience – who had been kept waiting for over an hour – were not in a very generous mood. Addison Cresswell, who was promoting the gig, told me not to panic, that I had fifteen minutes before I was due on. What neither of us realised was that the act before me – who was having a bit of a nightmare – was cutting his set down radically as he went. Less than two minutes later I heard myself being introduced.

It was quarter to two in the morning. I walked out to the centre of the stage, blinded by the light. The place was sold out – there were over three thousand people there.

To my surprise – and relief – my opening few gags went down really well. My set was designed to reel them in with some humdingers at the start, before the more theatrical, surreal stuff would start to happen.

But on this night – or rather morning – the stranger stuff left the audience cold. And they stopped laughing. I was only supposed to do ten minutes, and the first three minutes had been great. The next two were a little quieter and then it started . . .

'Get off!' came the voice.

As I hadn't had a laugh for a couple of minutes, I didn't quite have the authority to take this heckler down, especially as he was joined by a couple more and then, within seconds, a couple more. Also, with the spotlight so bright in my eyes, I couldn't see them, but I could hear that they were up on the balcony, miles away. Often in a small club you could wander over to the culprit, size them up and engage. Not here.

And now they could smell blood. There were maybe six of them in a room of over three thousand, but it was enough. They made so much noise that I was drowned out. To my credit I didn't hang about. I got off stage within seconds. But I couldn't pretend it had been anything other than a disaster, and a very public one at that.

For the rest of the evening – for the rest of the festival, in fact – comics and industry people came to commiserate with me. I'm sure the intention was to make me feel better, but each time it just confirmed that yet another important person had witnessed my humiliation.

It wasn't the first bad gig I'd had and it wouldn't be the last, but the scale of it felt enormous and very public.

Just a few weeks later, I faced another challenge when I was booked to join Blur on tour, as their support act.

I'd already met the band, having been asked to appear in the video for their single 'Country House'. Director Damien Hirst (clang, split in two, preserved in formaldehyde and sold for a million) wanted a bald guy to get chased by some sexy girls – in a reference to *The Benny Hill Show*.

My memories of the shoot mainly involve having several asthma attacks as I ran round and round for hours on a hot soundstage full of farm animals crapping everywhere (them, not me). Even now, whenever I hear that song, I suffer a mild panic attack.

I had a laugh with the band, though. Alex, the bass player, had seen me on TV a week or two before the shoot and remembered some of my gags. At the end of filming, I said goodbye and that, I assumed, would be that – but during our Edinburgh run my agent called to tell me that Blur had been back in touch. They were doing a mini-tour of UK seaside towns, as a warm-up for a big arena tour, and wanted a comic to support them. Was I potentially available and did I have a video recording of my act that they could watch?

Yes and yes.

My dad dropped me off on York Way in King's Cross where the tour bus was waiting. There would be eight shows in nine days. Usually the support act would travel separately, but as I didn't drive, the band had agreed to let me travel with them.

It was the week of the release of *The Great Escape* album. The battle with Oasis had hit its peak and the two bands, constantly sneering at each other, were the darlings of the tabloids. Each morning we'd eagerly sift through all the papers and see what Noel or Liam had said about them. Damon or Alex would usually have a pithy response. They knew it was a game and they played it well.

The band wanted to watch my set on the opening night, but I discouraged them, telling them it might take me a gig or two to work out what the crowd wanted. I should have let them see that gig, because it was probably one of the best ones I had on the whole tour – or rather, one of the only ones I managed to get through. Well, I say 'get through' – I had been booked to do half an hour but I never managed more than fifteen minutes.

The following night, in Dunoon, where Blur were not only the biggest band in Britain but the first major act to play there since the Tourists fifteen years earlier, I lasted a full two minutes, before the crowd dispensed with my services as one, gleefully shouting 'You fat bastard! You fat bastard!'

I couldn't blame them. There they were, a horde of frenzied teenage girls and there was I, a doughy, pudgy, surreal stand-up. While I had a warm response in a couple of the venues, I would say at least five of the gigs were calamitous – and that's me being generous.

While the audiences declared war on me nightly, the band at least took pity on me. I grew quite close to Alex James and Dave Rowntree, in particular – continuing to see them long after the tour was over – but any of my friends who came along would stammer in their presence. In Brighton, David Walliams came to visit and when I introduced him to Damon he was so starstruck he could barely speak.

After the show, the band and their crew would get plastered. I didn't drink much – preferring to smoke pot, as ever. It had become a real habit by then. In Bournemouth we went into the sea in the middle of the night, then Alex swanned around the hotel, naked. I was impressed by the band's lack of inhibition and their conscientious adherence to the rock lifestyle – all while absolutely killing it onstage every night.

Shortly after the tour ended, the first series of *Shooting Stars* aired on BBC Two (more of that later). I carried on gigging as Sir Bernard for another eighteen months – sometimes to audiences who heckled me throughout, calling for my TV persona George Dawes – but *Shooting Stars* was opening doors and I was keen to step through them. I'd slogged the circuit for four and a half years, doing hundreds of shows. I'd had the best of times and the worst. Now I was ready to move on.

I began eating
at a young age

E – Eating

I'm a bit peckish now, after all that. Shall we grab something to eat? What do you fancy? A sandwich? Anything in particular? Oh, you don't mind? Great.

What do *I* want?

Oh blimey, where do I start?

I've never tried cocaine, acid or even ecstasy. I haven't had a joint or smoked a cigarette in nearly twenty years. I have maybe six drinks a year. Baileys on the rocks, usually, but I can take it or leave it.

Food, on the other hand – that's my vice. This thing here ain't no beer belly. This is chocolate and chips, cakes and crêpes, croissants and croutons and copious amounts of crisps. When I'm eating breakfast, I'm wondering what to have for lunch. When I'm eating lunch, I'm musing on whether I'll make it through to supper without needing a snack along the way. In bed, cursing my aching tum after yet another Roman banquet, I'll munch a handful of Minstrels before dreaming of macaroons.

It wasn't always thus. I started eating *in earnest* around the age of maybe eleven or twelve. I'd had puppy fat until then, like many kids, but by the time I was heading for secondary school, I was a big fat pudding.

It was announced one day in assembly, a year or two before I left primary school, that the canteen was changing. Until then school dinners were free and you ate what you were given or you went hungry. It was the usual fare – corned beef or Spam, a scoop of salty mashed potato from a packet, veg that had been boiled for what tasted like hours and, for afters, semolina, sago or sponge in custard.

The government was privatising school dinners. It was sold to us as a positive thing – although we would now have to pay for our meals, we would get to choose what we wanted to eat. Obviously eager to turn a profit, the contractors simply served up junk food. And what ten-year-old wouldn't just choose nuggets or pizza or burgers for lunch every day? I don't think anything green ever touched my plate in that school again.

At my secondary school, Haberdashers', old-fashioned dinners were served – and again, you ate what you were given. Things should have calmed down a little then weight-wise, but unlike before – when I would walk from home to school and back – I was now heading up the road to catch the school coach from Stanmore station, where there was a kiosk. Each day on my way to school and on my way home, I'd stop there and buy something sugary.

At school there was a tuck shop. While the other kids spent their lunch break playing football, I would queue up, wolf down a jam dough-nut or a Marathon (as they were back then) and then head to the back of the queue and start all over again.

My parents' divorce, my father's imprisonment, my discomfort at being bald, my increasing unease at my growing attraction for other boys, my anxiety at my persistently low grades and the ever-increasing workload – I struggled to talk about any of this. Instead I just ate and ate and ate.

Back home after school, I would dissolve some chicken stock cubes in boiling water and add huge amounts of pasta, devouring the lot during *Neighbours*. A couple of hours later I'd be raiding the freezer and whacking some Birds Eye Steakhouse Grills and Alphabites in the oven.

Things came to an inevitable head. While I was out one day, my suspicious brother pulled my bed away from the wall to reveal hundreds of discarded chocolate-bar wrappers beneath.

It was decided that something *really* had to be done about it and so I enrolled in a weekly Weight Watchers class. My mum wasn't overweight but joined me in an act of solidarity. I was put on a strict diet and was thrilled to lose nearly half a stone in the first couple of weeks.

Each Wednesday evening we'd line up for the weigh-in – 'we' being about twenty-five women, one man and Matthew, the fat little boy with no hair.

The course leader was a bright, chirpy lady called Barbara, who would begin each meeting by asking if we had any 'noooooo members' – sound familiar? The longer you spent in the programme, and (hopefully) the greater the weight loss, the more the eating plan opened out to include previously forbidden foods. At the beginning I came to regard a slice of brown bread or a digestive biscuit as the height of naughtiness. Eventually I was permitted the occasional Hula Hoop or maybe even a Birds Eye Supermousse.

Over the next few months I stuck diligently to the diet and went from being a fatty bum-bum to – well, not quite stick-thin but certainly noticeably thinner. Throughout my teens I managed to stay just about the right side of chubby, but then eventually lardiness descended again.

And I've been there ever since. I go through phases where I get myself together, lose a couple of stone, but I always seem to return to my solace, my pleasure, my pain – food.

I think it would be easier for me if I wasn't such a fusspot when it came to food. I'm a bit like one of those freaky eaters you used to see on BBC Three. I'm not quite as extreme, but there are foods that most people love that I don't enjoy at all. For instance, fish.

Why don't I like fish?

Because it smells of fish. Also because people sometimes serve it with the face still on. Eeeeeuwwww.

Actually I quite liked fish as a nipper, but I had a traumatic experience with a fish finger when I was about fourteen and I've never got over it. I bit into one and it didn't taste right. I looked inside and there was this big hard green cube of something very icky-looking, about an inch long and an inch wide, and I haven't been able to touch one since.

There were two occasions in the last few years when I ate very high-quality fish, and I still didn't take to it. One was when I was on a date with a guy I really liked, and he ordered this very tender black cod with miso. It was the restaurant's signature dish. So I tried a bit, to make myself look all cultured and open-minded, but it wasn't for me.

The other time I had some was when I was on BBC One's *Saturday Kitchen*, and the chef cooked up some curried haddock. I couldn't very well say no because I was on live TV, so I had a little. What I would say is, if you like curried haddock then you would probably have really *really* liked this one, because it was the most curryish haddocky thing I've ever tasted. Fortunately they then cut to an insert which meant I had a chance to swan around the studio, telling everyone how wonderful it was and insisting that all the crew try some. Not only did I manage to return with an empty plate, but I also looked generous – even selfless – in the process.

I don't mind egg as an ingredient, but I would never eat just an egg. I realise that makes me sound ridiculous, but then I used to dress up as a baby on TV so I'm already fairly ridiculous anyway.

Condiments are in general a bit too much for me. Mayonnaise is an offender. Brown sauce, HP Sauce – all that stuff. It's got too much flavour. The worst is vinegar. I can't get past the smell of it. It makes me sad.

Not a fan of quiche. Ditto pâté.

Chocolate liqueurs are the ultimate act of betrayal. Ask any seven-year-old who picks one out of the box, expecting something lovely and caramelly, and ends up with their throat on fire.

Game is too red and small.

Truffle makes me gag. It's overly savoury. And pungent.

But the worst offender – and this might shock you, because for many it's their most favourite food in the world – is cheese.

I don't get it. I just don't get it.

Here's the thing . . .

We were born with taste buds and the power of scent to save us from danger.

Hence . . .

'Oh, what's that smell? It's a burning curtain' = run from house fire.

'Oh, I just bit into some chicken and blood gushed out' = decline undercooked poultry.

But then – even though we consider ourselves no longer primitive beings – unfathomably . . .

'Oh, lovely, some rancid mouldy yellow hardened fatty congealed liquid from the belly of a cow that smells of week-old socks and tastes of death' = eat lots of it, as if nice.

Seriously, cheese is the most disgusting thing on earth, bar none. I hate cheese: the taste, the smell, the texture. And don't try none of that 'Oh, but this is *goat's* cheese' nonsense on me, either. It's cheese, okay? It's CHEESE.

When I sit opposite you in an Italian restaurant and the man comes round with the block of parmesan and the grater, a part of me dies inside.

In fact, cheese upsets me even more than when you read in the *Daily Mail* about a spinster getting bludgeoned to death by a crack-addled teenager and it turns out she only had 12p in her purse. That's how bad it is.

I think I can figure out how cheese was invented. It would have been back in the days when almost everyone was poor and starving and no one dared waste anything. Every part of every animal had to be utilised. Even the bull's testicles were probably used for snooker.

And I can accept that somebody might have come down one morning and it was a hot day and the milk had turned. And they would have thought 'Right, I'll chuck that out, then', but then maybe they got distracted by, I dunno, a man playing a lute or a woman with bubonic plague walking past or something.

And so the next day, when they suddenly remembered about the milk, they would have looked at it and seen that it had now solidified.

And they would have had a sniff and gone 'Pooh, well, that stinks to high heaven. I'm definitely getting rid of that.'

And then the village idiot, passing by, might have spotted this and gone, 'I'll have it'.

And the other person would have said, 'Nah, mate, you don't want this.'

And the idiot would have said, 'Look, there's a famine on. I haven't eaten for months. It's either that block of stale milky yuck or I'll have to eat the wife. It's literally come to that.'

And so cheese was born.

Fine. Needs must, any port in a storm, and what have you.

But that was then. In the twenty-first century we are supposed to be a civilised bunch. We've developed in all sorts of ways. Smints, bubble bath, pyramid-shaped teabags – this is progress. So there is no excuse for the over-abundance of cheese that contaminates the Western world. It's everywhere.

The worst, by the way, is on a plane. Never have I been offered so much cheese as when I am flying over the Atlantic. I'm already trapped in a giant can of farts and now you want to walk around the cabin shoving some Brie in my face?!

I was on one flight recently where the guy next to me was fast asleep and blew off so much it was honestly like being inside a shit. Then they woke him up, served him a cheese sandwich; he wolfed it down, nodded off again and farted the whole thing straight back out.

Cheese. Is. The Worst.

Anyway (breathe in, breathe out, it's all going to be all right), rather than go on about the food I don't like, I thought I'd do a Gallup Chart-style run-down of the food I *love*.

Please note, while this is correct at the time of publication, things do *change.* For instance, I didn't get into mushrooms until my mid-twenties. Shocking, I know.

I should also add, this was not easy to compile. There are plenty of lovely things that didn't make it in. For instance poppadoms, a quarter crispy aromatic duck with pancakes, macadamia nuts, chicken gyoza from Wagamama and melon (cantaloupe and watermelon, not so much honeydew). It took me a long time to whittle it down, but whittle it down I did. Here goes . . .

In at number 10, it's fruity chews. I'm not talking Chewits – I find they get too hard in winter. I'm talking Fruit-tella and – a little more subtle flavour-wise but gorgeously waxy – the Moam or Maom or Maoaoaoam or however it's spelt. Not the hard balls – no, thank you – but the sticks and the flat strips. Wonderful. If I had done nothing else on this earth but come up with the raspberry one, I would regard myself as someone who has greatly enriched the planet. So synthetic it makes plastic look like kale. But who cares?

At number 9, down three places, it's ice cream. Baskin Robbins do a sort of frozen white and milk chocolate mousse which is creamy heaven and of course you have to eat it all at once because it'll melt before you get home and then if you re-freeze it you'll get botulism. Probably. The Cornetto is also a trusty friend. Häagen-Dazs is fine, but – and I know this may shock you – I would probably opt for a slice of Viennetta first.

Some of my most favouritest ice creams have come and gone, sadly. In the late eighties I used to enjoy Wall's short-lived Magnifico. It was part of the Cornetto family, but a lot bigger, which of course is always better. There was briefly a spectacular ice-cream bar around the same time called Sky. Inside the shiny blue wrapper you found a rippled choc ice with vanilla ice cream (but not yellow vanilla, the white vanilla, as in a Mr Whippy, only it wasn't whippy) and then, in the middle of the ice cream, an Aero-like piece of chocolate. It's greatly missed, as is the epic Wall's Romantica, a cake-shaped dessert that the family could enjoy together. It had vanilla and butterscotch, with a biscuit base – and if it was a person I would have married it.*

A little note on all ice cream: do be careful to store it in its own section of the freezer. Even a delicious Mini Milk can be rendered unpalatable if it has been sitting for days next to something savoury. It still sort of

---

* Also they should bring back Zoom lollies. In fact, I will do a free advert for Zoom lollies if they bring them back. That's how much I miss them. And I don't normally even like banana-flavoured things, but the Zoom was divine.

tastes okay, but it's no fun if – when you lick it – you get the unapologetic aroma of those Waitrose Frozen Beer Battered Onion Rings.

Also, sometimes people try and make their own ice cream. My mum makes coffee ice cream. Don't get involved. I love my mum and I know she'll be reading this and I apologise for the public humiliation and ingratitude, but even a Nobbly Bobbly tastes better than almost any kind of home-made ice cream. I realise a generation of budding Mary Berrys will be closing this book in disgust and hurling it in the fireplace – but remember, that fireplace doesn't work. It just came with the house. You use radiators. Look, all I ask is that you know your place. Big companies and shops *make* ice cream; we *eat* ice cream. You know I'm right.

At number 8, it's satsumas. Or clementines. Or tangerines. Or mandarins. God knows I love them all, even if I still don't know which ones are which. They used to be a winter treat. The clocks would go back and I'd experience my usual bout of seasonal affective disorder, only to be momentarily jerked out of it by the sweet tang of this orange citrus delight. Nowadays they seem to be in the supermarket all year round, but then again it's freezing cold all year round these days too.

When I moved to LA, I was able to live out my dream of growing lemons, oranges, limes and key limes, but it was the satsuma that excited me most of all. My Californian pals thought little of it – it's like living in Surbiton and boasting about the cooking-apple tree in your garden – but I would walk past the satsuma tree every few days, wondering when it would be time to pick off one of the fruits. A couple of years earlier, while house-hunting, I had stopped with a couple of friends in the lush neighbourhood of Los Feliz and naughtily picked a tangerine from a tree in the street. It looked and smelled amazing, but it tasted so bitter I screamed out in shock.

In my own garden I waited until the man who occasionally works there (I don't want to say 'my gardener' because it makes me sound a bit grand but clearly he is my gardener) finally gave me the all-clear to tuck in. I studied the tree. The fruits were all a bit odd-looking, mutant-like, different shapes and sizes.

I picked a large satsuma, peeled it and looked inside to discover something much smaller than expected. Still, it looked nice. But it tasted of nothing at all. I mentioned it to not-my-gardener and he told me he could get a special powder that would go into the soil and give it flavour. Ask no questions, I thought. All I can say now is that the satsumas that grow in my garden are the loveliest I've ever tasted. This might be partly because of their freshness – I will walk past the tree, pick one and eat it straight away – but also, let's face it, the gardener has done something with his magic beans. It did make me wonder, though, if pretty much every tasty, correctly proportioned piece of fruit I've ever bought in a supermarket has been genetically modified to within an inch of its life and perhaps I should be concerned about what this is doing to me health-wise. But then, let's face it, given that I've just written 391 words on the pleasures of store-bought ice cream, it's not likely to be an apple that kills me.

Actually, that's not true. It's quite possible that an apple could indeed kill me – because I am allergic to them and have to carry an adrenaline-filled EpiPen at all times.

It's the strangest thing. I ate apples continually growing up. There's even a photo of me on my bike when I was about six, with a Sooty puppet in one hand and an apple in the other, because I refused to put it down. I loved apples. Everyone loves apples. Then one day I suddenly realised that I hadn't eaten an apple for about three years. I bit into one and my lips swelled up and my throat started to get really tight. Eventually it subsided, but my doctor told me I should avoid raw apples, pears, peaches, plums and nectarines from then on.

The happy end to the story is that I seem *not* to be allergic to apples that have been cooked. Basically, McDonald's Apple Pies are fine. In fact, one could argue, they are vital – otherwise how else will my body get the nourishing appley goodness it needs? Think about it.

Bovril is at number 7, though not in drink form. No beef tea for me, thank you. No, I like to spread it on buttered bread. I'm sure I'm not the only person who does that. It's weird, because I have – as you may have gathered by now – a depressingly bland palette, so I shouldn't entertain this foul-smelling, pooey-tasting black tar at all, but about once a year I crave it and I *must have it*. Almost like a pregnant woman who wakes up and decides she wants to eat a book or some hair.

It goes back to my childhood, I think. On Sunday nights I used to make Bovril sandwiches and eat them in bed while watching *That's Life!* If you haven't had Bovril on your bread, it basically tastes like Marmite. Though I've no time for Marmite at all. Ugh.

I should caution you, though, if you haven't yet tried Bovril sandwiches for yourself and, on reading this, are now tempted, Bovril is, if you use even slightly too much of it, *disgusting*. So do please take care. I will not be sympathetic to anyone who has ignored me and gone and over-Bovrilised.

At number 6, a surprise entry – it's vegetables. Yup, who would have thought it? 'But they're healthy?', I hear you cry. Yes, shock-horror. I really like veg. Not all veg, obviously. That would be too normal, too fully-functioning-adult of me. Aubergines are a no. I think it might be because of the name. They sound a bit up themselves, don't they? I've never had an avocado and I'm not about to start now. They look too slimy and apparently they're quite fattening, so I'm simply looking after myself. I'm not wild about cucumbers, and tomatoes (strictly a fruit but clearly a vegetable) are something I will only entertain within a Bolognese. But peas – petit pois especially– and broccoli and onions and mushrooms and haricots verts are a staple part of my diet. I even don't mind a legume, if truth be known. Oh, and sweetcorn, which is almost too nice to be classified as a vegetable really.

BTW, I include chips as a vegetable and I hereby announce my campaign to have them recognised as one of your five a day. Oh, sorry? Is a potato not a vegetable? Do you know something I don't?

Incidentally, you may be surprised to find that chips – most people's go-to naughty food – do not have their own placing in the top ten. Controversial perhaps, but there is a very well-thought-out reason for this . . .

If chips were as uniformly delicious as we know they can be, they would be right up there at the top of the chart, but I've probably eaten seven billion different varieties of chip already in my short fat life and the quality is simply too variable for inclusion. To clarify, you never quite know what you're going to get with a chip.

I don't cook chips at home. Never have done. So if I have chips, it's usually in a restaurant. But the chips in most restaurants – or at least most restaurants I've eaten in – have clearly come from the freezer. And there is not much to them bar the glory of the carb itself. They have little taste, barely any aroma save for the stale fat they've been drenched in, and nothing much really to commend them. Without ketchup (and I always eat mine without ketchup – see above *re* tomatoes) they are dry. And when I say dry, imagine I said the word slowly, in a Jamaican accent, for added emphasis. Drrrrrrry. Well, hang on, actually maybe don't imagine *I* did the accent – because that might get me into all sorts of trouble these days – but imagine a Jamaican person lazily saying the word 'dry'. That's how dry a bad chip can be.

Not quite sure that was worth the effort, if I'm being honest.

Anyway, chips can be glorious. There's a place in Manhattan called La Masseria, in the theatre district, and their chips are long, thin and soggy. There's not a crunch to be found, but they're amazing.

My mate Alfie has a restaurant in Bray that does these triple-cooked chips. He'll tell you a long story about how they take days to prepare. Whatever, it's worth it.

And sometimes – usually in America – the chips have a light seasoning on them, and then it all comes together.

Chip-shop chips are frequently phenomenal, though I much don't like it when you leave the chippy and your clothes stink of cooking oil. Not only is it not an especially pleasant fragrance, but you can't then tell people, 'Oh, we went to Whole Foods and grabbed a pomegranate salad', because everyone knows you don't leave Whole Foods reeking of saveloy.

But overall, as much as I love 'em, you can't trust a chip. They're too unpredictable. That is why they're not in the chart. Sorry.

Oh, you see now I'm conflicted. Tell you what, I'll cut you a deal. At number 6, then, it's Vegetables feat. Chips.

At number 5, why wait till Sunday? Yes, it's the roast dinner.

Now, when it comes to a roast, most people have a tendency to focus on the meat. I understand that. I have to say that personally I tend to find myself preoccupied by the other components of the roast. That said, I like my beef medium to well done, thinly sliced and as fat-free as possible. This will leave some of you aghast, as you gnaw through big, thick chunks of red meat, blood dripping down your chin. You caveman, you! I bet you then nod off afterwards in your chair, farting in front of the hieroglyphics.

Actually, this does point to one of my big food-related issues, which is that I do eat meat but I struggle with it. It's mainly just unease at the reality of eating a dead animal. It's clearly both morally wrong and also a bit yucky. I can deal with chicken, but then what are those black elastic bits of string in the breast? Veins? Arteries? Eek.

The happy medium, I have found, is – wherever possible – to eat processed meat that looks like it has had nothing to do with any living creature ever. All hail the dipper! Vive la goujon! M&S Chicken Teddies, anyone?

Look at me. Like everyone else, I've become preoccupied by the meat, when everyone knows the glory of the roast dinner is that it is a compendium of many different foods. Bored of the carrot? Here's a sprout. Not a sprout man? Have some cauliflower. The possibilities are endless.

I'm not sure if I care all that much for the heavily buttered vegetable, which is something I've noticed has been creeping into the roast in recent years. Yes, a small knob on a steaming pile of peas is quite nice, but these carrots that slide all over the plate are unwelcome. Ditto these purple carrots. Let's not get carried away.

Parsnips sometimes make an appearance in a Sunday roast, I've noticed. Now I would normally reserve the parsnip exclusively for the Christmas roast, but others are keener and serve them regularly. I'd say they are fine as long as you accept them for what they are – a sweet diversion – but on occasion, early on in a roast, I might in good faith bite into some parsnip under the impression that it's going to be a roast potato. *Then there are problems*, because nothing compares to a roast potato, especially a crunchy one smothered in gravy. However, if you approach a parsnip with the knowledge that it is a merely a parsnip, then it can provide a nice sabbatical from some of the more senior elements of the plate.

To elaborate on my earlier point, roast potatoes in gravy are godly. They really are of God. Thinking about it, maybe that's why we have them on a Sunday. And I don't say that lightly. I've no desire to offend anyone on religious grounds, but I'm going to stick my neck out on this one because, let's face it, life is essentially pretty arduous, all things considered, so anything that brightens the day should be celebrated. And crispy, fluffy, garlicky, slightly oniony roast potatoes are definitely up there with the very best that life has to offer. Sex is nice too, but you know what I mean.

I've no idea quite why roast potatoes are so good. There's something fun about mashed potatoes. Fried potatoes we've covered, though we haven't mentioned the glorious sautéed potato, but then you don't come across them very often, do you? No one ever says, 'But, Joan, we've already had sautéed potatoes twice this week'.

Jacket potatoes are another cause for celebration, if served with lashings of melting butter – so much butter, in fact, that the potato in question is now sky-high in fat and calories and you might as well have ordered the chips.

As for boiled potatoes, what a waste! You must promise me we will never ever speak of boiled potatoes again.

BTW, the Americans do not have a clue how to make roast potatoes. It might be to do with the types of potato that grow there. Or they might just be too busy eating French fries and hash browns and mashed potatoes. They love mashed potatoes there. I get that. Like I say, there's something fun about mashed potato. I think it's because you can sculpt with it.

And of course we haven't even got to Yorkshire pudding yet.

The Yorkshire pud is not only the finest thing to have come out of Yorkshire (with apologies to Michael Parkinson), it is also clearly the most delicious (apologies again to Michael Parkinson). Beating stuffing hands down, this edible spongy cushion of blandness – if done right – is the highlight of any roast.

'If I ruled the world,' sang Harry Secombe, 'every day would be the first day of spring.' Well, if I, Matt Lucas, ruled the world, before I even unpacked I would give Yorkshire pudding a knighthood.

'Arise, Sir Pudding of Yorkshire.'

You'd see photos in the newspaper of a giant Yorkshire pudding posing happily outside the palace with his wife and kids, and then you'd see the photos again two years later, when – disgraced and stripped of its title – it gets sent to prison for tax evasion.

In short, I could eat Yorkshire pudding every day. In fact, lose the word 'could' from that sentence and you have a pretty accurate impression of how I live my life.

At number 4 – we're hotting up now – it's spaghetti Bolognese.

No veal ragout or none of that poncey nonsense, though. Minced beef, onions, mushrooms, maybe carrots. Proper English Bolognese.

And tons of spaghetti. Way more, in fact, than you would ever dare to put in any other pasta dish.

I think that might be partly why I like spag bol, to be honest. It's because you can somehow just eat loads of it and no one bats an eyelid. The key is to boil far too much spaghetti – 'Oh, I didn't realise how much I'd put in, it really expands, doesn't it?' – and then you sort of *have* to finish it, or someone will mention all the starving children in the world and make you feel bad.

It's the same with barbecues. You'd never go to a restaurant and order three chicken legs, four sausages and two and a half burgers, but somehow when it's a barbecue, you don't think twice.

At number 3, down one place, it's crisps and their kind.

Now before you think, 'Hold on. Of all the foods in the world – the oysters, the steaks, the sushi, the dim sum – and this pillock declares crisps as his number three?', just stop and remember how *violated* you felt the last time someone stuck their hand into your bag of Ready Salted without asking.

Right. May I continue now?

Thank you.

We have family friends who used to run a sandwich stall and, as a child, whenever I went to their house I was filled with wonder – Golden Wonder, in fact – for at the top of the stairs was a stack of maybe twenty boxes of crisps, straight from the wholesaler. You know, the same ones you see in the newsagent, with a hole punched out of the middle and forty-eight little bags inside.

I would stop and gaze unsubtly at the vast assortment in front of me, before my similarly-sized friend Paul-Simon – the youngest son of the family – would say, 'Oh, you can have a pack, if you like.'

And I did. Every time. And I made sure to make several trips past those boxes. I don't muck about, me.

This was back in the days of Smith's Crisps, of KP and Golden Wonder. Before Walkers greedily gobbled up the British market. Not knocking Walkers, by the way. There is a lightness and a flavoursome tang to the Walkers crisp that few of their rivals could offer. I found Golden Wonder crisps a bit greasy, in truth. But still, there's room for all of us on this planet, no?

How I love the crunch of the crisp, the snap, the grind, the final moment of sogginess and then the swallow. And then, without a pause, straight back into the bag for another, almost as if each crisp is merely an hors d'oeuvre for the next. Afterwards the tip of the tongue makes its journey inside each tooth in search of residue. Sometimes a finger is required to help prise out the final stubborn lump.

I've loved crisps ever since I can remember. After swimming lessons on a Saturday morning, I would linger by the machine in the hope that Dad would give me 9p for a bag of Salt 'n' Shake.

When we went to visit Auntie Katie in Amersham – not a real aunt but my grandmother's closest friend, from Berlin – we would always be given a bag each of Hula Hoops – or Hooly Wops, as she called them. We'd stick a hoop on each finger before devouring the lot.

Yes, I know a Hula Hoop isn't strictly a crisp. That is why I also include 'their kind' – which means all of those other yummy snacks that gather impishly in the crisps aisle. Your Quavers, your Roysters, your POM-BEARs.

Speaking of which, where have Frisps gone?

And Tubes. Tubes were nice. They were like a Square Crisp that had curled up and gone to sleep.

And the good thing about all of these snacks is that you can call up the Chinese restaurant, order your takeaway, eat three or four packets while you wait for the food to arrive and still not spoil your appetite.

Actually I don't know if that is a good thing, come to think of it.

Crisps and their kind are great. They just are. Not Monster Munch Pickled Onion crisps, which are obnoxious, the stench lingering about the fingers for decades after the bag has been scoffed. And not salt 'n' vinegar either, because they hurt my mouth. And not prawn cocktail or Worcester sauce. And not cheese 'n' onion for reasons I have already made clear. But everything else.

All right. Basically roast chicken, beef and plain.

In at number 2, it's matzo ball soup.

If you're an Ashkenazi Jew or you live in New York, I doubt this entry will need any explanation. For those of you who are scratching your little gentile heads in confusion, matzo or matzah ball soup is basically chicken soup with dumplings in it. Not quite the same dumplings they have in those scrummy M&S chicken casseroles. You know, the ones that every other supermarket is now doing an inferior copy of. But not far off.

This kind of dumpling – the matzo ball (or *kneidel* as it is called in Yiddish, just to confuse you further) – is made from a mixture of matzo meal, eggs, water and, usually, chicken fat.

Oh blimey – you don't know what *matzo meal* is?

Okay, so when the Israelites left Egypt they were in a bit of a rush. They didn't have time for their bread dough to rise, so they baked it and ate it unleavened. And they called this bread matzo. I don't know why. But they did. And because of this, during the Passover, when the Jews remember their freedom from slavery, they eat this unleavened matzo bread.

If you've never tried it, it looks and tastes a bit like Jacob's Cream Crackers.

No, I'm not keen either. Plugs you right up. It's like having a cork.

Aaaaaanyway, when you've fashioned these dumplings, made from the matzo meal, you boil them and add them to chicken soup and they are very very nice indeed. And you can throw in some noodles, chicken, carrot, swede, even a little boiled onion if you like.

If you live in New York City, you probably know at least half a dozen places in your neighbourhood that serve it. If you live in the UK, it's a lot harder to find anywhere that does, so why not do what *I* do and go to my mum's house on a Friday night? She makes a lovely matzo ball soup. I'll WhatsApp you the address.

And at number 1 – yes, you've guessed it – it's Chocolate.

Where do I begin?

Chocolate is like eating a smile. One mouthful of it makes my face feel tingly. It is a tonic. It is my friend.

I'm so enamoured of chocolate that, when I'm in a newsagent, I do sometimes find it quite hard to decide which bar to buy. My base bar – my starting-off point – is a Twix. I know where I am with a Twix. I'm not wildly keen on the variations – the white chocolate ones or the dark chocolate – because I don't really think they're necessary. They had a chocolate orange Twix for a while that was monstrous. Just get me a Twix. It's fine. I'll never complain about a Twix.

Ooh, here's a bit of celeb gossip for you. David Walliams likes Maltesers a lot. When we toured we had them in the rider (that's the list of items that each venue is requested to prepare and have waiting for you in the dressing room). I remember being a little worried at the beginning of the tour – not that we might get fat; I was already fat, as you know – that we might get a little bored of Maltesers every night. Well, I certainly didn't. And I discovered all sorts of ways of eating them. There's your bog-standard chomp, when you just shove it in and eat it. Then there's the slow nibble, where you peck off all the chocolate and then enjoy the light honeycomb ball in its own right. My favourite, however, is to put it in my mouth and suck it. The chocolate goes first and then the honeycomb melts – slowly, initially, and then it disappears in a flash.

I rarely go for a Mars bar, funnily enough. It is – alongside the Twix, the KitKat, the Dairy Milk and *perhaps* a Snickers – definitely one of your base bars, but I find them a bit too sweet. If I do have a Mars, I like it straight from the fridge, but I won't often buy one.

Milky Ways changed a few years ago, didn't they, when the filling went from brown to white, but I have to say, it was for the better. Double

Deckers, on the other hand, have never recovered since they made the inside more chewy. I would not have done that. I still eat them, though, obviously.

The Snickers v. Topic debate is something that I've given a lot of thought to over the years. The Snickers is longer, obviously, but I counter that the Topic is slightly taller. They both have much to commend them. Really, it's down to the consumer. Do you want hazelnut or are you going to stay with the safe old peanut? If it's the former, you're Team Topic.

Revels are a charm, apart from the coffee one, obviously. If you eat a coffee one, it's so horrible you have to have another Revel immediately to take the taste away.

Celebrations are nice, especially at Christmas. The order in which Celebrations are eaten are as follows:

The Malteser one
Twix
Snickers
Galaxy Caramel
Galaxy
Milky Way
Mars

And you just leave the Bounty bars and then eventually someone will have them.

Here's some other chocolate-related observations . . .

Thorntons' chocolate is too sweet.

Nestlé chocolate is nice but sometimes a bit powdery. And the Caramac is too sweet for grown-ups – even me. I had two recently when filming *Doctor Who* and I struggled to get through them both. I did try and palm one off on Peter Capaldi, but he wasn't going anywhere near it.

M&S chocolate-covered popcorn is whatever comes after delicious. Doublicious?

Kinder and Lindt are like sweet, elderly foreign aunts who visit occasionally. Always nice to reacquaint yourself with, but you don't want them to stay too long.

Oh, while I'm on the subject of the foreign stuff, Cadbury's in South Africa do a bar called Tempo, which is nicer than anything we have in the UK. I know this because whenever I visit a country outside the UK, I always try and find a supermarket so that I can inspect the local chocolate. And often they have the same bars as we do in the UK, but they taste a bit different because they use different preservatives in the milk or something. This kind of stuff really excites me, so you can clearly tell how much I've got going on in my life.

Overall, one of the great things about chocolate, though, is that, while the expensive stuff is usually very nice, often the cheap stuff is also pretty good. Which makes sense, given that chocolate in the form of a bar was created as a way of giving it to the masses, who couldn't afford the expensive drink.

And that, my friends, in a candy-coated nutshell, is my favourite food: chocolate. From the humble Crunchie to the unimaginably decadent Ferrero Rocher, I fear it will be the death of me. I mean it.

But what a way to go.

TL;DR – I have the eating age of a nine-year-old.

Filming the video for Fat Les's *Vindaloo*, 1998

F – Frankie and Jimmy

Tufnell House Halls of Residence, Tufnell Park, London. August 1990.

'He's over there. Go and ask him,' said Jim, a friendly lad from Newcastle, as he led me over.

'Hi. Sorry. Can you do it for me?'

Frankie rolled his eyes and sighed. Then he suddenly became animated. 'Ooh, no, missus. What? No, stop. Nay, nay and thrice nay. Titter ye not!'

'That's *amazing.*'

Frankie nodded. I wasn't telling him anything he didn't know already.

'Matt does Jimmy Savile,' said Jim.

'Oh yes. I've heard about you. Go on then,' said Frankie.

I did my impression. Frankie smiled wearily. It was a fair likeness, whereas Frankie's was uncanny.

He had a presence about him, did Frankie – an air of assurance – and I didn't get the sense that he particularly wanted to engage in further conversation with me, so I thanked him and went to the bar, ordering my usual Snakebite.

A couple of days later I bumped into him again and made him do the voice once more. Groaning, he obliged. A day later I saw him again. This time he said no. He said it was all anybody wanted him to do and he'd had enough now. Also he said his name wasn't Frankie, it was David.

I was staying at the halls of residence with lots of other young aspiring actors, all of us members of the National Youth Theatre. I was thrilled to be there. Unlike the National Youth Music Theatre (who I had been to Edinburgh with when I was thirteen), the National Youth Theatre focused on plays, rather than musicals. Now I was sixteen and I was an ac-tor. I decided I would play Hamlet, Lear, maybe even all Three Witches at once. There would be no stopping me.

For the moment, however, I was better known as Jimmy.

Actually I met Jimmy Savile a few times. In 1982, when I was eight, I went to watch *Jim'll Fix It* being recorded, thanks to a family friend who did the lighting on the show. Savile walked around the audience during a recording break and behind the back row, where we were sitting. He cracked some gags and patted my head. I went to see the show being recorded again a few years later. This time I was one of the lucky kids who were allowed to sit on the side of the stage, and was delighted when I spotted myself during the end credits, waving.

I was on a train on the way back from Newcastle another time in 1997 with some comedians in the smoking carriage. Suddenly we were choking on cigar smoke, waves of it, and we started to joke loudly that Jimmy Savile must be onboard. A few minutes later I walked past and saw that he was indeed sitting behind us, wearing his sunglasses.

I went to say hello and he actually recognised me from *Shooting Stars*. We chatted for the next half-hour, with him telling me how he had spent eleven consecutive New Year's Eves with Margaret and Denis Thatcher, and how he had Prince Charles and the Queen Mother's phone numbers.

He asked me what I was up to and I said I was heading home to write an article for *The Guardian*. He told me I should come up with ten 'life questions' and send them to him. He would answer them and they could form the basis of the article.

'How would I reach you?' I asked.

'It's easy,' he said. 'Sir Jimmy Savile, Stoke Mandeville Hospital, Aylesbury.'

I never did send those questions off. I felt that if I did, *The Guardian* would expect an ironic, mocking piece. I thought Jimmy was just a sweet old man and I didn't want to do that to him.

During that first summer in the National Youth Theatre, I did a two-week induction course. A year later, in 1991, I was part of the NYT production of *The Tempest* – as a magician's assistant.

Now it should be said that this was not your normal production of *The Tempest*. The director had studied under Lindsay Kemp and had made some unconventional creative decisions. There would be a chorus of fifteen Ariels and a homoerotic subplot between Prospero and Ferdinand (that disgusted my father so much he walked out after twenty minutes).

'Magician's assistant' sounds fun. The reality was that we were stage-hands, bringing props on and offstage. The show had Japanese influences and we were dressed head to toe in black, *koken*-style. Even our faces were concealed by black fencing masks. The background was black too, so the idea was that when we carried the props (which were luminous), you wouldn't really be able to see us. It would look as if they were moving by themselves.

The director had been charming at my audition, but in rehearsals – while he flirted with his actors incessantly – he made no attempt to hide his disregard for us stagehands, bullying and berating us at every turn. The bright spot was that David Williams – that guy who did the Frankie Howerd impression the year before – was playing Trinculo. In each rehearsal he would come up with bits of comedy business and I would cry with laughter. I had no doubt he was going to be a huge star one day.

David and I bonded over a shared love of comedy, both old – Morecambe and Wise, Laurel and Hardy – and new – Vic Reeves and Bob Mortimer. The despotic director was also a Vic and Bob fan and set up a TV in the rehearsal rooms so that he and David could watch *Vic Reeves Big Night Out* videos during lunch breaks. I'd tag along with a couple of others and we'd all laugh together, then rehearsals would resume and the director would be screaming blue murder at us again.

During the run, when I wasn't rushing around bringing props on and offstage, I would watch David from the wings every night. He spoke the Shakespearean text so naturally. I loved his routine and wished it was me playing Stefano opposite him. I only had one real ambition at seventeen – to meet Vic and Bob in person. I added a second to my list – 'to perform with David Williams'.

As I mentioned earlier, David had begun doing open spots on the circuit with his friend Jason Bradbury. I told him about Sir Bernard and how I hoped to do some gigs at some point too. He hadn't seen me do much more than carry a broom and repeat my naff Jimmy Savile impression over and over, but nevertheless he humoured me, as I spoke about my ambitions.

On the last night of the run, one of the bigwigs in the NYT arranged for us to have a party at the exclusive Browns nightclub in Covent Garden. I had heard of the club's reputation for attracting A-listers and I wasn't disappointed. At one end of the bar sat Michael Thomas and David Rocastle, who both then played for my beloved Arsenal (and yes, *of course* I went over to speak to them). At the other end, was MC Hammer and his entourage. That night I swapped addresses with David Williams. I was pretty sure he was just being polite. I really didn't imagine I would hear from him.

To my surprise, a few weeks later, I received a friendly postcard suggesting we get together for a cuppa. Over the next few years David and I developed a firm friendship, going to comedy shows and taking in arthouse films and plays. David ate far more healthily than I did, and so we'd meet at an organic café called Food For Thought in Soho and sit on uncomfortable wicker chairs munching on flapjacks and drinking peppermint tea, talking about our favourite comedy routines.

Sometimes I'd also go and watch him and Jason perform. Getting to know David and Jason changed everything because it meant I actually had *friends who were comedians.* That was the bridge for me. Watching them onstage gave me heart that, if they could somehow gain access to the circuit, perhaps I could do the same.

A year later I put my money where my mouth was, and started to gig as Sir Bernard. David and Jason would come along to my gigs, just as I had been to see them.

Two years after that, in 1994, Dorian Crook took his stand-up act to the Edinburgh Fringe Festival and invited me to do a guest spot in the middle of the show.

Some of my friends came to visit, including David. He and Jason had given up the comedy club circuit – Jason having decided he wanted to focus on TV presenting work. David had been appearing on kids' TV and writing for Ant and Dec – or PJ and Duncan, as they were still known.

One evening David and I were sitting in the busy bar at the Pleasance when we both realised we had had the same thought – that next year it might be fun to come to Edinburgh and do a show together.

London, 1995. There were ten people in the audience at the first preview of *Sir Bernard Chumley is Dead . . . and Friends!* at the Jacksons Lane Theatre in Highgate. Four of them had rung the venue a few minutes prior to curtain up to ask whether we might delay starting the show as they were watching *EastEnders*. We agreed.

The show went surprisingly well, given our inexperience. My usual stand-up set formed the backbone of the show, though David had made it a great deal better by thoughtfully adding some actual jokes to it. It made sense to focus on Sir Bernard, as he was becoming an established name on the circuit. David would play my sidekick – a psychopathic stage manager called Tony Rodgers, who had recently escaped from prison – and a few other characters.

Tony was a terrible misogynist and would tell awful sexist gags, following them with his catchphrase 'Nice one, lads, sorry, women!' It remains, to this day, my favourite of all our catchphrases.

'What's the difference between a radical feminist and a bin-liner? A bin-liner gets taken out once a week! Nice one lads, sorry women!'

We noticed that we could get a laugh out of the actual joke, then another laugh at how out of touch the character supposedly was for telling it. This is something that Alan Partridge did, that Ricky Gervais would go on to do in *The Office* and that we did throughout *Little Britain* and *Come Fly with Me*, with offensive characters like

Marjorie Dawes and Omar Baba – hopefully you laughed both with and at them.

Tony and Sir Bernard spent much of the show berating my course mate from university, Tim Atack. Tim was a brilliant musician and I thought he'd be a perfect foil for us. He had a rock band and mentioned once that he sometimes liked to shock audiences by casually wearing a dress onstage. With this information, David and I created a character for him – Miss Dorothy Cant. Tim sat at his keyboard behind us, with his long ginger hair and bushy beard, in a slinky black number, gallantly weathering a constant tirade of abuse.

Tony and Sir Bernard would also reprimand Alison Bell, the fictional lesbian stage manager who was supposedly at the back of the auditorium getting lots of the lighting and sound cues wrong.

'I suggest you spend a little more time thinking about the show and a little less time thinking about Sandi Toksvig!' Tony would bark.

We were a little surprised in that first preview when the *actual* stage manager starting responding, over the sound system, in character. As the show was in full swing we just had to go with it.

That night we also introduced David's po-faced performance artist character Simon Geiger and appeared – for the first and last time – as a Christian male stripper act called ResErection. The less said, the better.

The following week we had a couple more previews, this time in a smaller room at the same venue. We had a larger audience and had hastily rewritten some of the parts of the show that didn't work. The gag rate was higher but the show was still unhinged. We didn't just make a mess on the stage during the performance; we also started the show with the stage already not very tidy, sometimes with plates of half-eaten food left out as if no one had quite bothered to clear them away. We enjoyed going into the auditorium before the show and leaving screwed-up flyers, empty crisps packets and cigarette stubs – just general mess. Sometimes we would arrive and find a twenty-foot-tall steel tower on wheels – the type that stagehands might climb to change a lamp – and we'd just leave it unhelpfully in the middle of the stage for the whole show. We loved the idea that the audience was watching a sad, neglected bottom-of-the-bill act.

As well as Sir Bernard and Tony Rodgers, David also played Erik Estrada, a stunt porn actor from Bristol, whose private parts would appear onscreen in place of those of the stars.

'Now you may not know my face, but you will recognise my hot, veiny, throbbing penis,' was his opening line.

I had one other character in the show – Lindsay De Paul, an ageing Northern copper who spoke slowly and sternly, telling a long, convoluted morality tale about a teenage offender on his beat.

'Young black lad – young lad, black – and he's got a gun.'

Pause.

'Young black lad – with a gun.'

A further pause, to let it sink in. Then . . .

'Black lad – with a gun – and he's young too.'

Another pause, to add weight, as Lindsay eyed the audience.

'Young black lad with a gun. He's young, he's got a gun AND he's black! Aye, I didn't tell you he were black! That changes everything, doesn't it?'

The routine rambled on without making much of a point, other than that the copper was a silly old racist. Sometimes the audience waited politely for the next character to come on, other times they cackled like mad at the idiocy of it, the repetition, the pointlessness.

As well as all this, we would improvise, sing cover versions and perform a couple of original numbers we'd written, humiliate audience members and even get a couple onstage to play musical chairs – though the game would drag on and on, as neither Sir Bernard nor Tony realised that there was the same number of chairs as contestants.

At the end of the show Sir Bernard would pompously declare the evening a great success and bring the director onto the stage. The director (played by David) proceeded to give Sir Bernard some notes on various lines he'd got wrong and things that needed improvement, before inviting the audience to join him and Sir Bernard for a bite to eat after the show – 'some nachos and burritos and guacamole and shit'.

We'd ask for a show of hands to see who was going to come along, and of course not everyone would put their hands up, so then we'd get very offended and interrogate people as to what else they had 'going on that's so bloody important'. We would moan and whinge, until we were sitting in sulky silence. Any audience members who then laughed would receive a burning glare or a stern rebuke from us, which would only make them laugh more. They were disgraced, like naughty children.

We played with the silence for a while, as if all was lost, until Chris slowly started to sing the Nik Kershaw song 'I Won't Let The Sun Go Down On Me', to rouse Sir Bernard and the rest of the audience and rescue the night, before we took our bows.

We took the show to the Edinburgh Festival. We had a midnight slot in the Wildman Room at the prestigious Assembly Rooms venue and played to small audiences on the first couple of nights. Then we had a night off and I remembered something the comedian Boothby Graffoe had apparently done, where he'd put a sign reading 'SOLD OUT' on the door even though he hadn't, and after that ticket sales had risen. I went down to the Assembly Rooms and did the same thing – even though we weren't even performing that night – and the following evening, and from then on, we played to big crowds. As anyone who has put on a show at the overpopulated Edinburgh Festival will tell you, you need to pull any trick you can to fill the room.

We were delighted to perform to large audiences but our late start time meant that there were always a few people in the audience who were steaming drunk. Our style became more abrasive, more robust, louder, scarier as we realised we needed to claim and dominate the space from the start. We were rarely stumped by a heckle, because we'd simply shout abuse at whoever dared to interrupt us. I had good practice at this – Sir Bernard was used to screaming at hecklers.

Sometimes people needed to use the toilet, but such was the design of the room that the only way to get there was to walk across the stage. We'd bully and humiliate anyone who left and then stop the show and interrogate them on their return – had they flushed the chain? Had they washed their hands? Was it number ones or number twos?

We were back in Edinburgh the following year, in 1996, with *Sir Bernard Chumley's Gangshow*. We returned to the Wildman Room, though this time at the slightly earlier slot of 10.30 p.m. Content-wise, it was more of the same. We brought back some characters and introduced new ones. We sold out without any fuss – thanks in part to our success the year before, but also because *Shooting Stars* was now on air – though not all of the critics were charmed. Ben Thompson, writing in *The Independent*, had championed Sir Bernard previously, but didn't enjoy our latest offering, praising Harry Hill at the beginning of his review before adding . . .

Matt Lucas – known and loved by millions as George Dawes, *Shooting Stars'* Great Big Baby – emerged cooing and blinking into the crazy, mixed-up, post-Vic & Bob world at about the same time as Hill, but while the latter's talent continues to ripen, the former's currently seems in danger of dying on the vine. Sir Bernard Chumley's Gangshow (Assembly) finds Lucas and his equally gifted sidekick David Walliams skateboarding headlong up an anal/misogynist cul-de-sac. Their relentless scabrosity has torn free from its satirical moorings and is now floating freely in the lower reaches of self-hatred.

I wouldn't necessarily disagree with what Thompson said, and many others have echoed him over the years, though we did also receive a five-star review in *The Scotsman* for the same show. It became clear, however, that we were starting to polarise people.

The next year, 1997, saw a third series of *Shooting Stars* and *Sir Bernard's Grand Tour*, an amalgamation of the best of our previous two shows, with some new bits added – for which David, Tim and I went round the country in a minibus.

We were joined by Paul Putner, who I had met on Ivor Dembina's comedy course five years earlier. Paul was planted in the audience. About half an hour in, he would identify himself as the manager of the theatre and explain that the language we were using was unacceptable. He did this so naturally that he would often get abuse from other audience members, angry at him for interrupting the show. Eventually Sir Bernard and co. were deemed to have gone too far, and Paul explained he would have to close the show down. At his instruction, the lights and sound went off and, now in darkness, the audience would hear a violent struggle taking place. Eventually the lights came back on to reveal me with my trousers down, wrestling – not with Paul, but with David, who was on his knees, in front of me. One night we got an even bigger laugh than usual, and it took me a few seconds to realise that this was because I was wearing boxer shorts – rather than my usual Y-fronts – and my penis had slipped right out. Whenever I recounted this story, Walliams used to enjoy adding that it had slightly brushed his lips, though I can confirm this is not true!

We enjoyed the challenge of taking the show on the road, away from the parochial, arty confines of London and the Edinburgh Fringe.

One night we played the Wedgewood Rooms in Portsmouth. When we arrived, our faces dropped. It felt more like a rock venue than a theatre, with a large bar dominating the room. Grumbling, we set up our props, wondering how on earth we were going to win over the crowd, who had begun to pile in to this cavernous venue.

The show began and, as we had predicted, the audience were indeed restless and distracted. People were chatting at the bar, and walking around. They wanted George Dawes – they didn't expect this. Even those who were paying attention seemed to be stony-faced.

We knew we had a good show. We didn't give up. We dug our heels in, did our best to engage with the crowd. We managed to get them going after about twenty minutes and ended up doing the best show of the whole tour. Afterwards, as we walked through the bar, carrying our props back to the minibus, those who had stayed behind for a drink cheered and applauded us.

David and I had been working together for two years. Just like I had done with my stand-up, we divided audiences. But that night was something different. Whereas before we had either delighted or disgusted audiences from the off, in Portsmouth we found ourselves in what seemed like an impossible situation and turned it into a triumph. I decided that night – if we kept going – that one day we were going to be the biggest act in the country.

Who wouldn't be proud of a son dressed like this?

G – Gay

We drove round and round and round. We shouldn't even have been there. I can't think why the gates to my secondary school were open in the early hours of that Saturday morning in the summer of 1993, but they were, and my best friend Jeremy – then nineteen years old, like me – had already driven the pair of us all over north-west London for most of the night while I tried to say the words. I was petrified. I knew that once I'd said them, I couldn't unsay them, and I didn't know what the consequences would be. As we left the school behind us, I took a deep breath and told him, in the most excruciatingly contrived, self-conscious way possible.

'Well, what I'm trying to say is . . . I guess if it was a choice between Michelle Pfeiffer and River Phoenix, I wouldn't mind either way.' I felt the blood drain from my face.

'You what?' said Jeremy. He wasn't outraged. He was confused.

'I like . . . both. '

'You're bisexual?'

'I think so.'

'Oh blimey, I thought it was going to be something *awful*.'

'You don't mind?'

'Why would I mind?'

I didn't have an answer prepared for that.

'You know my girlfriend's bisexual?'

I didn't, actually.

'Yeah.' Then he mentioned someone else I knew. And then someone else. 'And Ian's gay, well that's pretty obvious. And you've met his friend David, right?'

Jeremy then went on to list various friends and acquaintances who were gay or bisexual and my relief turned to silent disappointment, partly with myself for having wallowed in pointless fear, shame and self-hatred for so long, and partly with everyone else on this endless list for stealing my thunder.

I had thought I was the only gay in the village.

Actually – before we go any further – that was Walliams's line and the character of Dafydd was based on Walliams's suggestion, inspired by a guy we'd both met. But we wrote the sketches together and I identified greatly with the irony of both wanting to be accepted and feeling less special as soon I was.

I wasn't entirely honest with Jeremy. There's a quip people sometimes use: 'Bi now, gay later' (a play on 'Buy now, pay later'). I know a lot of gay folk who came out in a similarly timid way, one foot still firmly in the closet, keeping up the insurance payments just in case. It's partly why some gay people sneer when someone tells them they're bisexual. They don't believe them. I believe them. These days it's even harder to come out as bisexual, it seems.

Let's go back. Because this didn't begin when I was nineteen.

When I was seven, I was playing some records with my friend Michael. I remember looking at the cover of a Shakin' Stevens single.

'Girls are pretty but boys are handsome, don't you think?'

Years later, when I mentioned in an interview that Shakin' Stevens was my first crush, *The Sun* newspaper called it an 'Exclusive'. They wrote about how I ogled photos of the star, even printing the word '**ogled**' in bold letters. Can you ogle at seven? Surely at seven you're just looking? To add to my embarrassment, they called the man himself for a quote. Years later I saw him at Rob Brydon's birthday and hid in the corner.

Oh. Sorry, I completely forgot. Two clangs (Shaky and Rob).

As a child I was relatively sociable, despite losing my hair. 'Doctors and Nurses' and various inventive adaptations were often played, with both male and female friends, but this kind of thing died out by the time I was about six, I suspect, when it no longer felt right to be dropping your pants and showing off your willy . . . er . . . willy nilly.

I started at a single-sex secondary school in the autumn of 1985, aged eleven, where I encountered boys, over a thousand of them – tall, short, fat, thin, clever, stupid, ugly, handsome boys. In the changing room after swimming, I noticed some of my classmates had hair growing down there and the talk was often of girls. I didn't have any hair down there yet or any interest in girls. I assumed the two went hand in hand and so I patiently waited to develop into a man.

'Do you know what "gay" stands for?' went the joke. 'Got AIDS Yet?'

Oh, how we laughed. Being gay was *hilarious*. Because none of us were, obviously. Like I say, I didn't fancy girls *yet*, but I was going to. *Very soon*.

In the meantime, just as I had stolen money from the charity pencil case, I stole a look here and there at the prettiest of my schoolmates. The blond ones, usually. Or the ones with dark hair. Or brown hair. Or red. Everyone with short hair, basically. And, of course, the long-haired ones. And straight or curly hair. And the boy in the sixth form who looked a bit like Glenn Hoddle. And . . . well, you get the picture.

You couldn't stare too long though, or someone would call you gay. Actually, someone would probably call you that anyway. People at my school seemed to be obsessed with outing each other. You were never asked. You were simply informed. And it could happen at any time for any reason – the smallest hand gesture, the way you pronounced a certain word, the colour of your new duffel coat. And that was it – 'Gay. You're gay. You are actually gay,' said someone, and as far as everyone else was concerned, you were effectively now lead singer of The Communards.

One poor boy in our class was sweet and sensitive, though he didn't strike me as particularly effeminate. No matter – one day it was his turn to be labelled gay, and it stuck. He got it the worst of anyone. I watched as he struggled in vain to defend himself against the taunts before finally giving way to weary resignation. After a few months things started to calm down. Then one evening it was announced on the news that a celebrity with the same surname had died of AIDS and the next day it started all over again.

Yet even when the star publicly acknowledged he had AIDS, he didn't mention being gay. There were very few gay role models – camp, yes, but actually gay?

Well, there was Colin and Barry, the groundbreaking but ultimately anaemic gay couple in *EastEnders*. Their gay kiss supposedly revolted the nation, prompting people who wouldn't watch rubbish like *EastEnders* anyway to write in to the papers to say that while they wouldn't watch rubbish like *EastEnders* anyway, they were extremely offended and *definitely* wouldn't watch rubbish like *EastEnders* now.

There were the people on *Out on Tuesday*, a 'queer' lifestyle series on Channel 4, who talked about things like gender roles and gay adoption. I couldn't make head nor tail of it.

There was Derek Jarman, who made very arty, impenetrable films, which I also didn't understand.

There was miserable *Maurice*, from the Merchant Ivory film of the same name, which they'd show late at night on Channel 4. I'd video it and label it something else, like 'Royal Variety Performance 1987' or 'The Muppets Take Manhattan' – something I knew no one else in the house would watch – and I'd put it on for maybe twenty minutes after school, until my mum got home from work, and then watch the next twenty minutes the following day and so on. Eventually I'd panic and tape over it, and then six months later they'd show it again and I'd repeat the whole routine.

There was Jimmy Somerville in Bronski Beat and then The Communards, who sang beautifully, though also a bit like someone was standing on his balls.

There was Frankie Goes To Hollywood, but they were banned from the radio by DJ Mike Read.

There were those lesbians who invaded the BBC News studio and who Sue Lawley sat on.

There were the Pet Shop Boys and Freddie Mercury, but they weren't really 'out' out, and there was Elton John who was so gay he married a woman.

Oh, and there was this actor who had come out at the age of forty-nine, Ian McKellen – who actually came to talk at our school one lunchtime about his career, but also about his concerns over the proposed Section 28.

Prime Minister Thatcher, in a speech given at the annual Conservative Party Conference in 1987, said it was the 'plight of girls and boys' that worried her the most in eighties Britain. 'Children who need to be taught to respect traditional moral values are being taught that they have an inalienable right to be gay,' she declared, to applause. 'All of those children are being cheated of a sound start in life – yes, *cheated*.'

Thanks to Section 28 of the Local Government Act 1988 – the first anti-gay laws to be introduced into Britain in over a hundred years – local authorities were prohibited from 'promoting' 'homosexuality as a pretended family relationship'.

Eh? How the hell do you *promote* homosexuality? Is there a two-for-one offer?

Because of this, I only ever heard homosexuality mentioned once by a teacher in five years at Haberdashers' – in a biology class, in a dry reference to chromosomes.

Sex education finally took place in the sixth form, by which time I'd already left, so I've still never been formally taught it. Even if I had been, it would not have included homosexuality in any way, as teachers were terrified that they'd lose their job if they so much as mentioned its very existence.

When Thatcher died, I mourned the victims of HIV and AIDS who had perished through helpless ignorance on her watch.

And me? I just threw myself into acting, both on and offstage. I joined in conversations in which we lusted after half the girls' school, despite me not knowing who any of them were or understanding quite why they were supposedly so desirable. At fourteen, I had appeared in a West End play. I boasted about losing my virginity in the dressing room, conjuring up a juicy tale about a hot brunette in the company who seduced me in between a matinee and evening performance. The event supposedly took place on the dressing table and we were so busy humping that I burnt my bare buttock on the light bulb. There was no truth in this, of course, but I think I sold it.

And yet, I wasn't entirely bereft of action in that department.

During a sleepover I had been wrestling with a friend on my bed – innocent, routine, laddish stuff. After a few seconds he looked down at my shorts in shock.

'Um . . . you've wet yourself.'

I had not wet myself.

Neither of us said anything more about it, but his visits became more regular as we started to explore our feelings. At the beginning we'd linger downstairs and I would offer him a drink of water. I'd wait for as long as I could until finally I could take it no more.

'Not much on TV. Shall we go upstairs?'

Before long we gave up any pretence that we were meeting for any other reason. If I called him, or he called me, that meant the coast was clear. However, we never ever kissed or had any kind of penetrative sex – we just 'fooled around'. Remembering it now, I realise we didn't even hug, not once, but it was – for me – a formative relationship.

This continued for four years, until I was eighteen. We had a couple of close calls, towards the end, when we nearly got caught. One time my mum came home from work unexpectedly early while we were both naked in the bath.

Soaking, I dived into the bedroom. As I heard my mum come up the stairs, my heart must have been beating even louder than her footsteps. My clothes were strewn on the bathroom floor, so I pulled on the only clothes I could find at the bottom of the cupboard – some ancient stone-washed jeans and a jumper I had last worn when I was nine! Patches of water flashed through.

Mum appeared. I stammered that the boiler at my friend's house had broken and that he'd come over for a bath. I expected him to come out of the bathroom at that point, but instead he walked out of the toilet, fully clothed.

He said a sheepish hello to my mum and left quickly. I got in the bath, shaking, beads of sweat teeming down my forehead. Forty-five minutes later I summoned up the courage to go downstairs.

This was the moment I had been dreading. I had been rumbled. This was it. There would be tears, recriminations, ultimatums.

Except there wasn't. Nothing was mentioned.

Had she not noticed? Or did she prefer not to say anything?

Somehow we had got away with it.

The next time he came over, he asked me if I was gay. The tone was surprisingly accusatory, as if *I* might be but he definitely wasn't. I mumbled something about 'liking girls as well'. He said he thought we shouldn't do this anymore, that he found it 'embarrassing'.

We saw each other a few more times after that, but then it started to fizzle out, until it was no more. I hoped in vain that things might resume eventually, but they didn't. I missed our sexual contact, though it had not carried with it any emotional weight. I wasn't in love with him. I had never dared think of him as a boyfriend, nor him me. Such things simply didn't exist.

Back at school, like most sixteen-year-olds, I became utterly besotted with someone. Unlike most sixteen-year-olds, it wasn't a girl or a teacher; it was, of course, rather inconveniently one of the other boys.

I'd vaguely noticed him before. He wasn't in my year so I didn't have much contact with him. I don't think we'd ever even spoken. But one day, something in me suddenly understood that he was the most breathtaking thing I'd ever laid eyes on.

From that moment on I could barely focus on anything other than the object of my obsession. If I saw him in a certain part of the school at a certain time, I'd make a note and be sure to engineer a way to be at that same place at the same time the following week.

I was so dazzled and dazed by his appearance that I found I couldn't retain or summon his image. It would drive me mad. I'd linger in the PE corridor where some of the school photos were pinned up, because he appeared in one of them. I'd pretend I was just passing through, lest anyone thought I was staring.

I hated going to school, but suddenly I hated going home each night even more. The weekends, formerly two days of glorious freedom, now conspired to bring time to an aching halt. Holidays were interminable, denying me those precious glimpses.

At home I thought of nothing and no one else, though, as besotted as I was, when I lay in bed at night, I didn't sexualise him, beyond a kiss. I wanted him in my arms, but this wasn't cheap or sordid, this was a love above any other, a coupling that rendered all others ersatz and inconsequential.

I knew a few people who seemed to know him, but I barely spoke to him myself. I assume he knew my name, though I can't be sure. I doubt I occupied a moment of his thoughts, but he was perennially in mine and I couldn't tell a soul (and certainly not the boy himself).

I left Haberdashers' after my GCSEs. I explained to everyone that I didn't like the teachers there, didn't like the other boys, wasn't going to get into Oxford or Cambridge anyway, so I might as well go somewhere else and take the A levels I wanted to take, like Theatre Studies and Media Studies, rather than the more academic ones I'd be obliged to take at Habs.

All of this was true, but I also knew in my heart that I simply couldn't continue in that environment. It was too intense for me, too painful. I was just too far away from what I needed, and from what so many of my classmates appeared to have. I had accepted that I would probably never have a boyfriend, never know real love, but being tormented on a daily basis by this almost ghostly apparition of unattainable beauty was making me feel more and more helpless, more dejected.

Weald College in Harrow. The autumn of 1990. A new start.

Thoughts of my crush remained; yes, they weren't going anywhere fast, the desire always there. We had mutual friends. I would see him around. I would buzz, I would jolt, I might even dare to talk to him for a few seconds, before withdrawing to comprehend, digest, assess. A hit and run. It would be a few years before the intense desire would fade, before I could say, hand on broken heart, that it no longer pained me to think about him.

At college I was able to express myself in ways that hadn't been available to me in the stuffy environment of my private school. The tutors at college dispensed with formality. No one called me Lucas. No one bellowed. They taught, but also listened. We appeared to connect on a more equal footing.

My lovely drama teacher Janet Harrison inspired the class daily and offered an alternative, more broadminded response to the world. One day she was discussing the virtues of a performance given by Derek Jacobi.

'He's gay, you know,' I said.

'Yes. Isn't it *glorious*?' she replied – the first time I had ever heard anyone express such a view.

Another episode sticks in the mind and no one comes out of it very well.

Our student union had invited a gay activist to speak at the college. Attendance at the talk was optional and, short of the whole college turning up, I doubt I would have gone along, despite being the target audience, as I would have presumed – correctly, I would say, this being Harrow in 1990 – that anyone's presence there would have been used as evidence that they were gay themselves.

But as soon as the posters and leaflets started appearing on campus, they were being rounded up by Harry, an indecently handsome, confident student in the year above me.

Harry was one of those guys who may have only been a year or two older than me, but who had the appearance and authority of someone ten or twenty years older. You know those guys? There's always a few of them knocking about. Taller, broader, smarter, sportier; hair longer and more flickier. We were still boys long after they became men. Like Kiefer Sutherland in *Stand by Me*. Only seventeen when he played the role, apparently, but he still scares the shit out of me today.

Incidentally, while we're talking about *Stand by Me*, watching that film shortly after it came out on video I found myself open-mouthed at the sight of River Phoenix. The night after I watched it, I had my first ever wet dream.

By the way I was thirteen and he was about fifteen or sixteen, so don't get all busy.

Anyway, Harry was a lad. The girls loved him. The blokes wanted to be him. In my first term at college I grew excited because Harry and his pals announced they were going to direct a production of *The Rocky Horror Show*. Harry had tipped me the wink that there'd probably be a part in it for me. Harry held auditions but the show never happened. He later admitted that he'd only done it to meet the new girls. We all thought this was funny. Like I say, Harry was a lad.

And Harry had decided that we weren't going to have a gay speaker at Weald College – not if he had anything to do with it. During the morning break he took the pile of posters and leaflets he'd collected, marched to the field by the canteen and dumped them in a large wire bin. He then asked for a light.

By now a twenty-a-day man, I proudly pulled out my prize bronze Zippo lighter and handed it to him. He set fire to the contents of the bin.

The talk was cancelled.

I participated in the ceremonial burning because I was sure that if people saw me there, then no one would think I was gay. I handed Harry the lighter because I fancied the pants off him.

I don't think anyone at college knew I fancied Harry, but I was known for a few other things – for doing Chris Eubank impressions, for boasting insufferably about my acting prowess and for my obsession with Queen.

When Freddie Mercury died, my mum couldn't understand why I was inconsolable.

'But he was a homosexual,' she said, not unsympathetic but mystified that I should even be surprised at the occasion – and the inevitability – of his passing.

The press pored over every detail of his life and death for days. I remember an *Evening Standard* editorial, not twenty-four hours after he had gone, which cited his decadence and debauchery as the reasons for his demise. Cause and effect. Crime and punishment.

I was beside myself with grief and grew deeply depressed. What hope was there for me? I could spend my days alone, celibate, loveless – or come out, be shunned, catch the plague, die.

Perhaps if I settled down, got married, had kids, maybe these feelings would go away?

No. I knew they wouldn't. They were just too powerful, too ingrained.

A problem shared is a problem solved, they say. I decided that the time had come to tell someone my dreaded secret.

I had set myself the task of 'coming out' to at least one person before I was eighteen. I missed my deadline by a few months, but at nineteen, I decided to confide in my friend Claire. Like my other friend Alex, we had bonded over a shared love of Reeves and Mortimer. She'd become my sidekick, always on hand to offer a loud, generous cackle at my daft antics.

I went over to her house, took a deep breath and told her I was bisexual. She said she had figured that might be the case. She was wonderful. I knew she would be.

After I told Claire, I told Jeremy, as recounted at the beginning of this chapter. I then told Alex, but this time I came out not as bisexual but as 'probably gay'. I was pretty sure Alex didn't have a problem with gay people. He'd fallen in love with the Billy Bragg song 'Sexuality' and we'd sung it often together, mimicking Bragg's unmistakable Essex drawl. He was great about it, said he hadn't guessed, actually, but that it didn't change a thing.

So I'd now told Claire, Jeremy and Alex. The only close friend I had yet to tell was another college pal, Nick.

Nick was one of the straightest people I had ever met. He was obsessed with Julia Roberts, Sylvester Stallone and *Die Hard*. He had made some offhand comments about gay people before – as had we all, in fairness – and I had convinced myself that Nick meant it. I was dreading telling him. Eventually I did so. He wanted to know when I was going to tell Alex or Jeremy or Claire. I confessed that they'd already known for a while. So Nick *was* horrified when I came out, though not because I was gay – he was actually incedibly supportive – but because he was the last to know. I love you, Nick.

With college over, I took my year off to work at Chelsea Sportsland and do some stand-up. After gigs I should have been taking myself off to gay bars, but I just wasn't ready.

'It will all happen at university,' I told myself. I knew there would be some gays there because a squeaky-voiced beanpole who worked in the office at Chelsea, and who had recently graduated, had mentioned, with a shudder, 'Oh yeah, university, mate – there's queers an' all sorts.'

Soon after my arrival at Bristol University in 1993 I read up on GLIBSOC – the Gay, Lesbian Including Bisexual Society. On a dark, wet, windy autumn night, with great trepidation, I showered, dressed and began the walk from my lodgings to Frogmore Street, home of the Queen's Shilling pub, where we were to meet for a drink before heading on to a club.

Being gay, Jewish *and* nervous, I took so long in getting ready that I was running very late. And – being gay, Jewish and useless – I had no idea where Frogmore Street was.

What's that? Why didn't I look it up on my phone? BECAUSE IT WAS 1993. We didn't have mobile phones. My dad had a car phone, which cost about a million pounds a minute to use and cut off after one syllable.

'Excuse me, do you know where Frogmore Street is?'

'It's up there, mate.'

'Thanks,' I said, scurrying off into the night.

The voice hollered after me, in its thick West Country tones. 'Oi! What you going up there for? There's queers up there! It's a queer place. You queer then?'

And the award for Shortest Ever Visit To A Pub goes to . . .

I walked in. There were maybe two or three shaven-headed men in there. I couldn't see any students. I ordered a Diet Coke, drank it *very* quickly, burped and left.

A couple of weeks later, GLIBSOC met again – at the Student Union. I had no excuse for getting lost on the way this time because I was living right next door.

There were a few of us staring at the floor. I knew one guy, Josh, who was in the year above me. His boyfriend Gideon was gorgeous, but taken! Apart from that, there was a *girl* there who I actually fancied a bit but I didn't bother trying to do anything about that.

Okay, so let's clarify. I was gay. I wasn't doing gay touching things with anyone at that time, but I was gay, and was now telling people I was gay or if I trusted them a bit less, bisexual.

So I was as surprised as you might be when, shortly after coming out, I then started to develop crushes on a couple of girls on my course. They both had boyfriends and I doubt I would have done anything about it even if they hadn't, but when I tell people this, they ask me if I am gay or bisexual.

And I've thought about it and I think the answer is this . . .

I'm 100 per cent gay. And also maybe about 20 per cent straight *as well*. I kissed a girl in a club once and I definitely liked it, but I kind of fancied her mate a bit more. And her mate was a bloke.

I've never slept with a woman, but I think I might quite like to at some point. Not just sleep with a woman, obviously. That sounds a bit mechanical. But talking of mechanics, I've no idea if the equipment will work. So, in a nutshell, unlike some of my gay or indeed straight friends, the idea of intimacy with a member of the opposite sex does not make me feel icky at all.

In fact, when someone (who themselves *hadn't* swum the Channel) recently pointed out to me that David Walliams had and therefore demanded to know what I was going to do for charity, I posited the idea of auctioning off my heterosexual virginity. And I was only half-joking.

Moooooooooooooooooving on . . . at university I started to assert myself. If anyone wanted to know, I was gay or bisexual, THANK YOU VERY MUCH, and if you had a problem with that, that was YOUR PROBLEM.

Yes, I became one of those. Among my course mates and the other folk in my halls of residence, that is. Elsewhere I remained cagey. It still felt like a risk to talk about it with someone you didn't know.

And nothing was more terrifying than shuffling into the news-agents and buying the *Gay Times*. I wanted to buy a copy so desperately, but it took me a long time to summon up the courage to do so. While I was at university *Attitude* magazine launched, and I found that a little easier to grab, having convinced myself that it was less overt, that the newsagent probably didn't know what it was about. Even so, I'd take it from the top shelf – where it sat next to the hardcore porn mags – and put it on the counter very quickly. I'd then dump loads of other things on top of it – *Shoot* magazine, the *TV Times*, a Yorkie, some Tooty Frooties – as if to suggest to the person on the till that this was something I just *happened* to be buying, rather than the main purpose of my visit.

Behind our halls of residence was a video rental shop which had an extensive selection of arthouse films and even a small but dedicated Gay and Lesbian section. On a Saturday night, while most normal students were in the pub, I would dart in, grab anything and check out as speed-ily as possible.

One film that made a big impact on me was Ron Peck and Paul Hallam's *Nighthawks* – the first truly gay British film, from 1978, in which people were out and, generally, matter-of-fact about it. I had read a lot about *Nighthawks* but when I finally saw it I was left quite down-hearted. This was no romantic coming-out movie, with handsome boys who find each other. The Everyman lead character wearily trawls the clubs for love and finds only sex. Away from the clubs, in the school where he teaches, he faces prejudice. He seems to be so lonely, so drained. There is no pot of gold at the end of his rainbow.

A few years later I returned to the film and saw it from a different angle, having, by then, become a regular at the clubs myself. I was refreshed by its lack of glamour, its mundaneness, its truth and its grim humour. The characters were real, just like the type of people I would come across, not only on the gay scene, but in life. I recommend it to everyone, not just as a seminal piece of gay drama, but as a remarkable piece of social realism. *Nighthawks* is barely known, yet I really think it's one of the greatest British films of the seventies.

Oh, by the way, this is NOT the same *Nighthawks* that stars a young Sylvester Stallone. Though that, I'm sure, also has its pleasures.

So while I was coming out of the closet, reading gay magazines, watching gay films, it would be a few years before I went to gay clubs or – God forbid – *actually met someone.*

You see, I had endured over a decade of inquisition and mockery with regards to my appearance. My baldness and my belly had made me so self-conscious about the way I looked that it did not occur to me that anyone in their right mind would want to date me.

I was also terrified that my family would freak out if I told them I was gay. They loved me and I loved them, but I had never ever heard the word 'gay' said in my house growing up. Queer, yes. Poof, yes. Faggot – my brother would use that one liberally. But not 'gay'. Never 'gay'.

Even my grandmother, who had left Berlin just before the war and who was what you would call in those days 'an intellectual', who loved opera and theatre and art, who doted on me, showered me with praise and taught me so much, found homosexuality deeply distasteful. I remember watching a news broadcast with her, which showed Ian McKellen delivering a petition about gay rights to Downing Street. She was very critical of him for 'taking up John Major's valuable time'. She was a kind, compassionate, wise woman, who I adored, but she was born at the beginning of the last century and it was one issue on which she was intransigent.

I'm not trying to paint my family as villains. They loved and supported me. I'm just making the point that that was how it was back then, not just for me, but for pretty much all of my gay friends. It was generational and societal. The best you could hope for was that someone would say, 'I don't mind what people get up to in the privacy of their own home just as long as they don't shove it down our throats.' That was, at the time, considered a liberal, *open-minded* response.

I could not tell them.

By the time I reached my early twenties I wanted to go to gay bars, to make friends, maybe even to meet that special someone, but I had become well known enough as George Dawes that there was a good likelihood that if I did, it might end up in the newspaper.

And so, maintaining that I must sacrifice my own happiness to protect my family, I just went about my life. I was sort of out – yes – but I told my friends I was too busy to meet anyone. I focused on my stand-up, then *Shooting Stars*, then my writing with Walliams. I occasionally had crushes – usually on straight guys because I didn't know that many gay ones – but I kept them to myself.

When I was twenty-two, my father died, suddenly. In amongst the enormous shock and grief was sadness that I had never been able to bring myself to tell him that I was gay. We were close on so many other levels, but I had remembered clearly, only a few years before, sitting in traffic in the back of the car while he moaned about shirtlifters. And it wasn't the only time.

On a more recent occasion, however, he had mentioned something about me hopefully bringing someone home one day – 'a girl, a boy, whatever'. Had someone said something? Had he finally mellowed?

There was to be more loss. Two years after my father died, my grandma passed away too. It was less of a shock and more of a relief for us all when she finally left us. She had been so smart, so proud, but at eighty-seven her mobility and short-term memory were rapidly and irreversibly failing her.

I knew that I had to wait for my grandmother to die before I could tell my family I was gay. We were all still reeling from my father's death and we had been busy looking after grandma. When she died, in January 1999, I decided I would give it about six months and then I would sit my mum down and come out.

But I was struggling – really struggling – and smoking loads of weed to try and blot out the pain of losing my father, my fears of being rejected by my family, and also I had something new to contend with – being in the spotlight. It wasn't quite as I'd imagined it – being pinched, poked and prodded by people, being followed in the street, being gossiped about.

I started to see a counsellor. We talked about all aspects of my life, my sense of failure – despite being already pretty successful, my grief for my father, my weight issues and my worries about what my family would think about me being gay.

'Why do you need to tell your mum?' the counsellor asked.

It seemed like a strange question to me. I figured that some people might be able to lead a double life, but in my position that would be trickier – and anyway, even if I met people secretly, I would not have been able to bring them back to mine. A few weeks earlier the family home had been sold. I had moved with my brother (who was literally homophobic, in that he seemed to have a *fear* of homosexuals) into a rented house in East Finchley. My life had become a lot busier since *Shooting Stars* had hit the airwaves. I was away a lot with work and also had a lot of fan mail. So as well as living with me, my brother was working as my assistant.

Despite our professional relationship, we still rowed sometimes, like most brothers do, and one night we were bickering away. He was a huge hip-hop fan and was singing the praises of a particular track. I had moaned that the lyrics were misogynist and homophobic. He cited his disapproval of the kind of music I listened to – stuff with a tune, that sort of thing – and I had started to extol the virtues of Queen and Freddie Mercury. The argument became more heated than usual and as he went to leave the room, he muttered to himself . . . 'Queer lover!'

'No,' I said. 'Just queer.'

He wasn't the only one surprised. I pretty much astonished myself with the response.

There was a pause. Then he looked at me, and started to laugh. Not a nasty laugh, more one of congratulation at having been fooled for a moment.

'I'm actually not joking. I'm gay.'

'Don't be stupid.'

'No, I'm gay.'

'This is a wind-up.'

'Nope. I swear on my life. I'm gay.'

A second for this to register, then 'Oh *great!*'

Just to be clear, this wasn't the 'oh *great*' someone says when they've just found out there's going to be a new series of *Curb Your Enthusiasm* or even the 'oh *great*' you fake when a nose-picking nine-year-old tells you they've made you some banana bread.

No, this was exactly the sort of 'oh *great*' that you say when you open the washing machine and realise you've put in all the coloureds with the whites.

Howard wasn't happy. At all. Nor was he especially convinced. Had I tried it with a woman? No? Ah, well, that was the problem. He told me he and his friends were going to hire me a prostitute.

'Great,' I replied. 'Can you get me one with nice pecs?'

Over the coming weeks my brother did his best to understand and accept what I had told him about myself, the content of which went against every fibre of his being. Having once told me with conviction (though I assume it's not something he learned first hand) that 'one man can't find love in another man's hairy arsehole', he had a bit of a journey to go on. To give him his due, we reached a sort of entente, which largely involved neither of us mentioning it too often, though he did make the occasional enquiry . . .

'So, do you, like, fancy David Beckham, then?'

'*Everyone* fancies David Beckham,' I replied. 'That would not be an indicator of whether someone is gay or not.'

On the face of it, things went back to normality for a bit, especially as Howard saw I was still the same twerp I'd always been, gay or not. For me, though, it was a major relief to stop having to pretend I was obsessed with girls. That kind of thing's exhausting.

The next thing I had to do was tell Mum.

A few months had passed since Grandma's death. Her house was going on the market and I had agreed to go there with Mum to help clear out some of Grandma's belongings. I knew it would be an emotional day, but rightly or wrongly I also knew that I couldn't keep my secret any longer.

After a few sombre hours, we left Grandma's house. Mum dropped me home and I asked her in. I made her some coffee, and brought it into the little dining room. I said I had something to tell her.

'. . . and that is that . . . I am gay. Oh wow. I can't believe I've actually just said those words out loud.'

Unlike my brother, there was no laughter, and no anger either, only tears. She was devastated. She said there would be no wedding, no grandchildren and no chance of me ever being happy. I would not find work. I would not meet anyone. And my friends – well, they would not react well.

I sighed – for her, not for me. 'They already know. All of them. Have done for years. Even Howard knows.'

More tears, including some from me.

'It was my fault. I smothered you.'

'No, no. It was no one's fault. It's not a fault.'

She did smother me, though. She is, after all, a Jewish mother. She wouldn't be doing her job without a bit of smothering.

'Didn't you know? I thought you would have figured it out. Lots of actors are gay. And I haven't exactly had a ton of girlfriends.'

She shook her head. 'Well, Rabbi Leigh doesn't agree with it *at all*.'

I helped her to the car. She seemed so racked with grief I wondered how she would even make it home. As she left, I composed myself, then called my stepdad.

'Mum and I had a bit of a . . . a tough conversation. She might be a bit upset. I'm fine and she will be. But just letting you know.'

That night I called up Ian, an old friend of mine, and asked him if I could come with him to the gay club he had been telling me about, Popstarz.

I was twenty-five and finally I was out.

And so it began.

I would go with Ian to Popstarz on a Friday night and Heaven on a Saturday night.

And on a Monday night.

And on a Wednesday night.

I became a fixture in the clubs, chatting with everyone – well, almost everyone. It was never easy to talk to someone I actually fancied, of course. I still doubted anyone would find me attractive, so I just tried to be entertaining instead.

And then one Saturday night, I was dancing upstairs in Heaven when a bunch of drunken teenagers tumbled and landed on me, clearly intentionally. As they helped me to my feet, one of them said, 'You're George Dawes, aren't you?'

I nodded, brushing myself down.

'It's our friend Sam's first time here. He's trying to snog as many boys as possible and he wonders if he can snog you.'

I rolled my eyes, then looked up to catch sight of an exquisitely pretty, dark-haired young boy. He can't have been much older than eighteen or nineteen.

'Um. I'll think about it. Is that okay?'

And I rushed over to Ian to tell him the whole thing.

'Well? What's the problem? He's beautiful.'

'The problem is that I've never kissed anyone. I don't have a bloody clue what to do.'

'WHAT?! You're twenty-five and you've never kissed anyone?'

'I've touched a dick.'

Ian sighed. 'Well?'

'Well what?'

'Are you going to kiss him? I don't think he's going to wait all night.'

'I probably should, shouldn't I?'

'I think you should, yes,' said Ian, still incredulous.

I gulped and popped a stick of Wrigley's into my mouth.

'Well, you can take that out of your mouth for a start.'

I walked gingerly over to the boy. He wasn't impressed by the wait.

'All right. I'll kiss you, then. If you still want,' I said, matter-of-factly.

'Yeah, all right.'

He was sitting down. I was standing up. There was no room on the packed bench for me to join him.

'Do you want to . . . get up . . . for this kiss?' I asked.

'Nah.'

And we kissed, his tongue flapping around the inside of my mouth, like the desperate, final throes of a trout on the deck. I didn't feel anything in particular. My heart didn't soar. Maybe I was just concentrating too much. After a while I put a merciful end to the whole thing.

'You really ought to give up smoking, you know,' I chided him. I'd recently given up myself and had become the most insufferable bore about it.

We arranged to go and see The Bluetones in concert. I spent the two weeks prior to the gig completely over-thinking things. Was it a date? Were we now lovers? Eventually I sent him a ridiculous text message a few hours beforehand, saying he was welcome to stay over afterwards, if he wanted. He didn't reply. I went to the concert alone, this time chiding myself over my impatience.

Well, I say 'impatience'. I hadn't had any sexual contact since I was eighteen. It had been seven years. I wanted to meet someone and fall in love and all that, of course, but by now I mainly just really really wanted to have sex.

Eventually I did, a few weeks later, with a lad I spotted dancing, topless. He was a fan, and was happy to chat with me. We ended up back at mine. He wanted to . . . um . . . go the whole way, but I was a bit old-fashioned, and so we did some other things instead, before he scampered off to catch the night bus. I saw him around a few times after that, but he just wanted to be friends. I was gutted, but at least I had finally broken my duck.

I still had to overcome one obstacle, though – my conviction that I wasn't good enough for any of the guys I took a shine to. I wasn't alone in my dysfunction. I soon learned that there was a lot of arrested development out there on the gay scene. It's hard enough for young LGBTQ+ folk these days, but back then so few of us were out to our families or at work, and even fewer had felt able to come out at school, so we hadn't dated in our teens like our straight classmates, we hadn't made the mistakes. By the time we came out, we might have been adults, but it was like a playground out there.

One of the things I noticed was how many gay men criticised other gay men for being effeminate, how they described themselves as 'straight-acting' as if it was some great virtue. I could understand how guys might be more physically attracted to other guys who were more masculine, but I could not see how this translated into the ritual social belittlement and estrangement of more effeminate men. After all, we all knew that same-sex attraction was not a choice. If it had been, none of us would have chosen it, in the face of all the abuse we suffered. Therefore why couldn't people also see that effeminacy wasn't necessarily a choice either?

There were two large clubs to go to in the West End on a Saturday night – Heaven and G-A-Y. The former was the biggest gay club in Europe and, in theory, more sophisticated, offering different floors and different styles of music on each – club, R'n'B, indie etc. – while G-A-Y was at the Astoria, with one huge room blaring out cheesy pop music. At G-A-Y the joke was that everyone was either fifteen or seventy-two. The clientele at Heaven seemed positively cosmopolitan in comparison.

I'd go to Popstarz on a Friday night, but Heaven was my place, my local. I spent my evenings in the VIP Room – not through snobbery but because I preferred to sit and chat rather than to dance. I didn't chat all night, though. Every so often my friends and I would do a circuit of the whole club. And it wasn't just a bunch of pretty boys. There were all types in there – posh chaps visiting from the country, gangsters, geeks, tourists – all coexisting (relatively) peacefully.

I was pretty surprised to see such a variety of types, shapes and sizes. And I was also surprised to discover that gay relationships came in many different forms too.

Plenty of people had partners significantly older or younger than them, and often those partnerships were happy and healthy.

I learned, too, about open relationships. There were sometimes rules about using protection outside the relationship, or only doing certain things with other people.

Others were in partnerships that had strong dominant and submissive overtones, and explored the idea of ownership and obligation. One of my friends used to go to a bondage class at night school and would relay to me how happy he was that he had learned a new knot, but how miffed he was that his partner was the one who always wanted to be in control.

I met people who were in polyamorous unions. It seemed utopian on the face of it, but they were often burdened by vast numbers of rules and regulations, with rosters determining who slept with who, on what night, in which bed, and who would do the washing up while the other two were getting jiggy. I was exhausted just hearing about it.

Despite what you may read in the papers, however, the majority of those who weren't single were in much more conventional relationships, ones that mirrored those of their straight friends.

Yet this was a world in which there was no gay marriage, no civil partnership, no equal age of consent even. In fact, any attempt by a gay couple to adopt children was assumed by many to be a front for something far more sinister.

So it was left to us as a community to define for ourselves what a relationship was. And, years on, even with societal acceptance, I believe this is still the case. I noticed recently there was a furore in the papers about a high-profile gay couple who, it turns out, are in a happy, consensual open relationship, but who have decided that that is their business and nobody else's. The press had a field day, calling them hypocrites and demanding the right – denied by the courts – to 'expose' them. Expose them for what? For not conforming to what some straight columnist has decided is a permissible relationship?

For years we have not been allowed to be. We have had to forge our own pathways to express and explore a love that the majority have deemed unnatural and undesirable.

Finally, now that gay marriage is legal, do we all have to go and buy our morning suits?

Sorry. It doesn't automatically work like that.

What's the point of 'coming out' if you're then going to go straight back in, in terms of what shape you actually want your relationship to take? That's not being out.

As a closeted teenager in the suburbs, the relationship I had dreamed of having – an impossible dream, I was quite sure – would be with a guy roughly my age, and it would be forever, and it wouldn't involve anyone else.

But on the gay scene I learned quickly that while some shared my ideals, others rejected them, seeing them as a pale imitation of what straight people do.

In fact, thinking about it, when I was growing up, not only was there no gay marriage, there wasn't even the *concept* of gay marriage. People weren't really even lobbying for it.

On the Valentine's Day 2001 edition of *This Morning*, Richard and Judy presided over a 'gay wedding' live on ITV (their inverted commas, not mine). The country found it not so much disgusting, as *hilarious*. That's how recent a concept it is.

I'm not David Cameron's biggest fan but I do thank him for pushing through gay marriage, despite the efforts of many in his party – and other parties too, it has to be said – to block it.

Things don't move for an age and then suddenly they move almost too fast to take it all in. It seems absurd now that gay marriage was so opposed, so feared. The sun still rises. There haven't been ten new plagues. I'm baffled by the Church's arguments about the 'sanctity' of marriage being between a man and a woman. The institution of marriage long predates the existence of the Church.

Back in Heaven at the end of the last century, defining any relationship would have been a luxury for me. I was just trying to get into those jeans that fitted me perfectly six weeks ago, and still trying to catch the eye of each gorgeous guy that walked by.

And, inevitably, whichever lad I'd taken a shine to that week had a girl with him – the fabled fag hag – who I'd appear to take more interest in, pumping them for information about their pretty friend, with the aim of getting their endorsement in the process.

One girl always used to pop over for a chinwag, a chirpy Cockney-type, black hair and wild make-up around her eyes. Years later David and I were on a TV show and she came up to me and started talking about the old Heaven days. I was gobsmacked – I had never put two and two together. It was Amy Winehouse. (Better put in a clang there.)

Sometimes my efforts to charm a lad were successful. I spotted one boy, a model so handsome my jaw dropped. We spoke briefly, but I didn't dare try to chat him up – I knew I stood no chance. I bumped into him again a few weeks later and to my surprise we ended up back at mine. Again I became quite smitten, but he wasn't looking for anything serious. It took me a while to get over it – he seemed so perfect. One night, when I was still pining for him badly, I decided to go out and have a drink to cheer myself up. I got off the Tube at Oxford Circus, stood on the escalator as it took me up, and was mortified to see his face looking back at me from every second poster. There were hundreds of him. I fixed my glare on the ground, only lifting it once I had exited the station, whereupon I saw his mug again, in a different campaign, above the giant Next store!

Another lad was more proactive in chatting me up – a shaven-headed artist, a hipster, actually, if such a thing existed back then. He drank a lot, though. I gave him my number and he emailed me the next day – this was a relatively new thing, emailing – and apologised for being so drunk. He wanted to take me to dinner. This he did, and we ended up in bed. We saw each other a few times, but it became clear that he had a drinking problem. When he was sober, he was sweet and intelligent and *present*.

On our last date I took him to the theatre and then to a bar, and we agreed to go back to mine, but he wanted to go to a club first.

'Just one more drink.' That was his mantra. 'Just one more.'

On this went, until it was about 3 a.m. Eventually I muttered that I was leaving, and that if he didn't come with me, then that was probably it.

He looked at me. 'Yeah, you're right. We're not really a match. Bye.'

Off into the night I went, feeling very sorry for myself.

I woke up to a string of voicemails . . .

'Matt. Matt! God, I'm such an idiot. Shit. Why do I drink so much? Matt, you're amazing. You really are. I've been a complete dick tonight. I really like you, Matt. Really. I'm so sorry. Would you give me one last chance? Can I meet you tonight? Can I take you for dinner? Can I *cook* you dinner? No drink. I just want to see you.'

I sat through a match at Highbury that afternoon feeling conflicted. Should I ring him? Would it be a loss of face if I did? But then I *did* like him.

I got home around 6 p.m. Enough time to shower and change and then head over to his.

I called him . . .

'Hey.'

'Hey.'

'How are you doing?'

'Good. Good . . . Sorry, who's this?'

'Matt.'

'Matt? Oh. Hi.'

'Hi.'

There was a pause.

'So, um, what time should I come over?'

'Matt . . . This is kind of embarrassing, but I thought we agreed last night . . .'

'Well, yes, but your voicemails . . . ?'

'What voicemails?'

'. . . the ones you left on my phone at six this morning.'

'I didn't leave any voicemails this morning.'

'You did. You said –'

'Look, Matt, I told you last night I wasn't interested. I actually think it's kind of weird that you're calling, to be honest. I'll see you around.'

I realised I'd had a lucky escape.

Finally, in February 2000 I was outside Heaven with my friend Tom when a cute lad started tagging along with us. He was cocky, shaven-headed, a bit rough, but steeped in designer clothes and reeking of expensive perfume. He was also utterly bewitching – but dangerous, I could tell. He was lurking near the front of the queue, hoping to get in without paying, I think. My celeb status meant that I was always granted free entry, along with my friends, so I nodded to the doorman to let him come in with us.

Once inside he offered to buy us drinks and then a couple of his mates appeared – one a big burly guy, who eyed me with suspicion and whisked the lad away. I swiftly surmised that whoever was paying for the Prada clothes and Hermes belt probably wasn't doing so for my benefit and decided not to get involved.

Half an hour later he found us again. He was pretty upfront, wanting to know if I was seeing anyone.

'Ha, you're not in my league,' I said.

He looked hurt. 'That's not very nice.'

I suddenly realised that I'd jumbled my words. 'No, no, NO! I meant, I'm not in YOUR league.'

We swapped numbers and then the burly guy reappeared. I slipped away.

Later that night the lad left a voicemail, suggesting I call him.

I called him the next day and we chatted. And the next. And the next.

I was on a tour of *Troilus and Cressida* at the time and we were in York, with rotten reviews and barely any audience. His text messages were cheeky and flirtatious and kept my spirits up. I'd come offstage and hurry to my phone, hoping there'd be a new one there.

A couple of weeks later we were in Manchester and he came to see me. He didn't want us to sleep together straight away. I booked a swanky room in a nice hotel with – at his request – separate beds.

We went for dinner and to a club and then spent the night chatting, watching TV and having a few drinks. At the end of the weekend, just before my twenty-sixth birthday, we decided we were *boyfriends*.

He didn't want me to go to his hometown because he wasn't out, so he came to London to visit most weekends. By now I had appeared in some Cadbury's Creme Egg commercials and was able to buy a nice flat in West Hampstead. Again, my brother had moved with me. It was only a few months since I'd come out to him, and he was clearly unnerved by the sight of a topless, tattooed skinhead wandering about the place, munching on cornflakes. I, meanwhile, was buzzing.

However, beyond the physical attraction we had for each other and the sheer *wonder* I felt at *actually having a boyfriend*, we didn't quite have enough in common for it to develop any further. He drank brandy, smoked cigars and took cocaine, none of which held the remotest appeal for me. He loathed football to the extent that he refused to kiss me if I was wearing my Arsenal shirt, wasn't fussed about musicals and couldn't fathom why I didn't find motor racing the most exciting thing on the planet. Three and a half months after it began, it was over. I suspect I knew all along that it might not last, but it ended amicably and I felt a sense of achievement that, however briefly, I'd managed to make a connection with someone beyond just a one-night stand. There was hope.

Meanwhile my mum, like my brother, was also having difficulty coming to terms with me being gay. I was sympathetic to a point – after all, it had taken me twenty-five years to tell her, so I reminded myself that I had to be patient. My stepdad suggested she see a counsellor and gradually she came to accept things. 'You're still my son and I still love you,' she told me.

That Christmas my mum, brother, stepdad and I went to my step-mum's flat for lunch. (Yup, we all get along. Very modern.) My stepsister gave me a bundle of presents. One of them was a teddy bear in a black leather hat, with a moustache. Everyone laughed.

Except me. I wasn't ready.

Not long after, I called up Auntie Sheila, my late father's sister. I wanted to tell her what I had now told the rest of the family.

'I know, Matt,' she said.

'Who told you?' I asked, wondering which family member had spilled the beans.

'Your father.'

I didn't know what to say.

'He'd figured it out. He was just waiting for you to tell him. He said that he loved you and just wanted you to be happy.'

Right. That's more than enough gayness for now. Even gay people probably found this chapter a bit over-gay. I know I did.

I'm going to have a Snapple and then walk the dogs. And while I do, I might ponder whether, in maybe twenty-five years' time, the notion of dedicating an entire chapter of an autobiography to being gay might actually seem – in Britain, at least – rather quaint.

My first day at Haberdashers', Sept 1985 aged 11. As you can see, I was painfully shy

H – Haberdashers' Aske's Boys' School

To this day I have not the slightest idea how on earth I got into Haberdashers' Aske's Boys' School – or Habs, as it is known.

Habs was supposedly the best school of the lot and certainly the toughest to get into. By 'the lot', I mean the collection of private schools in and around north-west London that those who could afford it battled to get their children into.

I noticed a year or so before Howard was due to leave our primary school, Aylward, that the conversation had turned to where he'd go next. I had assumed he (and eventually I) would attend either a local comprehensive or JFS – the Jewish Free School.

Our parents, like many of their friends, were keen for us to have opportunities they felt they had been denied. Neither of them had been to university. In fact, although my father had passed the entrance exam at a top school, he was informed that there wasn't actually a place for him as they had already filled their quota of Jews.

Howard had been for extra tuition with Mrs Madeley who lived, conveniently, on the way home from school, and I subsequently did the same. Although I would generally prefer to come straight home after school and park myself in front of the telly for the rest of the night, I didn't actually mind the extra workload Mrs Madeley gave me. We were rarely given homework at primary school and I enjoyed the extra stimulation. Also, Mrs Madeley was nice. I know that sounds like a small detail, but I always worked harder for teachers who were just nice.

At the age of eleven I took entrance exams for John Lyon School, University College School, City of London and Habs. Everyone told me that John Lyon was the easiest of the bunch. Well, I failed that.

I actually took the exam for University College School twice – a year early 'just to see' and then again when I was the right age. My overriding memory is of having a tumultuous head cold and only one tissue, and having to blow my nose constantly and then wring the tissue out again. I can't recall if I got round to answering any questions.

I passed the exam for City of London School but failed the interview when, ironically, the teacher conducting it had a cold himself and seemed more interested in the contents of his tissue than anything I had to say.

The scene was set, then, for me to go to JFS.

Plusses?

It's a state school so it wouldn't cost my family anything.

Darren and Barbra – my dad's girlfriend's kids – went there.

And you got to leave early in the winter, so that you could get home before the Sabbath came in (i.e. before sunset).

Minuses?

It was in Camden, which meant a fifteen-minute walk to the bus stop, a ten-minute bus ride, a twenty-five-minute Tube ride, and then a further walk to the school. As an eleven-year-old I found the prospect daunting. Folklore had it that kids from other local schools would beat the crap out of you if they saw you in your bright blue uniform.

All boys had to wear a kippah – the small, round skull cap. Having no hair meant that mine would invariably slide off with the slightest head movement, and even if I stood still and it stayed on, I looked like the Pope, which wasn't very Jewish.

And they taught Hebrew. I already took Hebrew classes on a Sunday morning and was soon to start them on a Tuesday evening, in preparation for my bar mitzvah. I hated Hebrew. I thought it was impossible to learn and I was amazed that even people from the Bible – who had no distractions like *Grange Hill* or Teletext – could speak it.

The remaining exam was for Haberdashers' – the best school of the lot, I was repeatedly told – so no one held out much hope. I let my friends know that I was probably going to JFS – or Joe's Fish Shop, as Darren and Barbra called it.

There was no entrance exam but my mum and dad still had to take me to JFS for an interview. Despite having been told that it was a cinch to get into – unlike the other schools, it taught pupils at all different academic levels – I still got quite a grilling, as the teachers stressed that hard work and application was expected of all pupils.

As we left, my mum made it clear that she was surprisingly impressed by the place. 'Weeeeell, that wasn't quite the cakewalk you were expecting, was it?'

No, it wasn't. Because I didn't know what a cakewalk was. I still don't. In fact I've never heard anyone even use that expression before or since, and that includes my mum. But if a cakewalk means a walk where they give you a slice of gateau at the end, I'm in.

Anyway, somehow I passed the exam for Haberdashers'. This meant I was to go in for an interview.

I told the English teacher that I was an avid reader of John Buchan novels, which was a lie that one of my better-read friends had suggested I tell.

I informed the Maths teacher that I wasn't the best at the subject, but that I was *very* keen to learn.

The first half of the previous sentence was true.

When a letter arrived notifying me that I had won a place there, the family's jaws dropped. This was not expected. Imagine Kevin the Gerbil getting into Oxford to study Molecular and Cellular Biochemistry. It was about as likely as that.

Two other boys from my primary school had also got in, but one of them couldn't afford to go. My parents couldn't afford for me or my brother to go either, but my grandma paid for him and I was eligible for an 'assisted place'.

The snob in me was delighted. And I was really pleased for my parents, my mum in particular. It is one of the great pleasures in life for any Jewish mother to be able to *kvell*, to *schep nachas* – to feel happy and proud. Anyone who could tell their friends that their son – *both* of their sons, *noch* – were at Haberdashers' . . . well, we were as good as a doctor and a lawyer already.

Haberdashers' was a wonderful school, everyone told me, not just because of the great teachers but because of the *marvellous facilities*. Boy, did people go on and on about these *marvellous facilities* (I've put them in italics because that's how people said it). There was a swimming pool, a music school with *syu-perb acoustics*, thanks to these giant mushroom-like objects that hung from the ceiling, designed by the man who'd done the same thing at the *Royal Albert Hall*. There was a brand new *one-million-pound sports hall* – no one ever just said 'sports hall' – with cricketing practice nets and a weights room. There was an *all-weather sports pitch*, with an expensive gravel-like surface, perfect for those freezing-cold winters. There was a dedicated *Drama Studio*, a separate *Art and Design Centre*, endless playing fields, a cricket pavilion, an athletics track, a room full of *BBC Model B computers*, a lake with swans . . . the list was endless and it was all set in over one hundred acres of lush green-belt countryside. It was as impressive a sight – and site – as you can imagine.

What I had also been told repeatedly – but hadn't really truly considered – was that everyone at Haberdashers' was very very clever and the workload was immense.

'You are the top five per cent, the cream,' the stiff, stern Junior School Head Mr Wilson informed us, as we assembled in the main hall on that first morning.

He was right. Except about me. With the exception of English, I was stumped by the contents of the school syllabus. Physics, German, Chemistry, Geography, Biology – all of it. I couldn't understand what anyone was going on about at any point. I would write notes copiously during lessons and do my best to remember them, but I had no idea what anything actually meant.

I didn't so much fall behind as miss the race entirely.

I wasn't just overwhelmed by the high expectations placed upon us, I was also intimidated by the confidence and ease exhibited by some of my classmates, many of whom had already spent four years being moulded, tweaked and polished at the Habs prep school.

New to me also was the unrelenting formality, the poshness of it all. It was so strange and manufactured, so disconnected from the outside world that I'd come from and so much importance seemed to be given to it. I didn't understand the purpose of it all. Why did I need a fountain pen and why must I write in black ink and not blue? Why did I have to stand up when a teacher entered the room and wait to be allowed to sit down again? Why did no one call me by my first name? Not even my friends.

And why was everyone so damn competitive?

Every time there was an exam, it wasn't enough for those who did well to be happy for themselves, they also seemed to delight in everyone else's failure. Results were displayed in the corridors for all to see and I was usually informed by some boy or other of my low marks mid-waddle, long before I'd arrived at the noticeboard.

'Lucas, you got thirty-eight per cent,' someone would yell. Eventually, when the crowd cleared, I'd study the results myself. I never started at the top, always the bottom. I would find my name much sooner.

This place wasn't for me.

I was already struggling with my studies and distracted by my parents' acrimonious separation, which had left me heartbroken. I was not prepared for what would follow.

One Saturday morning, early in 1986. I was still eleven and in my second term at Habs. I was watching TV at home when my father popped by to see me. He'd moved about twenty minutes away and would try and visit on the weekend, usually while Mum was at work.

We chatted as usual and then, just before he headed off, he mentioned to me that he had a court case coming up in a few days. It was something to do with the business he used to own, that had since closed down.

I asked him if he was going to win some money.

'No, actually, it's some other people who say I owe *them* money.'

He seemed pretty relaxed about it and told me that he didn't believe they had a case. The conversation was brief. As he left, I pondered on it for a minute or two, and then forgot all about it.

A couple of weeks later and the weekend came and went. I hadn't seen Dad that particular Saturday but it hadn't really registered with me. I'd spoken to him a few days earlier on the phone. I didn't see him every single weekend, as sometimes he was working.

I came home from Hebrew classes as usual on the Tuesday evening to find a tense, heavy atmosphere at home. My mum was there, with Grandma Margot. Howard was sitting in the morning room – a rather grand name for what was just an extension that led from the kitchen – and I went in there as usual, ready to watch *Grange Hill* before starting my homework.

Mum and Grandma came in and sat me down. They had something to tell me.

'We've already spoken to Howard,' said Mum. I looked over. His brow was furrowed. He didn't meet my gaze.

'Do you know,' she continued, slowly and nervously, 'what happens when people do bad things?'

Huh? What on earth was she going on about? Why was she talking to me like I was five?

'I have some bad news. I'm afraid to tell you your father's gone to prison.'

Tears. Many tears. Many many tears. Shock. Sadness. Humiliation. Above all, concern for him.

My dad. My poor father.

We were a middle-class suburban Jewish family. I did not know of anyone who had been to prison. I had no frame of reference.

I watched *Grange Hill*, did some homework, pushed some food around the plate and went to bed in a daze.

The next morning Mum drove me into school. I was crying. One of the other boys in my class noted this.

'Why are you crying, Lucas? Did Darren Lewis beat you up?'

I shook my head.

'Why are you crying then?'

A small crowd gathered. I couldn't speak.

'Darren Lewis beat him up. Why did you beat him up, Lewis?'

Lewis shrugged.

Meanwhile my mother went to speak to my housemaster, who summoned me to see him at morning break. As I sat in his office shell-shocked, he addressed me in that posh matter-of-fact English stiff-upper-lip way.

'Well . . . Matthew . . . I've heard your news. You're not the first boy it's happened to in this school and you won't be the last, I'm sure. My advice to you is not to tell any of the other boys. You know what they can be like. Any problems, see me.'

My father John Lucas was sentenced to nine months in prison for fraud, with the possibility of three months off for good behaviour. He was sharing a cell with a heroin addict in Wandsworth, the crumbling Victorian shithole that train robber Ronnie Biggs had escaped from. I wondered if my dad might be able to do the same. He wouldn't allow us to visit him there, but he sent me and Howard a remorseful letter in which he imagined we must be disappointed in him.

He couldn't have been further from the truth.

My dad was my hero. I loved him dearly, still do. He was kind to us, warm and funny. He was loved by many. When he died, over four hundred people came to the funeral. He was no career criminal. In the mid-eighties he made a stupid mistake, borrowed some money in an attempt to save his ailing business. He hoped to pay it back, but his debts spiralled and he wasn't able to. I can't argue that that shouldn't involve a prison sentence, but I didn't and don't think any less of him. He was human. Humans err. I do little else.

After ten days he managed to engineer a move to Spring Hill open prison and a few weeks later, our application to visit him was accepted. My dad had been dating a lady called Andie, who was recently widowed. Many would not have stood by him, but she did. She was to take us to see him, along with her kids and also Grandma Margot. Andie was only a recent addition to our lives and I can understand my mum wanting someone else to join us, though how glad my dad was to see his former mother-in-law is something I'm less sure of.

We arrived at the prison and waited with various other families until we were taken to the canteen. There, sat at a table, was my dad.

He was tired. He was ashamed.

And he was wigless!

WHAT?!

It was the first time – apart from that brief moment in the bathroom when he had pulled his wig back a little to show me – that I had seen him like this. He had some hair at the back and, having not yet seen the prison barber, wild, wavy wisps growing out of the sides of his head. He joked that he looked like a mad professor. And that broke the ice.

We talked less about his life and more about ours. He wanted to know how we were doing at school and how the Arsenal were getting on. Andie's son Darren told him about a funny new show on BBC One that had just started, called *Dear John*. He sang the theme tune in a loud falsetto voice and we all laughed.

We would go to visit Dad every few weeks. I did my best not to tell people at school what had happened, but I couldn't help confiding in one or two, as people were wondering why I had become so withdrawn. Soon the whole class knew, but not all of the teachers. One afternoon in the large locker room, with the whole year gathered, my biology teacher – who also picked the cross-country team – was loudly bemoaning the lack of pupils who were willing to turn up at a weekend and represent the school. His particular bugbear was the *Jewish boys*, because they had a ready-made excuse not to come in and compete.

'You, Lucas. You can come in and run on Saturday.'

'Um, I can't, sir,' I replied, in panic.

Such a response from a first-year pupil to a master was not generally welcomed. We were to do as we were told.

'Why not?!' snapped Sir, bristling.

'He's Jewish,' offered someone.

'Well, you don't wear one of the little hats, do you?' he replied, as if that meant I wasn't. 'You'll come in on Saturday. It'll do you good.'

I waited for the room to clear, before telling him quietly that I was visiting my father on Saturday.

'Can't you see him another day?'

Oh, for fuck's sake!

'Mr Yeabsley can explain,' I mumbled, shuffling away as the tears started to roll.

Spring Hill prison didn't look to me like a prison at all. It looked more like a fifties holiday camp, more *Hi-de-Hi!* than *Porridge*. My dad told us this was because it was an open prison, where many of the inmates were either petty offenders or were at the end of long sentences. He could, if he wanted, walk right out of the gate. Nobody would stop him, but when they caught up with him – and they would – he'd be sent straight back to a much tougher unit.

But one day, in the middle of his sentence, he did leave. It was an authorised exit – something to do with the divorce, I think – which required him to go in person to central London, to meet with some lawyers and attend a hearing.

My brother and I took the day off school so that we could see him afterwards for lunch. We caught up with him and Andie, as arranged, in a restaurant in a large department store, where they were waiting for us.

Suddenly our father was here with us – not in prison – but here, now, in this shop, at this table, like normal. We're eating a meal, like normal. He's checking my manners, like normal, telling me not to interrupt when Howard is talking, and not to eat with my mouth open. We're having chicken. We're having ice cream. We're Dad and Andie and Howard and Matthew and we're just out for a meal. It could be any day, any moment.

But this moment, in those six God-awful months – and I'm crying as I write this, as I remember this moment – was the greatest moment I ever got to spend with him. If I could ever see my father again, I would see him there.

An hour later, it was time to go. Andie took Dad back to Springhill and because he arrived on time he was rewarded with a job in the prison library. I was proud of him when I heard this.

In the summer, after six interminable months inside, John Lucas was released from Spring Hill prison and *E.T.* was re-released in the cinema. Dad took us one evening. I'd seen it many times before, though only on pirate video. In a year of many tears, I cried again when E.T. went home, even though I knew it was going to happen.

By the end of the first year at Habs, my academic results had been so worrying that my future at the school was in the balance. In the first term of the second year I was therefore put 'on report', meaning that I had a timetable card which had to be signed by the teacher at the end of each lesson, denoting how well I had applied myself. It was an indignity afforded to perhaps one or two members of each school year, and one that felt so public, such a topic of interest and amusement amongst my classmates, that I might just as well have gone to school in only my underpants like in all those dreams I still have (it's okay, my therapist knows).

And slowly . . . things got a little better. Even when my academic results were low, I at least got credit for applying myself. It was a patronising but effective way to work with someone in my situation.

At the end of the second year I lost all that weight and got the part in *The Roman Invasion of Ramsbottom*. The year after, I made my West End debut and my confidence continued to rocket as I took parts in other school productions, playing Mr Hardcastle in *She Stoops To Conquer* and Mr Thwackum in *Tom Jones*.

In the third year, young Mr Rossotti – now my English teacher – made a bold decision to set aside the recommended reading list for a term and allow us to choose our own reading matter. While my classmates selected Dickens, Orwell, Tolkien (anything that might impress), I plumped for an altogether less salubrious option.

My stepsister Barbra, four years my elder, had recently been championing the works of Jackie Collins. Indeed, her shelf had begun to groan as her collection of Ms Collins' novels grew, such was her admiration for the author's work. I took her sage advice and brought

Hollywood Husbands with me into the classroom. Mr Rossotti was a little surprised but, as he had encouraged us to pick whatever we liked, he probably felt it would be unfair to ban or even criticise my selection.

None of us were prepared for the revolution that would soon take place. I devoured the contents within a handful of days (and the same number of sleepless nights) and handed the book with a glowing recommendation to a classmate, while I graduated to *Hollywood Wives*. *Lucky* followed, then *Chances*, then *The Bitch*, *The Stud*, *The World Is Full of Married Men* and *The World Is Full of Divorced Women*. By this time, nearly half the class had set aside C. S. Lewis and William Golding so they could learn about the lurid sexual exploits of Gino Santangelo, Sadie LaSalle and Muffin.

It all came to a head one Monday morning when an exasperated Mr Rossotti decided enough was enough. He excused himself for a couple of moments, then reappeared in a sweat, carrying a tower of books – each one a copy of Graham Greene's *The Third Man*. The experiment was over.

Outside the classroom, no matter how many school plays you performed in or orchestras you joined, the school was most proud of its sporting achievements – though my attempts to contribute didn't work out too well.

In the first year I had volunteered as scorer for the cricket team, though I was summarily dismissed from my duties after a single match for putting down nicknames in the log book instead of surnames.

A couple of years later I found, to my surprise, that I rather enjoyed playing hockey. I started outfield, where my low centre of gravity actually seemed to work to my advantage. My asthma and my generally poor level of fitness, however, soon led me to become a goalkeeper.

I was quite fearless and, with padding on, was happy to dive all over the place. Had I finally found my sporting métier? My pal Jake Moore was taller and broader than me, and so it made sense that he would be goalie for the A team and in early practices I was goalie for the B team. I was delighted and actually I was pretty good, though I say so myself. Mr Talbot himself would holler encouragement from the corner flag – 'Lucas! Great save!'

And then Jayesh Makan happened.

Jayesh Makan came along one day to hockey practice, picked up the goalkeeping pads, put them on and took his place in goal.

Eh? Had he not got the memo?

Worse, he was really good. The bugger.

By the time we started to play competitively, against other schools, Jayesh was the B team goalie.

No one told me I wasn't required at practice anymore and so I continued to go along. I'd sit on the sidelines until Jake or Jayesh had decided they'd had enough and then I'd quickly put the pads on for the last few minutes.

One day I arrived at practice before any of the other boys and sat patiently in the changing room as usual. In walked one of the younger teachers, who assisted Mr Talbot in running the sessions.

'Come on then, what are you waiting for?' he asked.

'Jayesh, sir,' I replied.

'Never mind Jayesh. If you're here first, you get to play.'

I liked this new rule.

I put the kit on and was fully dressed by the time Jayesh arrived. He took one look at me and went to inform Mr Talbot, who then came in and screamed at me in front of the whole squad.

'How dare you?! HOW DARE YOU?! Who do you think you are?! You know that Jayesh is in goal! Take those pads off immediately! Disgraceful behaviour! Outrageous!'

On and on he ranted. I looked at the younger teacher and waited for him to step in.

'Ah, sorry, Mr Talbot. Yes, I told Lucas that as he was here first, he could play in goal today' . . . is what he should have said. But he didn't say a bloody word. I can only surmise he was as petrified of Mr Talbot as the rest of us.

With everyone else laughing their heads off, and Jayesh the victor, I peeled off the kit and handed it to him, head bowed.

A few weeks later I got my revenge – on Mr Talbot, that was. Not on Jayesh, nor the younger teacher (who still teaches at the school, which is why I've not mentioned his name!).

Well, I say revenge. It was actually accidental. One of the sixth-formers tapped me on the shoulder one lunchtime. Their keeper was away and they were about to practise on the all-weather pitch. Would I be up for going in goal that afternoon?

Absolutely. I had a couple of free periods and some boots in my locker. I managed to borrow some mouldy old kit thanks to Jim, the avuncular Irish caretaker who lived in a cupboard in the PE corridor.

I jogged up to the all-weather pitch and took my place in goal, impressing all with my prowess. Like I say, I wasn't too bad.

At the end of the session I went to collect some balls that had been left behind. Looking down, I made the dreadful discovery that my rugby boots had ripped up about a third of the surface of the pitch.

Now, let me say, that all-weather pitch was Mr Talbot's pride and joy. Nothing meant more to him than that pitch. Its surface was state-of-the-art and had cost tens of thousands of pounds. It was ours to play on, to improve, to enjoy, *but whatever we did*, we were NEVER to go on it with the incorrect footwear.

'Talbot's looking for you. Have you seen him yet?'

'Did you hear Talbot's asking where you are?'

'Did Ken catch up with you?' (He was called Ken sometimes because he was the spit of Ken Dodd.)

This question – and various other incarnations of it – was asked of me several times a day over the next couple of weeks, as I sought to avoid the raging, track-suited fireball that was Keith Talbot.

I did everything I could to steer clear of the PE corridor, but one day in the playground I turned around and he was there. I braced myself, ready for the hairdryer treatment. Alex Ferguson had nothing on Keith Talbot. He could see the panic in my eyes. I saw him pause and then he spoke very calmly.

'You've been avoiding me, haven't you, son?'

I nodded.

'I was very upset to see the state of the pitch. That's going to cost an awful lot of money to repair, Matthew, and the lads won't be able to play on it for a while now. They're very disappointed. But I know you didn't mean it.'

And with that he walked off. He was full of surprises, that man, but even when he was boiling over, I still thought he was great. Unlike some of the other staff, years of teaching a bunch of entitled brats had not made him weary or cynical. He cared.

I left sport to the big boys and went back to doing plays and banging drums in the orchestra.

I stumbled through five years at Habs. I want to say I came out relatively unscathed, but I don't think I can. There were pockets of humanity there, moments of humour and warmth – but not enough. Some flourished; I didn't. Not really. I believe that nowadays the school is not only focused on academic results but that it engages more with the wellbeing of its pupils and has a greater appreciation of their differing abilities and needs. But back then, despite my achievements in the school plays and my contribution to the various bands and orchestras, I felt weighed down, and not just by my own physical bulk. Where did my childhood go? Maybe it was exacerbated by difficulties in my home life, but nonetheless that place never became a refuge.

We were constantly told how we represented the school wherever we went. Well, the school represented us too, and not always helpfully. Years later, at university, I learned that Haberdashers' was almost a national byword for arrogance, a sense of superiority. Despite being somewhere near the very bottom of the pile there, it still took me a long time to learn humility – years and years, even, to understand what it was. I simply hadn't been exposed to it very often.

The school was, however, a hotbed of creativity. I was far from the only voice. A small number of us left Habs and disregarded expectations of becoming a doctor, lawyer or hedge fund manager, and made our way instead into the world of comedy.

David Baddiel led the charge. I followed. Close on my heels was Sacha Baron Cohen.

Sacha had been in my older brother's class. Sacha, my brother and a couple of others had bonded over a shared love of hip hop. There was lino on the floor of the kitchen at Sacha's house and my brother had gone there to practise some breakdancing. I remember visiting the Baron Cohen residence with my mum in 1982, aged eight, to collect Howard. I was very impressed, having never met someone with a double-barrelled name in real life before.

Dan Mazer, who co-wrote and produced much of Sacha's work, was in the year below him. Robert Popper, who created *Friday Night Dinner*, was a few years older. Dean Nabarro, Dean Craig, Chris Little, David Tyler and Steve Hall were all alumni and have also gone on to either write, produce or star in TV comedy.

The last mention goes to Ashley Blaker, a wittier man than I'll ever be and one to whom I owe a great debt. He's co-written and produced much of my work, but these days you'll find him selling out synagogues and theatres both here and in the US, as Britain's only orthodox Jewish comedian.

Some nice clangs there, you'll agree. In fact, Steve Hall used to be in the comedy troupe We Are Klang, so maybe I should change the spelling.

My final year at Haberdashers' started out being the easiest and probably ended up being the hardest.

In the summer holiday I had grown friendly with some boys from my year that I hadn't known very well before. One balmy hot Saturday afternoon four of us decided to go up to the West End. We smoked, cheeked passers-by and mooched around the shops. Day turned to night and we were out for hours, just laughing and idling away the time. There was a chemistry, a sense of freedom. We were independent in a way we hadn't been before.

A little clique formed, with the four of us at the centre, then grew and grew until it contained about a third of the year. Suddenly fifty of the boys – the sporty ones, the street-wise ones, the good-looking ones – would gather at the home of the ringleader – a diminutive blond boy I will call JJ.

JJ lived with his mum, a former TV presenter; his stunning brother, a hairdresser who whizzed around on a motorbike and told us he had had trials at Arsenal before injury put a stop to his career; and their pretty sister, who looked a bit like Patsy Kensit.

They were great fun, and they seemed to be so much more chilled out than my family. They had big dogs everywhere, Sky TV and their fridge and freezer was full of all sorts of delicious processed food that we saw advertised on TV and which my mother would never buy.

It was there that I had my first ever Mars ice cream bar.

It was there that I smoked my first ever joint.

And it was there that we generally assembled, most Saturday nights, drinking and partying. Sometimes JJ, our pied piper, would lead us to the local park, where we'd break in, neck rum and spin on the roundabout until we puked. Back at the house we'd blast music so loud that the police would come round, then return half an hour later, while JJ's mum, roll-up hanging from her lips, would nod obediently, before shutting the door, waiting until they were out of earshot and shouting 'All coppers are bastards!'

JJ's parties were the talk of the school. Everybody would be angling for an invite. And the four of us at the centre of the clique would decide on a whim whether to grant their wish. Our influence and popularity seemed to grow by the day, as we wielded this new power malevolently. We spread gossip, created drama, respecting and fearing no one. We were fifteen and we were horrible, basically.

And for the first time, socially, I was thriving. My crowning moment had come at one of the parties. I had already gone to bed, but someone had drunkenly remembered I could be vaguely amusing on occasion. I was irritated to be woken up at first, but then I saw that I had an audience, including some of the handsome, sporty boys.

I seized the moment, sat in my sleeping bag on a chair in the living room and improvised for an hour, impersonating the teachers, pupils, staff and anyone else who came to mind. It was probably the funniest I've ever been. Everything I said brought the house down. Looking back, maybe that was the moment I realised I might have a gift – not just as an actor, but as someone who could come up with the funnies too. On the Monday back at school, I was congratulated again and again, and made to repeat the impressions. I was flying high.

And then – rather to my annoyance – I turned up at JJ's the following Saturday to discover someone had invited some *girls* along.

Oh.

Suddenly everyone's attention was on these girls, and they now became a permanent fixture in the group. Even my friend Robert, who I had assumed was as gay as a daffodil, couldn't stop putting his tongue down that Helen's throat.

As ever, I was still waiting for those straight feelings to arrive.

I started to become a shadow at the party. Week after week we'd all be getting along fine, and then after a few drinks everyone was just sort of kissing and touching each other. I would wander around the house, petting the dogs, nicking another choc ice, rolling another joint. Sometimes I even just put myself to sleep in JJ's bed, while everyone else was downstairs having a love-in.

One Saturday night I was a bit under the weather and I stayed at home. I turned on the TV and a film came on that blew me away. I couldn't get over how funny and fresh it was.

The following weekend I arrived at JJ's house, later than usual, clutching a video tape I'd just bought in town.

'Guys, you *have* to see this.'

No one was interested, but I insisted. Prising apart various kissing couples, I turned off the music and made everyone gather around the TV. I put the cassette into the VCR, dimmed the lights and waited for the others to be converted, like I had . . .

. . . to the magic of Charlie Chaplin's masterpiece *Modern Times*.

'What the hell is this?'

'No, trust me. Trust me.'

'Charlie fucking Chaplin?'

'Seriously, this is amazing. Trust me on this.'

I had them for a minute or two, but no more. They wanted to drink, to smoke, to screw – and I wanted to watch a black-and-white film. What was I thinking of?

I still love that film today, but whenever I watch it I am reminded of that night in 1990. It was the beginning of the end for me.

I should have seen it coming. I had, after all, been pretty instrumental in helping to create the monster.

In our group had been a guy called Richard who, predictably, we'd labelled as gay.

The conclusion had some basis in fact. At a sleepover a few years earlier, when we were maybe just twelve, he had been caught cuddling up to and stroking one of the other boys and I had recounted this tale to the group. I outed him, basically.

I hadn't necessarily thought that it would haunt the boy as much as it would go on to do – like I said, everyone was constantly outing everyone anyway, with little evidence. But this time it stuck, and – unlike the other poor kid who had been taunted mercilessly a few years eariler – we didn't ever really *say* anything directly to this boy. No, this was a more cowardly, insidious form of bullying. We badmouthed him, turned him into a pariah, exiled him from the group without ever explaining why, or even telling him that he wasn't wanted.

The group had started to flourish on this kind of behaviour, to define itself by it, almost. There was a faint whiff of *Lord of the Flies* about the whole thing, to be honest, a brand of cruelty particularly distinctive to that age, that time in our lives when we are perhaps at our least empathetic.

We were so drunk on our power that sometimes we even just informed someone at random that the party was going to be at their place the next Saturday.

'But my parents are going to be in.'

You might get a sympathetic shrug but you wouldn't get a reprieve.

We would arrive at the house, raid the fridge and guzzle the contents of the cocktail cabinet. We'd put metal objects in the microwave and watch the explosion. Whoever's house it was would be running around tearing their hair out. We thought it was funny.

After we'd banished our friend from the group for being gay, it was another boy's turn. This one's crime? He exaggerated things too much. In our eyes he had become the biggest liar the world had ever seen. No matter that he had been a friend I often met up with outside school, whose mum had welcomed me and my pal Robert to their home. Sorry, mate.

And then it was my turn.

One night, midway through the school year, the four of us were sleeping in the garage at JJ's house. We were discussing plans for the summer. It had been suggested months earlier that three or four of us might go inter-railing around Europe together, to celebrate the end of our GCSEs. Over the coming weeks the size and scale of the trip had grown – there were now a dozen of us intending to go, and we often found ourselves talking about it.

Then the topic of conversation took a turn. I think it might have been planned, actually . . .

'Why don't you have a girlfriend, Matt?' asked JJ.

I was silent for maybe a second too long.

'I dunno really. I guess I'm not very confident with girls.'

'But the girls love you. They all think you're hilarious.'

I wasn't sure that was true. But I just wasn't ready to give anyone the actual reason.

The next day we went to Wembley Market to hunt for bargains. In the car, in front of JJ's mum, I was ridiculed, pushed about a bit, even. When we arrived, the others tried to give me the slip. We'd always mucked about, but this – this was different.

I got it. I got the hint. I'd given the hint often enough. I knew what was going on.

A week or two later and I got the tap on the shoulder.

'Party at yours on Saturday.'

Usually I was one of the ones giving the order, now I was merely receiving it.

I didn't want a party at my place. I knew full well what would happen to the house. I didn't want to put my mum through that. I also knew that my next-door neighbours had an elderly family member who was lying there ill, and not going to get better. I'd gone out of my way not to play music too loudly, as I knew how the sound carried.

I arranged for us all to meet in Harrow town centre, a few miles from my home, in the hope that we might get distracted and find something else to do. Within an hour we were on the 340 back to Stanmore.

My prized copy of *Sgt. Pepper's Lonely Hearts Club Band* was blaring out loudly when we got a phone call from the neighbours. They asked for the music to be turned down. I did so, and JJ turned it back up. I turned it down again. It got turned up again. A scuffle took place and I yanked the needle off the record, scratching it.

The mood couldn't have been more sour. As one they departed, angry at me, embarrassed for me. Any hopes of redemption I might have had were dashed.

The following Sunday morning my mum and I awoke to a string of messages on our answerphone that had been left the previous night, during a party to which I had – of course – not been invited. The phone had been passed round, with many of the boys I was supposed to have gone inter-railing with taking it in turns to tell me how happy they were that I would not now be joining them on their trip. That's how I learned I wasn't going, though it didn't come as a surprise.

The last few months of my time at the school were spent with me just counting the days till I could get away. Lunchtimes were spent chatting with Ashley, the funny lad from the year below. My hell-raising days behind me, we spent Saturday evenings at his, talking about football, watching *The Flintstones* and making prank phone calls to the teachers.

With the summer approaching, I wondered how I might occupy myself during the long break, now that I was no longer welcome on my own trip around Europe. My closest friends from outside school were all going on a tour of Israel but, believing I would be inter-railing instead, I had missed the deadline for that.

Then, finally, some good news! Following an audition a few months earlier, I learned that I had been accepted onto the National Youth Theatre's junior course. That would have been a tough call – go inter-railing with my friends or further my acting ambitions. As it was, the choice was made for me.

After five years, I left Habs with no fanfare. I walked almost unnoticed towards the school exit – not to the coach park where I normally went, but to the car park near the girls' school, where – if I remember rightly – my brother came to collect me.

Those last few months were a real test of my resilience. I had been pretty unpleasant, it's true, but, hidden in that large group, I had been blind to the harm I'd caused. Later, when I became the focal point of its aggression, I learned the hard way what it was like to be rejected.

But guess what?

If I hadn't been excluded by the group, I probably wouldn't have cultivated that friendship with Ashley. Years later, when David and I were struggling to interest TV producers, it was Ashley who believed in us and who invested his time in *Little Britain*, producing it for radio.

In fact, if I had still been part of that gang I might even have felt duty-bound to go inter-railing instead of doing the National Youth Theatre course, in which case I might never have met David Walliams.

So if it wasn't for them, I doubt you'd be reading this book.

And funnily enough, if it wasn't for *me* they might not still be talking about Haberdashers' unrivalled academic excellence either.

You see, my year went on to collectively score the *highest A-level results of any school in the country*.

And I like to think that, by selflessly opting to take my A levels elsewhere, I played my part in allowing that average mark to be as high as it was.

You may applaud.

I – Idiot

I'm genuinely thinking of setting up an organisation called Idiots Anonymous, where people like me – members of the unintelligentsia – can gather and share stories of poor judgement and general haplessness.

'My name's Matt and I'm an idiot. It's been two hours since I last smothered my roast beef dinner in chicken gravy.'

I'm clumsy, muddled, neurotic, socially awkward and useless at everything other than being useless, something at which I rather uselessly excel.

And I've always been this way. I was born a berk. I probably even stubbed my toe on the way out.

I over-dress and babble away endlessly on first dates, causing even the most mild-mannered to run off screaming into the distance.

I buy expensive clothes which don't fit in the hope that they'll spur me on to get thinner, and then instantly go and get even fatter.

I'm always late apart from the very rare occasion when I'm about an hour and a half early, and then I just traipse around the shops buying more clothes.

And sometimes I run baths and just forget to get in them.

Trust me, I'm a twerp.

Don't believe me? Here's one for you.

We filmed parts of *Come Fly with Me* at Stansted Airport and stayed at the big hotel connected to it. After filming I had got into the habit of stopping at one of the kiosks at the airport and grabbing a burger or some snacks for myself, as room service usually took a while and we had to be up early for filming.

One night I returned to my room after we'd wrapped, showered, dried myself and looked for the bag of goodies I'd picked up the night before. I couldn't find it anywhere. I searched and searched and reasoned that it had either been stolen or – more likely – accidentally put out with the rubbish by one of the chambermaids. I was incensed that I could leave something – anything – in a bag in my room and it could be thrown away so carelessly. Furious and exhausted, I called down to the front desk.

'I'd like to speak to the manager, please. In fact, have him come up to my room *immediately*!'

'Is there a problem, sir?'

'Yes, there is a problem! One of my bags has gone missing!'

'I see. I'll send the manager up right away.'

'Yes, I think you should. I don't know what kind of hotel this is!'

Within a couple of minutes the manager appeared, to be greeted by the sight of the fat bald one from *Little Britain*, with just a towel around him.

'I'm very sorry about this, Mr Lucas.'

'So you should be! It's a disgrace!'

'I just need to fill out a report. What kind of bag was it?'

'It was one of those cheap white plastic bags you get in Smith's!'

'Right. Can you tell me where you left it?'

'Over there,' I pointed. 'Right next to the bin.'

'I see. Yes, well, it does seem possible that one of the maids might accidentally have mistaken it for rubbish and thrown it away, I'm afraid.'

'Well, that's just not good enough, is it?' I yelled. 'I bought a whole load of food at the airport yesterday and was going to eat it tonight and now it's gone!'

'Right. Well, if you'll tell me what was in the bag I'm sure I could send someone out and we could replace the contents.'

There was a pause, as I slowly recalled what had been in the bag.

'Um . . . some Monster Munch. The yellow ones, not the pickled onion.'

'Okay.'

He started to make a list.

'But it was a grab bag. They were on special offer. A chicken and mushroom Pot Noodle. A Curly Wurly. Two Boosts. A Toblerone. A white chocolate Kinder. A croissant from Pret, but that probably would have been hard by now so don't worry about that. A bottle of caffeine-free Diet Coke, a Ribena and a Chomp.'

'. . . and a Chomp,' he repeated to himself, as he finished writing it all down.

He apologised again and said that he'd be back shortly.

About an hour later, as I was nodding off, still with the towel around me, there was a knock at the door. The manager handed over a new cheap plastic bag. I thanked him, half-asleep.

I looked inside at the stack of chocolate and crisps. I told myself that I was going to put on about two stone if I started tucking into that, freaked out and promptly put it all in the bin.

See? Told you I was an idiot. In fact I'm at least eight idiots in that story alone.

Honestly, I could fill a volume with tales which confirm my general foolishness, but I'd only leave it in the taxi on the way to the publishers, so here's one more – quite literally off the top of my head – to illustrate my point and then we'll get on with the rest of the book.

Once or twice a year I like to go to New York City to catch up on some Broadway shows. I usually go on my own – because, like a lot of idiots, I'm single, and even my friends quite wisely give me a wide berth when it comes to things like being seen out with me in public.

Not long ago I was on one of my loner/theatre geek trips, where I'll often pack in two shows a day. I'd been to a matinee and had a couple of hours to kill before the next show, so I sat in a nearby hotel lobby for a bit, sipping Sprite and writing my diary.

I then decided I would grab something to eat near the theatre. I asked for the bill and pulled a handful of notes out of my pocket, putting them temporarily into the crown of my upturned white Nike cap on the sofa next to me, as I switched off my laptop and packed it away.

I paid the bill and walked down past the theatre where *Fun Home* – the show I was about to see – was playing, and stopped in at the cheap'n'cheerful Cosmic Diner. As I ate my matzo ball soup (of course), I noticed the stares of some of the other diners.

This sort of thing isn't entirely unusual. I frequently get recognised in the US, mostly for my brief appearance in *Bridesmaids*. Sometimes people look at me quizzically, while they try to figure out why I'm so familiar to them, and then the penny drops and they smile and nod.

And I smile back, because I'm a really great guy.

And that's what was happening a fair bit in the Cosmic Diner while I was busy souping. (I've just invented that term right now. I like it. I'm going to use it.)

Soon it was time to head to the theatre. I collected my ticket at the box office and headed up some stairs towards the auditorium, when a lady tapped me on the shoulder.

'Hey, you're gonna lose that money in a minute.'

I put my hand in my pocket but there wasn't anything in there.

She then tapped my cap (which was on my head) and I put my hand to my head. There – in the hole in the back of the cap – was a large bundle of notes, sticking out like a ponytail. I realised in that moment that when I had put my cap back on earlier, as I left the hotel, I had absent-mindedly forgotten to remove the notes first.

'Oh,' I stuttered. 'Yes, um, oh, um, that's funny! Yes! Someone played a practical joke on me.'

Which I thought was at least a vaguely less embarrassing thing to say than 'Thank you. I have been walking round with dollar bills hanging out of the back of my cap because I am mental.'

The lady looked at me blankly.

I continued. 'Yes, yes. *Very* funny joke. We often do it to each other. Plant money on each other. Yes. But the joke is on him because I am of course now richer than I was, ha ha! Because it was his money. This money. And now it is mine. Ha!'

'Well, somebody would have snatched it, I'm sure, especially given who you are.'

Great, I thought. Not only does she think I'm mad, but she recognises me too. Brilliant.

I settled down to watch the show, which was an engrossing, profoundly beautiful piece about sexuality and bereavement. It had been running for at least half an hour when I noticed that I was getting quite hot. I took off my cap, only for another sweaty five-dollar bill to fall from my head slowly into my lap.

See? *Idiot*. Told you.

Right, let's crack on. I've already taken up too much of your time as it is.

The bar mitzvah boy, April 1987

J – Jewish

I don't remember a time when I didn't know I was Jewish.

When I say 'Jewish', I should mention there are several different types of Jew in Britain. These are the main ones . . .

1. There are the people who are Jewish by birth but don't even know it, or who know it but are not observant in any way.

2. There are Liberal Jews, sometimes called Progressive, for whom much of the service might take place in English and there's often an informality about the whole thing. You might even have a woman rabbi or people in jeans playing guitars. Oh, and many people would agree you can break the rules that decree you can't 'work' on the Sabbath and will therefore drive to synagogue.

3. There are Reform Jews, whose services may be half in English, and in which men and women are allowed to sit together. They might drive to synagogue – which strictly speaking they oughtn't to do, because it's the Sabbath and driving could be interpreted as 'working' – but to make themselves feel less guilty, they'll spend half the journey at least talking about the fact that they shouldn't really be driving.

4. There are Orthodox Jews, who belong to an Orthodox or United synagogue, where most of the service is in Hebrew and lasts for ages. Men and women sit separately. They'd never have a female rabbi. One or two might drive to synagogue, but park around the corner and walk the last bit so that no one sees.

5. And there are the Really Orthodox Jews – not their official name but I'm not sure what else to call them. They're the ones you see with the black hats, coats, curly sideburns and long beards. The women wear wigs and when they go to synagogue they sit upstairs or even behind a curtain,

so as not to distract the men from prayer. Really Orthodox Jews definitely don't drive to synagogue on a Saturday. They can't even turn on the TV to find out the football scores because that too would violate rules in the Torah, even though the Premiership wasn't formed until 1992.

There are also some other types, but those are the main ones.

My dad was brought up in a traditional Orthodox synagogue. My mum's family were members of Belsize Square, a synagogue set up in 1939 by refugees, mainly (like my maternal grandma) from Germany. While three of my grandparents were born in the UK, either their parents or grandparents came from further afield. I'm as British as you like, but all of my blood is Eastern European – from Poland and the Ukraine. The family name on my father's side was Solotsky, until it was anglicised to Lucas at the turn of the twentieth century by a border official.

Both my mum and dad's families were observant and kept kosher homes. When my parents married, they decided to join a Reform synagogue, so my brother and I were brought up as Reform Jews.

By the way, neither of my parents – and definitely not their parents – would have dreamt of marrying someone who wasn't Jewish. We lived among other Jews and I went to a Jewish kindergarten. Then, when I was a little older, much of my life revolved around the synagogue.

We would often go to the Shabbat service on a Saturday morning; I would go to Hebrew classes on a Sunday morning, youth group on a Sunday afternoon; more Hebrew classes on a Tuesday after school and even cub scouts at the synagogue on a Thursday evening.

Saturday morning services seemed to go on forever, and involved lots of standing up and then sitting back down again on hard wooden benches. My brother and I would pass the time browsing the back of the *siddur* – the prayer book – and chuckling at the funny names of the ancient rabbis whose lessons were quoted. At the end of the service we'd go to the hall next door for the *Kiddush* blessing, willing it to be over with quickly so we could stuff our faces with dry cookies and *challah* bread and sip weak orange squash.

At youth club on a Sunday afternoon we would play games and sing songs in Hebrew. We'd also go on trips with the synagogue – to

Amsterdam and to Paris, where I saw a ghost – but usually to Manor House in Finchley, the home of RSY – Reform Synagogue Youth.

Much of what we learned through RSY was about the idyllic land of Israel. We were taught much about the historic persecution of the Jews and the need for a homeland, but never of the complexities and issues involved with the formation of the state. There was no nuance, no understanding of the concerns of the other side, because we didn't even know there was another side.

I've only been to Israel once – in 1980 – when I was six. Dad said that the Western Wall was the holiest place I'd ever visit and so I quietly kicked it, daring God to do his worst. I loved the sights, sounds and smells of the souk and enjoyed riding a camel, but found the endless sightseeing a bit much, preferring to stay in with my grandma's friend Auntie Chava. We also spent a week on a kibbutz, and I cried because of the number of flies in the hot, humid dining room. I constantly got lost trying to get back to the little box house we were staying in, because there were so many little box houses and they all looked exactly the same.

From the age of about seven, I started taking Hebrew classes on a Sunday morning. These were split into two one-hour lessons – Hebrew and History. The latter was more engaging; the former was just a grind.

We were taught in the Barnet Hall, a decaying prefabricated building next to the main synagogue, which was temporarily separated into a dozen classrooms by corrugated dividers, through which we could still hear everyone else. We were taught in large groups, so we didn't get to know or respect the teachers in the same way we did at school. There were no detentions, no real way of punishing us other than a rebuke. When that happened – and there was always someone being shouted at – we just rolled our eyes or sniggered.

At break-time we gathered in the synagogue car park. I remember my friend's older brother picking me up one day and putting me in a bin, but I got off lightly compared to one boy, who also happened to be in the year below me at primary school. He had a crowd of kids around him one week, and I saw that he was wearing nothing but black school shoes, socks, white underpants and a vest. When I asked why, he told me that his parents had warned him repeatedly that if he continued misbehaving they would send him to Hebrew classes like that – and he had and they did. It seemed to me an unimaginably humiliating thing to do to someone, even then. If you did it now, you'd probably have your child taken away from you.

As if Sunday mornings weren't enough, on a Tuesday evening for the two years prior to my bar mitzvah there were additional Hebrew lessons at the synagogue, in which I learned my *parsha* or portion of the Torah. This was the part of the Bible which I would be singing for my bar mitzvah from the handwritten scroll in front of the congregation. When learning this section, we also had to memorise different Hebrew vowel sounds and precise discordant musical phrases. The vowel and musical notation appeared in our study books alongside the Hebrew text to help us, but not in the actual scroll we'd be singing from on the day, making the task seem even more remote and impossible.

I hated going to Tuesday evening classes. I would arrive home from school with mountains of homework to do and resented the extra burden of bar mitzvah classes. As I walked down the road from Stanmore station towards our house, I would start practising whatever limp, cough or sneeze I would try to deploy as an excuse that week, to convince my mother that I wasn't well enough to go. Sadly I'm not that good an actor, so I was rarely successful.

Despite two years of dedicated bar mitzvah lessons, in reality I ended up learning my entire piece parrot-fashion, just three weeks before the big day itself. This was thanks to even more lessons on a Sunday after-noon at the home of Mr Lawrence, who had also taught both my brother and mother before me.

At Habs there was a large percentage of Jewish students and so we had special Jewish assemblies once a week. They were often a shambolic affair, taken in the classroom and run by the older boys. Sometimes we all gathered more formally in the music school and listened to dreary sermons from a visiting rabbi. The exception was Rabbi Wilschanski, a jolly old soul who spoke with a thick Yiddish accent, played the fiddle and told jokes about Jewish people eating too much.

We had the option at school of studying Jewish RE, instead of the multi-faith syllabus. Our teacher was a glamorous Orthodox lady who also had a lucrative sideline giving more advanced lessons at her home to some of my classmates. She was always more engaged with them than with the rest of us, calling them by their first names and asking after their mothers. She would sit at her desk majestically, rubbing in hand cream and expressing disapproval at Reform boys like me. I was used to this kind of snobbery. It was not uncommon to be lectured by some of the more Orthodox boys, many of whom piously refused to recognise Reform Judaism as a legitimate movement.

I found Jewish RE a drag. I'd already been taught much of the syllabus at Hebrew classes, so one term I decided to switch to the multi-faith class. I was the only Jewish boy there and found it much more interesting. We were taught in the chapel by the school chaplain, Reverend Lindsay, a warm, gentle soul whose glass eye fascinated me. His lessons were much more interesting, but my father was so alarmed when I recounted to him how I had taken communion that I felt obliged to switch back again.

As my bar mitzvah approached, my mum took me to Jeffrey's in Edgware, where every boy went to get their bar mitzvah suit. The choice was limited, however, as I had grown so fat. From the few available outfits I picked a black jacket with thousands of golden specks.

We were not usually given to being flash in my family – we couldn't afford to be, for a start – but the jacket I chose that day was the epitome of ostentatiousness. It was the sort of thing Ben Elton wore on *Saturday Live*. My dad (who had split from my mother a couple of years before) arranged to come over to the house to see me in it. I slipped it on and waited for his arrival.

As I opened the door excitedly, his face dropped. He said the jacket was ridiculous and ordered my mother and me to take it back. The shop would neither refund nor change it, and so my father, grumbling, took me one Saturday morning to Regent Street. We traipsed around the department stores, until we found a much more low-key jacket and trousers. I remember the handsome young shop assistant measuring my inside leg, and even though I was only twelve I felt a rush of excitement.

On my bar mitzvah day in April 1987 it rained and rained. The service went by without a hitch and I managed to get through my piece. My parents were still at war and, while they could just about sit proudly either side of me in the synagogue, there was no prospect of them throwing a party together for me. Therefore I waved goodbye to my dad as I left the synagogue and went back to our house, where my mum had arranged a large lunch for maybe twenty-five family members. In the evening she threw a party for me, also at home, and, in typical Jewish fashion, everyone made such a fuss of me you'd think I'd won an Oscar.

A week later it was my father's turn.

I'd been to a number of lavish bar mitzvah parties. The majority of my friends at Habs had parents who could afford to hire out huge function rooms like the Glaziers Hall, or at swanky London hotels like Carlton Tower or the Intercontinental. There would be a big band, a DJ, a toastmaster, endless speeches, helium balloons – the contents of which we would inhale – and even special guests. I was never at one where this happened, but I heard many stories of Arsenal and Tottenham players turning up to surprise the bar mitzvah boy. I always thought that was the kindest gesture of all – never imagining for a moment that the players were almost certainly given an envelope full of cash for their troubles.

Having lost his business and been to prison the year before my bar mitzvah, my dad didn't have much left in his coffers. Three years earlier my brother had had his bar mitzvah at Melanie's nightclub in Hendon, where the DJ – who called himself the 'Black Prince' – had ignored our repeated requests for Abba, Wham! and the Beatles, and had played only the latest underground soul releases, plugging in the mic to sing along. After the party was over, my parents complained about the DJ and remonstrated about the scarcity of food, leading to an almighty row in the corridor in which the manager struck my father. The four of us left the venue in shock, with my parents instructing me never ever to tell Grandma what had happened.

When I arrived for my bar mitzvah party at the run-down community centre in Wealdstone, I thought there had surely been some mistake. I went to the cloakroom and hung up my coat on one of the few remaining pegs. In the main hall were a few tables, with paper tablecloths and some plastic chairs. My dad and stepmother's friends brought the food. A couple of fifteen-year-olds were providing the disco.

My school friends started to appear in their expensive suits. They were doubtless as confused as I was. There was no silver service, no Ray McVay and his Big Band, no pink chocolate almonds all in a bow.

In the echoey hall my dad gave a speech, as did my brother. They both paid tribute to my resilience and fighting spirit. Howard said, 'When the chips are down, Matthew eats the chips,' which got a big laugh. I had written a speech, which I gave at my house the week before but had forgotten to bring with me, so I mumbled a few words of thanks into the microphone.

My bar mitzvah party was thrown with great love by my father and stepmother, but it was so different to anything else I had experienced, and I was not prepared for it. To my eternal shame, I was embarrassed by its humbleness. Looking back, I've got a horrible feeling I showed little gratitude.

These days I don't really go to synagogue very much, unless there's a specific reason. My religious belief hasn't so much wavered as disappeared entirely. It was on a visit to Ethiopia with Comic Relief some years back, as I met a man wasting away from AIDS in a tiny hut, an image of Jesus on the wall, that I figured there were three possible answers to the big question of whether or not God exists.

1. Yes, but he's not very nice.
2. Yes, but he's not very good at it. Like Aston Villa.
3. No.

I wish I could believe. I might be able to look at the suffering in the world differently, but I just can't see it. And yet, despite being an atheist, I always look forward to Jewish holidays with the family and enjoy much of our rich culture. I love the feeling of being part of something. I'm not sure I've experienced anything else comparable to it.

K – Kevin

On Friday, 16 August 2002, I met a man who would change my life.

His name was Kevin John McGee.

It was impossible not to fall in love with him.

He was handsome and smart and kind.

And he was funny. Oh, so funny.

When he was happy, I felt a warm glow inside. When he was sad, I was sad too.

I wish he was here with me now, but some things are not meant to be, I guess.

I think of him every day and I'm thankful for the time we had together.

Because Kevin John McGee was beautiful.

And here are some photos of him, so you can see for yourself.

L – Little Rumblings

20 August 2002. Late afternoon. BBC TV Centre, top floor.

Jane Root's assistant popped her head around the door to remind her boss that she needed to leave imminently for the opera. The Controller of BBC Two nodded and continued to gaze into the distance, deep in thought. David Walliams and I sat opposite her, trying desperately to read her face, looking for a sign, something, *anything*.

Nothing.

Jon Plowman, one of the Comedy bigwigs at the BBC, broke the silence. 'Jane?'

She blinked, as if waking from a dream. 'I've just cancelled *Big Train*. If I say yes to this show, I have to be able to justify it to everyone who was involved in that.'

She returned to her trance. David and I shared a look. The seconds ticked by.

But more of that later. All in good time.

Patience.

Following on from our first Edinburgh show in 1995, we were asked to put together a series of sketches for the Paramount Channel – all TV parodies, directed by twenty-one-year-old prodigy Edgar Wright – which had gained us a cult following. We filmed a few more, for Channel 4, and then we made a six-part series of ten-minute films for BBC Two starring Sir Bernard and Tony Rodgers (again directed by Edgar).

I'd had a rude awakening before *Sir Bernard's Stately Homes* was even broadcast, when Reece Shearsmith came over to my house one night. We'd become firm friends with the *League of Gentlemen* team at the Edinburgh Festival a few years before.

I was going to show him some of our series, but first he was going to screen a couple of episodes of *The League of Gentleman*. As soon as it began I realised that we were occupying different universes. We had made a mildly-amusing-if-you-like-that-sort-of-thing bunch of short films. They had made something groundbreaking, a masterpiece, perhaps the greatest comedy series of its time. I was blown away by its originality, its confidence, its command. It looked and sounded like no other comedy show. Two episodes turned into six – I didn't want it to end.

Then it was time to show Reece our offering. He was very polite and positive about it, but the ground had shifted. Not long afterwards both series were screened. *The League of Gentlemen* rightly received every plaudit – and award – going. Our first episode was greeted with a muted response – and that's putting a gloss on it. The critics labelled the show juvenile and flat. Victor Lewis-Smith, whose radio show I had been an avid fan of as a teenager, suggested, in his *London Evening Standard* review, that, instead of broadcasting the second ten-minute episode, the BBC would be better off having ten minutes' silence, in memory of our careers.

I remember Bob Mortimer telling me how you must always launch with your strongest episode, because that was the one the critics were going to see. Because our series told a story, we were locked into an episode order. I thought that it started to get a lot better by episode four, but by then it was too late. David and I had an idea for a second series but there was no hunger from anyone for that.

After the disappointment of *Sir Bernard's Stately Homes*, TV execs' interest in us seemed to wane. The considered opinion was that we were great onstage but weren't really ready for TV.

We were rescued by Myfanwy Moore, who had been at university with David and who had commissioned us a few years earlier to make the Paramount sketches. She was now running a new cable channel – UK Play – which would feature pop videos introduced by comedians.

Myfanwy asked us and a few comedians to record some links. We decided that, rather than doing Sir Bernard and Tony again, it would make sense to spoof pop stars just as we'd spoofed TV shows. They weren't accurate impressions – in fact, we delighted in being inaccurate. We had loved how Vic and Bob had almost gone out of their way to misrepresent celebrities. Bob's Noel Edmonds wore a strange distorting bodysuit but somehow it seemed to capture the host perfectly. We would adopt the same approach as them, just as we had done at Paramount, by taking a kernel of truth and then magnifying it dispro-portionately. For instance, Brian May and Anita Dobson famously had similar hairstyles. In our parody they were a two-headed monster, sharing a specially made two-headed silk shirt and speaking in unison. Björk, to us, was like a little puppet – all squeaky and childlike – so when I played her, she was a ventriloquist puppet, with David dressed as Keith Harris, operating her.

Myfanwy thought we'd seized our opportunity and really made some-thing of it, so she asked us to come up with an idea for our own series. It had to be at least 50 per cent music, because that was the channel's remit, but we could pretty much do what we wanted with the other half, as long as it didn't cost very much. In fact, the budget for the first series was so small it was shot on Mini-DV (i.e. video camera!).

It made sense to us to make the music a feature of our series, rather than try to fight it, so with *Rock Profile* we decided to spoof *The O-Zone*, a popular magazine interview show which ran on Sundays on BBC Two, hosted by Jamie Theakston. Luckily for us, we managed to snag Jamie himself to host our spoof. He had been in the National Youth Theatre before he'd become a presenter, but even so, it isn't always easy to play yourself. We needn't have worried – Jamie was spot-on at sending himself up, really easy to work with and a great laugh.

Each episode needed about twelve or thirteen minutes of original material from us. We'd film two episodes in a day so we had plenty of lines to remember. We had to keep the shows relatively simple visually, because of the time and budget constraints. In a nod to *The Chart Show* we wrote five or six 'RockFacts' for each video, which scrolled across the screen as they played – though ours were completely made up.

Just like Paramount, who repeated us endlessly, UK Play showed *Rock Profile* again and again. It became their highest-rating show and it seemed a no-brainer for all of us to do a second series. We brought back some of the impersonations and created new ones. Most merciless was Gary Barlow (me), who was reduced to living in a bedsit with Howard Donald (David), railing against the global success of his former bandmate Robbie Williams. In the first series we had filmed the characters in David's flat and despite the best efforts of the team to repaint, I could still make out some faint Take That graffiti on his living-room wall for years afterwards. Now, bringing the characters back, we filmed on location and even shot on proper cameras!

By the end of the second series of *Rock Profile*, we learned that some of the people we had played – Robbie, George Michael, Geri Halliwell, Boy George – had become fans of the show. We wondered if we'd been too cruel – in the case of Gary Barlow, we definitely had and I've mumbled my apologies to him many times since – but at the time we were the underdogs, still on the outskirts, tucked away late at night on cable telly, and it felt cheeky and subversive rather than mean-spirited. We were still punching upwards, as they say.

Whenever we met TV execs, they told us that the show deserved to transfer to BBC Two or Channel 4. In the end it was bought by BBC Two, re-edited and screened at 11.25 p.m. on a Sunday night. We hoped this might lead to an original *Rock Profile* commission, with the type of slot and budget given to other comedy shows, but there was no further interest, despite positive reviews. Meanwhile Channel 4 launched Avid Merrion and his *Bo' Selecta!* show, which also spoofed pop stars in a surreal way. It became clear that *Rock Profile* had gone as far as it was going to go.

We turned our attentions instead to radio. We recorded a couple of pilots – one starring Sir Bernard, with *EastEnders* star Letitia Dean as special guest. It went down a storm with the live audience but the people at Radio 4 were less convinced. They declined to commission the show, though it was – and I'm not making this up – a full fifty weeks before they got round to telling us.

We had another go, this time producing a sketch show. I had got it into my head that we would do better without the audience there, that we could be more experimental and make something more intimate in the confines of a recording booth. I was right – it was more experimental and more intimate, but it still wasn't what Radio 4 were looking for. At least we had a much quicker response this time from the BBC, albeit not the one we wanted. It came in the form of just two words – 'Lacks conviction'.

In 1998 David and I rather optimistically wrote a TV script for a sketch show. We toyed around with different approaches and came up with the idea of asking the question 'Who is Britain?' Within a day or two, this had morphed into *Little Britain*. We liked the title. It felt distinctive.

The League of Gentlemen's stunning TV series had raised the bar, in terms of sketch comedy. It had worked not only because it was funny and original, but also because it had such a clear identity. Most other sketch shows seemed just to be scattergun – a film parody here, a spoof advert there, a historical sketch, some stand-up, a song. We'd already produced so many TV and pop parodies, we knew we didn't want to go straight back down that path.

Little Britain had rules. All of the sketches were fourth wall, in that the characters never knew that they were on camera. This meant no monologues down the lens and no talking directly to the audience. Also there were no parodies or songs or animation. The only aspect of the show that was different was the framing device, because there was a narrator who could be heard speaking directly to the audience. We liked the idea that he or she would be able to provide information for the viewer before each sketch had begun, allowing us to start the sketch at the latest possible point, without loads of boring set-up.

We thought the *Little Britain* script was probably the best thing we'd written, but we just couldn't convince BBC Two Controller Jane Root to invest in us at that level. In fact, we couldn't even get a meeting with her. I only knew what she looked like because I'd seen a photo of her in *The Guardian*.

A chance meeting in the street was to change everything. Not with the elusive Jane Root – yet – but with my old school friend Ashley Blaker. We hadn't seen each other for a few years. He told me that he'd recently been taken on by the BBC as a trainee radio comedy producer.

He wondered if we had anything we might like to develop with him. I spoke with David and he was understandably reticent. Radio seemed like a closed shop to us. However, we saw little harm in dusting off the *Little Britain* script and modifying it for radio. After all, most of the work had already been done. We had a few new ideas, so we penned some more sketches and we made the narrator more pompous and provocative, more of a character. He would provide the listener with useful information, but it was often governed by his old-fashioned, bigoted or just plain unhinged attitudes. While there was a sense of reality about the sketch characters, the narrator himself was simply not to be trusted.

As for who would provide the narration, we had a wish list. There were only three names on it, if I recall correctly. Tom Baker was first choice. Second choice was Michael Sheard, who had played the terrifying Mr Bronson in *Grange Hill*. In third place was Harold Pinter. We thought Pinter was about the longest of shots imaginable, but it amused us to have his name on the list. We approached Tom first, assuming he'd be too busy, expensive or picky. To our delight he said yes.

Tom was everything we hoped he'd be, times ten. Friendly, garrulous, eccentric, mystical, ungovernable, maybe even slightly delirious. He was also magnificent. Maybe for him it was just a nice change from the daily grind of dreary commercial voiceovers, but for us it was magical. He lent his iconic voice to our material and gave it authority.

With the voiceover in the can, we gathered at the Drill Hall in London – now RADA Studios – on 20 January 2000 to rehearse and record the pilot, alongside Paul Putner, Samantha Power and Jean Ainslie. We'd worked with Samantha in our Paramount series and seen Jean in *The Day Today*. As the audience took their seats, we waited anxiously at the back of the room, by the stairs.

I turned to Ashley . . . 'This needs to work tonight. This is the last roll of the dice.'

Well, luckily for us it did.

In that pilot alone, we featured Emily Howard, Jason (who falls for his friend's nan), Dafydd Thomas, our take on Dennis Waterman and Marjorie Dawes.

Marjorie had already appeared on *Shooting Stars*, but not as a weight-loss course instructor. This new incarnation of the character was much more demonic and there was never any mention of her son George, who didn't feel like he'd come from the same universe as *Little Britain*.

Dennis, in a way, was unusual because it felt more like something we would have done in the Paramount series or on *Rock Profile*. It was another of our 'un-impressions'. We took a tiny grain of truth – that the real Dennis Waterman sometimes sings the theme tune to shows he's in – and turned it into his obsession. In actual fact the real Dennis didn't even write the *Minder* theme, but it amused us no end to imagine he refused to accept jobs unless he could 'write da feemtoon, sing da feemtoon'. This obsession turned him into a child (or at least someone who spoke like a child) and turned his agent Jeremy almost into the role of a pleading parent, trying to reason with their kid.

Emily Howard was David's idea. He once told an interviewer he'd like to live the last ten years of his life as a woman and I'm not entirely sure he was joking. When I first met David he'd think nothing of going out for the night in a skirt, black lipstick, fingernails painted and a clip in his hair, often with his then-girlfriend Katy on his arm. He revelled in the shock he created. I thought he was nuts.

Emily was a straight male transvestite who wanted to pass herself off not as a woman, but as a *lady*. The fun for us was that she thought that to do so she had to subscribe to outmoded Edwardian ideals of femininity, like the dainty heroine of a Barbara Cartland novel – ideals that were barely even attainable for women, let alone burly men. It was as much about her being out of her time, as out of her gender.

Sometimes I receive complaints on Twitter about Emily from members of the transgender community, who say that the sketches led to them being teased and alienated. Initially I was surprised. In our minds we saw a clear distinction between our character – a man who wears women's clothing for gratification – and someone who was born into the body of the wrong gender. We wouldn't have made jokes about the latter, but we considered the former fair game. It makes me sad to think that what we thought of as harmless might have had a negative impact on people who were already suffering. I think there are lot of characters and themes we'd approach very differently if we were doing the show now, and I'm sure Emily would be one of them.

Dafydd was inspired by a very sweet guy we'd both come across in the National Youth Theatre. David recalled how this man had just come out (as bisexual, actually) and was convinced he was the only one in the group. He often lamented feeling so isolated, but seemed to enjoy it at the same time, because it made him special and different. Walliams realised this was a great starting point for a sketch. As ever, I marvelled at – and benefited from – his ability to pinpoint a defining characteristic and guide us as we turned it into almost a living person.

And when it came to Dafydd, I could at once empathise with the dichotomy of the gay man when he comes out – you want recognition, respect, understanding and of course companionship, but as soon as you have those things you no longer feel like a martyr, you're no longer the keeper of the all-powerful secret. You gain so much when you come out, but, to your surprise, you do also lose something as well.

Dafydd's coming out turns his small Welsh village upside down – but not in the way he has anticipated. No one bats an eyelid. Instead of bigotry he finds an absurd matter-of-factness from even the blokiest of blokes. In fact, it seems as if the whole town has been at it themselves all along.

The sketch in which teenager Jason falls in love with his best friend's nan was actually something we'd written in an afternoon for a TV pilot for Paul Kaye. David had worked with Paul on BBC Two's *The Sunday Show* – which saw Paul's alter ego Dennis Pennis terrorise celebs as they strode unwittingly up the red carpet – and Paul and I had become firm football friends, often going to Arsenal games together.

We were excited to give the sketch to Paul, but when the production company told us that the few hundred pounds we were getting paid for the sketch meant they retained complete ownership of the idea, we paused before signing the contract. We'd heard how Harry Enfield's character Tim Nice-But-Dim had been written originally by Ian Hislop and Nick Newman, and that the writers had an option not only to write further instalments of the character but to get a piece of the action if Tim Nice-But-Dim ever appeared in, say, a film or as part of a tour or on a T-shirt etc. In short, they kept a share of the IP – the intellectual property. We were more than happy to accept a nominal fee for writing the Jason and Nan sketch, but when we asked what we might get in return if the sketch ended up spinning off into sequels or into an advert, there were no guarantees or obligations. Even though Paul was a friend of ours, would have been perfect in the sketch and I'm sure had not the slightest idea at all about the business deal being proposed to us, we felt we had no option but to take the sketch back.

And I'm glad we did. Jason and Nan were *naughty* in a way that would come to define *Little Britain*.

Vicky Pollard was inspired in part by one of the vox pops in a short film I had made at university with some of my course mates. We had been put into groups of four and set the task of producing a six-minute documentary. I came up with a simple idea, called 'How Are You?', which involved putting the question to passers-by in Bristol's Broadmead shopping centre. It was the natural response of almost everyone to say 'Fine, thank you', but then we'd delve a little deeper – asking if they'd answered truthfully, if not why not etc.

One of the contributors was a young lad, who replied in a sweet but bumbling manner. When I showed the film to David, we started to impersonate him and his thick West Country accent until it escalated to the point where he had become the least articulate person in Britain. Along the way he became a she – one of those petrifying teenage girls who stare you out at the bus stop – and, working backwards, we reasoned that Vicky's staggering inarticulacy was the result of her buying time as she tried to conjure up an excuse for whatever misdemeanour she had committed on that particular day.

Often when we created characters, David would start at the beginning and I would start at the end. By which I mean he would think of the central comic conceit first, summed up in just a line sometimes, and I was able to help flesh it out, give it nuance, make it distinctive.

An example of this was his idea for a character, Mr Mann, who goes into a shop to buy something incredibly specific without even knowing if such a thing even exists. He suggested someone looking for 'a pirate memory game called Yo Ho Ho, suitable for ages six to twelve'.

As we began writing and rehearsing the scene, I started to add the strange, archaic, parochial Northern tone. The sketch evolved and we began to mess around with long pauses. When we transferred to TV, we figured that if we didn't ever see Margaret (the woman who Roy the shopkeeper shouts upstairs to), we could continue to release ever more unlikely nuggets of information about her. For instance, we learn several sketches in that she is not able to help look for something because 'I haven't got any arms or legs'. This got us a big laugh – not only because it was a surprise, and because the information was delivered in such a matter-of-fact way, but also because we didn't actually have to *see* the horrible reality of it!

Whereas David would usually arrive with a line for a sketch that we'd then flesh out, often my ideas for a character or sketch came from just a phrase someone might say or even an odd vocal mannerism, and then we'd work backwards to figure out how and why someone might say that.

I remember suggesting a situation where a government adviser was relaying the results of the latest inane round of market research back to the prime minister. We came up with various faddish ideas of what people might have said when questioned. One of them was 'People would like to see you in shorts more'. David immediately seized on that, and we worked back until he figured out that actually this might have more comic mileage if these weren't real market research results but instead just a ruse by a smitten aide to try and get the PM into a skimpier outfit for his own pleasure. Thus Sebastian was born. Any similarity he might have had to Peter Mandelson, then a close ally and trusted adviser to the real prime minister, may or may not have been coincidental.

But occasionally I had the clarity myself to sum up a character in a single line before we put pen to paper. One example was smooth-talking Kenny Craig. 'A hypnotist who uses his powers offstage but for very small gain,' I wrote. The example I gave was of him being at the counter at McDonald's – 'In a moment I will ask for *six* chicken McNuggets. You will place *nine* chicken McNuggets in the box.'

Incidentally, though we were confident Kenny would work in the radio show, there was uncertainty about Sebastian and the PM. David was a bigger fan of the sketches than I was, but neither of us was wholly sure that they'd get laughs. We wrote them quite late in the process, but wanted them to appear across the series, which meant that even though we'd never performed the characters before, we'd have to record three Sebastian sketches in a night. We were nervous enough about the response to ask our producer Ashley to leave the outside broadcast truck where he'd be listening and come into the theatre and give us a hand signal if he still wanted us to record the third sketch. However, the audience laughed so wildly at the first two that he didn't need to bother.

The first series of *Little Britain* was a success, in the way that a Radio 4 show can be. Which means you don't really hear much from anyone at the top – or even the middle – but that they let you come back and make some more.

The Drill Hall wasn't available, so this time we recorded at the BBC Radio Theatre in Portland Place. When I listened to the episodes back afterwards, I was a bit disappointed, as the sound was flatter, slicker and somewhat muted. The studio was purpose-built for radio, but to me it sounded over-processed and – because so many other shows record there – the same as everyone else's show. The Drill Hall definitely had more of a live feel.

In the second radio series we introduced the character that became Ray McCooney, the Scottish hotelier. Here he was just a chef, but he had the same distinct brogue and infuriating manner. We had a lot of fun writing that character, coming up with weird riddles and ridiculous olde-worlde sayings.

From the radio pilot onwards, we made no secret of our ambitions to transfer to television and often started sentences with 'When we do this on TV . . .' as if it was a foregone conclusion. It wasn't. Despite the success of the radio show, we still couldn't command an audience with Jane Root.

We did, however, manage to attract the attentions of Stuart Murphy, who had recently taken over the reins at the soon-to-be-launched BBC Three. The channel was going to be aimed at viewers in their teens and twenties. It was going to have lots of money invested in it and a great deal of promotion. Stuart wanted to commission us to make a pilot of *Little Britain*.

It might sound crazy now, but we were resistant. BBC Three was going to be a cable channel. We'd already made shows for Paramount and UK Play and were worried that if we made *Little Britain* for yet another new cable channel we'd be blowing our big chance to reach the wider audience we felt this show deserved. It was said that some BBC Three programmes might get a transmission on BBC Two or even BBC One, but there was no assurance.

We met with Stuart, whose enthusiasm and support was rousing. He said we should go big, and have cameras swooping over the landscape. We liked the sound of that. He also wondered if we might have a funky music soundtrack running beneath the sketches. I could see why – the BBC audience was going to be young, and Dom Joly had had music embedded in *Trigger Happy TV* to great effect, but we said we thought that it might distract the audience and he said that was fine. We appreciated his support – he had strong ideas but wasn't using his position to force them on us. He was just a fan of the show and wanted to pitch in and get the thing made.

We were very flattered by Stuart's interest, but we were adamant that if we made *Little Britain* for TV, we needed a proper budget and a guaranteed slot on a mainstream channel. Stuart told us that if we made a pilot for him, he'd show it on BBC Three's launch night – which was being simultaneously broadcast on BBC Two.

Meanwhile Graham Linehan, who had co-written *Father Ted* and *Big Train*, had become a big champion of the radio shows and offered to produce and direct the TV pilot. Graham was a big, bold, brilliant shock to the system.

We had promised Stuart and anyone else who would listen that we were not simply going to make a radio show on TV. We would do our best to defy the programme's radio origins and make it as enjoyable to watch as it had been to listen to. For me, that meant costume and make-up, and fancy camera work. As for everything else, I still believed that if a sketch had been successful on radio, we had effectively earned the right to pretty much just stand it on its feet and point a camera at it.

However, from day one, Graham was insistent that this was not just a lazy approach, it was also missing a real opportunity. He set about reworking everything. I was resistant at first. I was being over-reverential towards the material. For Graham it held less of a mystique. Often he just wanted to use it as a launch pad to see what else we could do.

There were tensions in the room, and within a day or two David and Myfanwy – who was producing – made it clear to me that Graham wasn't obliged to spend his time on our pilot. If I didn't toe the line, he'd be gone.

My unwillingness to explore wasn't to do with ego – I was just genuinely fearful of changing something that we knew already worked. However, I didn't want to lose Graham's brilliance, not to mention his passion and positivity. Also, of course, I didn't want to jeopardise the pilot. Who knows whether Stuart might have pulled the plug if Graham left?

I took a deep breath and joined Graham, David and Myfanwy on the trip. And what a trip it was. Over the next few weeks we experimented and played around with the material, and wrote some brand new stuff too.

The first thing Graham wanted to do was to get rid of Marjorie. He felt that she was too similar to *The League of Gentlemen*'s 'Pauline' character. We saw his point – a woman bullying a room full of people – but we really liked the character. It had been one of the most popular sketches in the radio series and we argued that none of the jokes were the same as Pauline's. The compromise was that Marjorie would remain, but we'd change the setting to make the sketch appear – cosmetically, at least – less similar. Thus the scene in the pilot takes place in Marjorie's sitting room.

One of the stand-out sketches from the pilot was our take on Dennis Waterman. It might have been Graham's idea – I don't remember now – but we decided to shrink Dennis, literally making him the size of a child onscreen. We knew that we could use CGI to achieve the effect but we were adamant that the sketches would be more fun if we used more innocent, old-fashioned techniques. Two replica sets were built – one in each size – and the action cuts between the two. The props were made twice and often we'd defy the rules of ratio in pursuit of the biggest laugh.

When it came to making the series, my favourite Dennis moment is when he is terrified by a mouse – which is actually played by a man in a purposefully ropey costume. As if to play up the shameless stupidity of the moment, the mouse actor simply opens the door and walks out of the office.

Incidentally, it might amuse you to learn that the animal handler who brought along the real mouse that day flinched and shuddered as she placed it on the desk. When I asked if she was all right, she told me she was terrified of mice. To which I thought, well, if you're terrified of mice, there are literally tens of thousands of jobs in the world which don't in any way involve handling mice. Just putting it out there . . .

Also, please notice, if you will, the correct use of the word 'literally' in the above paragraph. Yes, believe it or not, I have opted to use the word 'literally' to actually mean 'literally', rather than 'figuratively'. A novel move, you will agree. Millennials – take note.

In the radio show I had played the prime minister in the Sebastian sketches. When we were casting the TV pilot, we all agreed that we would need someone far dishier and more authoritative (and, I like to think, older) to play the prime minister opposite Sebastian. We decided to look for a 'Tony Head-type'. For some reason, it wasn't until we were quite far along in the casting process that some bright spark actually suggested we approach the man himself. We doubted he'd be either available or interested, as he was then happily ensconced in Hollywood, playing Rupert Giles in *Buffy the Vampire Slayer*, but by chance we caught him during the show's hiatus and he liked the script enough to say yes.

We didn't actually meet him until he'd already accepted our offer. Lucky for us, then, that he was not only perfect in the role, but also warm and friendly and a great team player. The farcical nature of the sketches meant that they continually evolved during rehearsals, sometimes even being rewritten on the day of filming. Tony was either at ease with this, or he simply didn't let on! Either way, we could not have found a better prime minister. He made him Blair-like, without ever doing a distracting impersonation. He understood exactly what was needed, and knew how to make the character authoritative yet strangely vulnerable, and always real.

For TV we had to decide what our teenage delinquent Vicky Pollard would look like. We'd seen the cover of an issue of *Time Out* magazine some years earlier that had featured two feisty teenage girls from

Brighton, all pigtails, snarls and too much eyeliner, glaring provocatively at the camera. I'd shown this page to David and we'd kept it, rather optimistically, for reference should it ever come in handy.

In a costume-hire store we came across a bright pink Kappa top. It amused us to think that this was what Vicky would wear in court – which was the setting for the pilot sketch. It didn't occur to us that she would wear this as frequently as she did, but we never found anything else that seemed to work as well. Ditto Marjorie Dawes, with her royal blue jacket and purple culottes. Incidentally, years later I was at the Wynn Casino in Las Vegas when a man approached me with an angry look on his face. He told me he was head of Kappa in the UK and that the company blamed the fact that Vicky wore a Kappa top for a sharp downturn in the brand's fortunes! As I write this, a decade or so later, I'm delighted to see Kappa has been reborn.

On the night of the BBC Three launch we went to Television Centre and were interviewed by Johnny Vaughan. The following day we had a few reviews and it was generally well received – no raves, but no drubbings either. Stuart called and said he'd love us to do a series. BBC Three would put up half the money . . .

Which brings us back to 20 August 2002 and that glass-walled office, where Jane Root continued to stare into the distance. We watched patiently.

We were used to being patient. It had taken eight patient years of patient slog and patient graft just to get into the BBC Two Controller's office.

'We've got Tom Baker,' I proffered.

'Yes, and Tony Head,' David added.

'Well, that just means I can't put it on after *Manchild*.'

And then, again, silence.

Jon Plowman turned to her. 'Jane, I *urge* you to commission this show.'

The assistant reappeared at the door. Jane really would be late for the opera if she didn't leave now. Root sighed and mumbled a few words. And with that, we were ushered out.

And I really wasn't sure if *Little Britain* had just been commissioned or not.

I turned to David. 'Did she just say yes?'

'Um . . . I *think* so.'

'She did,' said Jon.

'You sure?'

'Yup,' he replied.

David and I turned to each other. 'YAHOOOOOOO!!!' we screamed, as we ran along the corridors of TV Centre, hugging and kissing strangers in our path. 'We're gonna be the biggest fucking stars on the planet!!!'

No, of course we didn't. We just got in the lift and went down.

Words by
Matt Lucas
Music by
Matt Lucas and Alicia Witt

Music Arranged,
Performed and Produced by
Kevan Frost
Vocals Performed by
Matt Lucas

Middle of the Book

To hear the song please visit middleofthebook.com

still a way to go so much to talk a-bout, I know. I've made a list of what I must im-

part so if you like to read those books a-bout the biz, there's

Doc - tor Who and Pom - pi - dou and don't for-get Les Mis... But

first the____ mid - dle of the book is here, it's plain

may - be you should go and Skype your mum. Some

ex - er - cise would do you good. The dog needs tak - ing out. But hur - ry back be -

cause there's more to come.

N – Nearest and Dearest

My dad John was born in 1944 and my mum Diana a year later. Dad grew up in East Finchley and Mum not far away in Golders Green. He was with a group of lads that gatecrashed her birthday party. They started dating and before long they were engaged. They married in 1968 and moved a few miles further out to the north-west London suburb of Stanmore. You'll find it at the top of the Jubilee line.

Dad's father Harry had been a respected figure in the community. He was a successful accountant and once stood as a Labour candidate. My father was expected to follow him into the business, but chose instead to forge his own path, starting up a company that traded in aluminium.

Mum worked for the BBC World Service. She'd been George Melly's secretary at one point. On one occasion she interviewed her father Maurice Williams, one of Britain's most celebrated philatelists and, with his brother Leon Norman Williams, a prolific writer and a regular face on TV.

When they married, Dad felt it was no longer appropriate for his wife to make the long journey into town every day, so she quit and took a part-time job at a travel agent's instead.

In 1971 my older brother Howard was born, and then I came along in 1974. Home life was typical, middle-class, English and Jewish. Our parents would go out once or twice a week in the evening to see friends – they had many – but otherwise Howard and I would sit in front of the TV, then Dad would come home from work and we'd squeal with laughter at a Laurel and Hardy or Harold Lloyd short together while Mum cooked, and then we'd all eat together.

At night the landing light would be left on and the door ajar, as my brother and I lay in our bunks, squinting at Roald Dahl and *Ponder and William* when we should have been asleep. It was no surprise that we both soon had to wear glasses.

Howard enjoyed the benefits of being the older one. He had the top bunk and would tell me he had sweets for me, so I'd climb up to see him repeatedly, only to find it was a wind-up. At school he'd protect me; at home he'd terrorise me – the usual brotherly stuff. When we played in the garden on a see-saw (which went round and round as well as up and down), Howard would swing it round at speed, and as his legs were longer than mine I was at his mercy, growing dizzy. He'd stop suddenly, then stand on his seat so that I was suspended in the air. When he was ready he'd step off and I'd come crashing down helplessly to the ground with a thud. The most elaborate prank he played on me involved a letter he'd faked from Matthew Corbett, which left me sitting patiently on the stairs in my best clothes, waiting all afternoon for Sooty, Sweep and Soo to arrive and take me out for the day.

At weekends we'd see our grandmothers – both now widowed. My dad's mother Fay was far less strict than Mum's mother Margot, who doted on us but made clear her disapproval if we were ill-mannered or not paying attention.

In the school holidays we went to Golders Hill Park or were taken into central London to see the sights, visit exhibitions, even to attend classical music concerts. Fun tended to have an element of education attached. We went to the Science Museum, the Natural History Museum, the Imperial War Museum and many more. My favourite was MOMI, the short-lived but rather wonderful Museum of the Moving Image, situated on the South Bank. They had actors there who would wander around in character, interacting with the public. One, in Soviet military uniform, attempted to usher us onto a train carriage which was screening an Eisenstein film. Grandma pulled me away tightly – 'We are *not* being ordered around by a Russian!'

We'd swim whenever we could. At Harrow Leisure Centre we'd enjoy the outdoor pool in the summer, or the two indoor ones. My head was always turned by the line of arcade machines that formed a path towards the changing rooms, but they were usually occupied by older, more confident boys. If I was lucky enough to get a go, they'd chew gum next to me impatiently, rolling their eyes and swearing quietly as they endured the short wait it took for me to lose my pennies.

There were three pools at Copthall: a main pool, a kids' pool and a diving pool. An oft-repeated rumour went round that someone had belly-flopped from the top board and their stomach had split open and they'd died instantly – but that didn't stop us.

Sometimes Dad would take me and Howard to watch Arsenal. My father had flipped over the handlebars of his pushbike when he was fourteen, causing serious injury. The surgeon who operated on him also happened to be surgeon to the Arsenal team. My father spent the best part of a year recuperating and was very kindly given Arsenal tickets while he did so. He passed his love of the club on to Howard, who passed it on to me. I was excited when we made the trip to Highbury every few months to see a game, though it would be a few years until I found myself able to follow it. As a youngster I thought the matches themselves crushingly dull and impenetrable, but the sense of occasion, of being part of something, and of being with my family appealed to me greatly. I couldn't wait to get dressed up in my red and white top, scarf and hat, and chant with the others.

When I was seven we holidayed in Corsica with some family friends. The mums cooed over the royal wedding of Charles and Diana on TV, which bored us kids and our dads rigid. Mum would talk of little else for weeks and even bought a souvenir videocassette case to house the tape she had recorded the wedding on. Dad had set the video, because Mum could never work out how to do it.

I thought the video recorder was extraordinary. I'd first come across one in 1979 when some family friends went away for a couple of weeks and let us borrow theirs. I sat in the lounge and watched *The Wizard of Oz*, nearly wetting myself in terror. I was desperate for the loo, but didn't realise the film could be paused. I also assumed if I walked in front of the TV while it was playing, my image would be superimposed onto the film, ruining the tape forever.

A year later we hired our own video recorder. It came with a free copy of that most ghoulish of disaster movies, *The Poseidon Adventure*. I watched it endlessly, gradually becoming immune to the suffering of the characters, their fate already clear.

Childhood seemed to involve having the same books read to me and watching the same TV shows and films over and over again. It never bothered me that I knew what was going to happen. Like many children I found reassurance and comfort in familiarity. When we rented films from the local video shop, I'd usually watch them twice in twenty-four hours, and more often than not I'd already seen the damn thing in the cinema anyway.

At Christmas I would commandeer the video recorder, buying the *Radio Times* and *TV Times* at the earliest possible opportunity, highlighting what I would be watching and what I would be taping. It was a military operation, with charts drawn up and clear notices stuck on the recorder – 'MATT IS RECORDING! DO NOT TOUCH!' For my birthday each year I'd ask for blank videocassettes.

I've already mentioned my parents' separation. It was during the school holidays in 1984 that Howard and I were sat down and given the news. Dad said he would move out shortly, but wouldn't go far, and said he would still come and see us often. He confessed he'd been sleeping downstairs in the living room for a while, putting his bedding away each morning before we woke up.

I was gobsmacked. I had heard of couples splitting up, and of rows and shouting, but there hadn't been any of that, to my knowledge. They told us that we weren't to blame and that we would not be affected by the split. The former might have been true, but the latter was a naive, unsustainable promise, given the anger and recriminations that were soon to rise to the surface.

Once separated, battle lines were drawn. Our parents generally maintained a frosty civility when they came into contact, but when not in each other's presence, neither of them hid from my brother or me their disdain for and frustration with each other. If I was with my dad, sentences would often angrily begin with 'Thanks to your mother . . .', and she was the same towards my father.

My parents had been very sociable and had had a seemingly endless supply of friends – mainly other Jewish couples of a similar age. In the separation, many of them were also divided, like belongings. Sometimes one parent would express disappointment over the loss of a particular friend or relative, whom he or she felt had unfairly taken the side of the other.

Divorce was not common back then. I only knew one friend, Jeremy, whose parents had been through it. He said it would be all right, that I'd get used to it. Meanwhile I harboured hopes that the separation would be temporary and that things might one day get back to normal. However, my hopes failed to materialise. The relationship had broken down irretrievably. My mother had fallen in love with someone else.

After Dad left, our house went on the market, so it became the norm to have people come to view it. One Saturday he mentioned to me and Howard that a lady called Andie was coming to look at the house, and it so happened that she was a friend of his. He said she also went to our synagogue and we should be nice to her. Of course she was already a good deal more than a friend, but this was a clever, less pressured way of introducing us. He told us later she had been the only woman he had dated, following the end of his marriage. He said he had gone to a singles group – where everyone had looked glum, except for her. She was smiling.

She didn't actually have all that much to smile about. Only a year or two earlier she had lost her husband to a terrible illness. She had two kids, Darren and Barbra, a little older than my brother and me. The first time we met them, at their house, I groaned – and so did Darren. I knew him from Hebrew classes. He was one of the kids who'd teased me for not having any hair, so much so that his parents had been called in to see the headmaster. However, all former rivalries were instantly forgotten and we got along famously – despite his love of Tottenham Hotspur. I was always happy to spend time with Barbra as well. She thought I was cute as a button. She always made a fuss of me and we'd sit on her bed, listening to Duran Duran, George Michael and Phil Collins, playing with her kittens and chatting about our favourite TV shows.

Dad had been planning to buy a small house, but before long he moved in with Andie, Barbra and Darren instead; and soon he and Andie got married. Andie was gregarious, outspoken, an extrovert, always busy, often cooking. She could be strict with us too. While Howard and I were pleased that our father had met someone else, our mother and grandmother were quite strict already and there was an interminable amount of being told what to do from our teachers at school, so neither of us particularly wanted to have yet another figure of authority in our lives. Once we were a little older, we got along better with her. We were less brattish, and she was able to relax and not feel any obligation to be parental. A relief all round!

My father set up a new business as a high-end cab driver. He got hold of a second-hand Mercedes, worked tirelessly and built up contracts with regular customers. He would frequently drive Lord and Lady Caledon, whom he was very fond of. He also regularly drove the singer Lynsey de Paul and she once sent him to deliver a bouquet of flowers for a friend. He knocked on the door and out came Freddie Mercury, in a dressing gown. My two favourite men just met each other, I remember thinking to myself, though I scolded him too for not returning with an autograph.

I loved hearing of the celebs he'd driven – the Pet Shop Boys, TV-am weather girl Wincey Willis, Trevor McDonald, Jools Holland, Michael Fish. He arrived early once at the home of Paul Daniels and Debbie McGee, who kindly invited him in for breakfast. He drove Roy Orbison, who he had been a huge fan of, and also – most surreal of all – spent a weekend chauffeuring the Afrikaner white supremacist Eugène Terre'Blanche, who expressed gratitude that my father could voice vastly opposing political views without resorting to abuse.

One job sticks in my mind most of all. One day my father mentioned that he was now regularly driving one of the boys in my year to school. I was surprised that news hadn't already got back to me. The boy in question knew that it was my dad who was driving him and he never mentioned it to me or – as far as I know – to anyone else. I was grateful for this. Other boys at Haberdashers' would have sneered at me if they knew that my father drove one of the other boys to school for a living. The main thing I felt, however, was envy. I wished I could spend as much time with my dad as this boy.

Things didn't work out with Mum's relationship and she soon found herself on the singles circuit. Ever the hostess with the mostest, Saturday nights frequently saw a trail of fellow divorcees arrive at the house for tea and sympathy. I enjoyed the company of my mum's battle-worn new friends, who'd doll themselves up to prove they still had it, and who'd make a fuss of me. I'd nosily sit in on their conversations, following their dramas for as long as I was allowed, before Mum would send me off to do my homework.

Every so often Mum would introduce me to a new beau. I liked some more than others, but none compared to the man she met a decade after the split, and who she would eventually marry – Ralph. They've been together for over twenty years now. He's warm, kind and smart – what we Jewish people call 'a proper mensch'. We don't have a father anymore, but we do have a loving stepfather, and another stepbrother, stepsister and their kids too. We're spoilt. Mum and Ralph are very happy together. They play bridge. They watch *Strictly*. They go on countless cruises and always return having made new friends.

My mum – like all good Jewish mothers – enjoys cooking. She loves to serve up roast chicken and roast potatoes and tell you that there's plenty more, insisting you have seconds, and then, as you leave, pointing out that you could really do with losing a bit of weight.

She likes some of *Little Britain*, but not the rude bits. She didn't mind *Come Fly with Me*. She doesn't understand *Doctor Who* – but then who does? If it was up to her, I'd probably still be in *Les Misérables*. Oh, and she read an early draft of this book and said it was 'all a bit Tears of a Clown'.

My brother and I speak or message most days. It's usually nonsense – silly photos we've seen online or football-related stuff. If he's at work and I'm watching the match on telly, I'll point my phone at the TV, film the goals on it and WhatsApp them to him. The bickering of our childhood has long since faded.

My father was surrounded by a loving family and had many friends, but he worked all hours, day and night, just to make ends meet for the last decade of his life. His efforts, and the accompanying stress, not to mention his heavy smoking habit, eventually caught up with him.

In November 1996 I was on tour, doing the *Shooting Stars* live show. Dad had driven to Reading on a Sunday night with Andie, Barbra and Darren to see the show. I hadn't seen him for five weeks as I'd been on the road and I was astounded by how skeletal he looked. He even had a walking stick – maybe two, if memory serves me right. He told me that he had a doctor's appointment the next morning. I was extremely shaken to see him so thin and frail and barely slept that night.

While on the tour bus the following morning, I received a phone call from him. He explained that the doctor had told him he'd had a virus but the good news was that it had gone. Now he needed to get his strength back and put on some weight again.

The following day we travelled through the night from Cambridge to Glasgow on the tour bus, and had just arrived at a hotel around 9 a.m. It was a rare day off and I was looking forward to having a kip and then catching a film.

My phone rang. It was my stepbrother Darren. He told me that my father had died. I made him repeat himself five or six times, because my brain wouldn't take the news in.

He'd had a massive heart attack in the kitchen of his home, causing him to fall. Darren and Barbra heard the noise and rushed downstairs. Darren tried to give him the kiss of life, but he was dead within a minute or two. We wondered if the fall had contributed to or even caused his death but the post-mortem revealed that the heart attack itself would have been fatal.

The tour was suspended for a week and a half. I flew straight back to London, meeting my mother, brother and grandmother at the airport.

I was too distressed to give a speech at the funeral, though Darren – who had already lost his own father – spoke eloquently about lightning striking twice.

I was so traumatised by my father's sudden death that my brain instantly locked away almost all of the memories I had of him, as if to protect me, I guess – or them. I still don't know where they are.

As I mourned, I realised I was not just grieving for his death, but also for much of his life. I spent the next few years lost, outside things, utterly bereft and refusing to believe that I could ever heal. Despite the love of my family and friends, it wasn't until 2002, when I met Kevin McGee, that I started to experience happiness again.

I finally met Sooty, Sweep and Soo!

Fascinating paparazzi shot of man rifling through satchel, must have fetched millions

O – Oh Look, it's Thingy

When I was six years old, my mum and dad took me and Howard to the London Palladium to see the Christmas pantomime *Dick Whittington and His Cat*. It starred Jim Davidson, Mollie Sugden, Windsor Davies, Lionel Blair, Melvyn Hayes and Clive Dunn. I was breathless with excitement at the prospect of seeing these big stars in real life and I wasn't disappointed. The show was delightful and I laughed like a drain. Throughout the performance I could scarcely comprehend that 'little me' was actually in the same room as them, and yet it felt logical too. I watched these people frequently on TV. They were my friends.

I enjoyed going to the cinema, but theatre became my true love. Often my Grandma Margot (she was from Germany so you pronounced the 't') would take me into central London to see matinees in the school holidays. At her prompting, we would hover at the stage door afterwards. As the actors appeared in their civvies, I'd hesitate, and then she'd push me forward towards them. 'Tell them you are an actor,' she'd say. I met Su Pollard, who chatted like we were old friends, and later Michael Gambon, Judi Dench, Topol and even a quiet, shy Gene Wilder. Bernard Hill kindly invited us in from the rain.

For my tenth birthday outing I went to see *Singin' in the Rain*. I dearly wanted to meet the star of the show, Tommy Steele, and went to speak to the stage doorman before the performance to ask if Tommy would be signing autographs afterwards. He gruffly told me not to get my hopes up. I spent the whole evening feeling sad and rejected.

After a matinee performance of *42nd Street* I was hoping to meet Frankie Vaughan, but the company manager told us he always had a sleep between shows. He did sign my programme, though, and it was sent back out to me. I was chuffed to bits.

Mum took me to see the musical *Time* and afterwards we joined a line of maybe twenty fans waiting to get Cliff Richard's autograph. Mum had told me many times how she'd been at an exhibition in her early teens, waiting for hours to meet the harmonica player Larry Adler, when an announcement was made – Larry was ill and instead an aspiring pop star named Cliff Richard would be appearing. My mum took one look at the spotty little imp, screwed up her face and left. He went on to become a megastar; she became a dedicated fan and spent the next thirty years kicking herself. Finally we were going to meet the man himself.

The first lady in the queue asked for the autograph to be personalised to her, and Sir Cliff apologised. He politely explained that he had a reservation at a restaurant with friends and last orders were in half an hour, so he hoped we'd understand if he just signed his name. The lady accepted this, and Sir Cliff signed.

The second person in the queue, either having not heard the conversation or just pushing her luck, also asked for a personalised autograph and Sir Cliff patiently took maybe thirty seconds to explain again why he was only signing his name tonight.

The next person made the same request and Sir Cliff gave the same reply, and was made to do so again and again, to everyone in the queue. I guess he couldn't have said no to the first few people and then yes to the others.

I watched with fascination as he diligently repeated this refrain, and couldn't help but think that he could have written *The Mahābhārata* by now and be round the corner tucking into coq au vin and a glass of Shloer. You will know by now that I can be a bit of a shitbag, so it won't surprise you to learn that I too couldn't resist making the same request. I wasn't too fussed as to whether I got a personalised autograph or not, but by then it seemed like a rite of passage just to be on the receiving end of Sir Cliff's glazed-eyed mantra. Of course, any right-minded non-celebrity would surely have turned to the third or fourth person and said 'Didn't you hear what I just said? No! I'm not writing your bloody name. I've just done a show. I'm hungry!' and then probably written 'You are a twat' instead of their name, but you can't do that when you're famous. No matter what the provocation or what's going on in your life, you are expected to just grin and bear it. Still, I guess patience and professionalism are part of what makes Sir Cliff special. That and the fact that he lives with a former priest, which only adds to his mystique.

Actually I did meet Sir Cliff once more, years later. Walliams and I were guesting on the Steve Wright radio show. He tends to pre-record his interviews so it's common to bump into other celebs when you're waiting to do yours. Last time it was Nick Clegg. Another time I spotted Jeremy Vine, but I didn't speak to him because he once slagged me off on *Points of View*.

Anyway, our publicist that day – Jackie Gill, one of my favourite people on the planet – is also Sir Cliff's publicist, so we begged her to introduce us to the great man himself. We were there to promote our first ever release, a CD compilation of the best bits from the *Little Britain* radio shows. I asked Sir Cliff for a *personalised* autograph for my mum and at the same time gave him one of our CDs. I don't think he had a clue who we were. He used the CD case to lean on as he signed a photo and then gave both items back to me in return.

Don't assume, by the way, that I don't think much of Sir Cliff, because I think plenty of him. And I'm not just saying that because my mum is going to be reading this book. 'In The Country' is one of my shower-time singalong standards, and it's easy to forget now but if you've ever seen the 1961 movie *The Young Ones*, you'll know that Sir Cliff Richard was once the sexiest man in Britain.

I digress.

In 1989 my school friend Andrew Bloch wrote to Russ Carvell, the cartoonist at a teen pop magazine called *Number One*. Andrew had subsequently been invited to visit the magazine's offices for a tour. He asked me and our pal Jason to join him. We met the magazine's editor, who couldn't have been friendlier and filled our open satchels with magazines, posters, badges and stickers.

On our way out we noticed a large gaggle of teenage girls chattering excitedly. Curious, we joined the queue and within minutes found ourselves in a nearby studio, watching Bros perform. I considered myself far too cool to be a fan of theirs, but they were the biggest band in Britain at the time, so I was happy to watch them as they sang 'I Owe You Nothing' for a live satellite link-up with Japanese TV.

After the song ended, one of the managers came out and said the boys would stay and meet the fans on the condition that we didn't all go crazy. Within seconds, Matt, Luke and Craig's clothes were being yanked at by a horde of screaming girls and they were ushered away, but not before I had been over to each of them and shaken their hands.

On the way back to Waterloo station that day I spotted Buster Edwards at his flower stall. He had recently been the subject of an entertaining biopic starring Phil Collins. I got Buster's autograph, which he signed 'Why me?' – 'Well, because you robbed that train, I suspect' was what I wanted to say, but that would have been ungracious.

I loved celebrities. I couldn't get enough of them. I read about them in the papers incessantly and tuned into every chat show. But why didn't it stop there? Why did my friend Robert and I spend a whole day handwriting fan letters to anyone who we thought might respond? Bananarama did, *Moonlighting* singer Al Jarreau didn't. And why did I feel the need to actually seek out and meet as many celebrities as I could? I knew that these stars and I weren't actually friends and most likely never would be, but for some reason I needed to feel as if I meant something to them – just as they did to me – even if only for a few seconds. In the short time I had in the presence of the famous people I encountered, while I shook with nerves, I felt both small and large, insignificant and yet elevated. I knew I wasn't on their level but I also knew – or at least believed – that I was now at least on a level above those who had not met them. And that was enough for me, for the time being.

Of course I had experienced a kind of fame myself since the age of six – the fame that goes with being the boy in your town with no hair. Unsurprisingly no one asked for my autograph or said they admired my work, but they stared at me and pointed and sniggered as I walked past, which does bear some similarity to what I experience these days.

Shooting Stars made me a fair bit more famous. Some would smile at the mere sight of me and shout 'What are the scores, George Dawes?' Others would squint at me – where did they know me from? Those who did recognise me, and came over to say hello, were usually more interested in the other four people on the show. Were Vic and Bob as *mental* in real life? What was Mark Lamarr's problem? And did I have Ulrika's phone number? It was recognition, but I had no gravitas. No one shook with nerves, like they sometimes do now.

Little Britain changed everything, in that it was everywhere, and so were we. Well, I was less everywhere than Walliams, who was single and enjoying the nightlife and the premieres, while I tended to stay in with Kevin, but the show was so big for a while, and so widely embraced by the tabloids and broadsheets, that the paparazzi would linger outside my house for hours on end, regardless of whether I was there or not. I remember Walliams once saying, 'You know you're famous when they print a photo of you not even doing anything'. He spoke from experience, and that was something we shared. We reached such a level of recognisability that, if I walked into a room, it was reasonably safe to assume at least someone in it would know who I was and, unlike a few years earlier, people now asked me questions about myself and the work, rather than about my co-stars.

These days it has calmed down a little. Mainly I spend my time in the US, where people once again ask me what it is they've seen me in. I am then obliged to list my credits. Each title is invariably followed by a 'no' until I get to *Bridesmaids*, a hugely successful movie in which I occupy perhaps six minutes of screen time. 'Oh yes! So what's Rebel Wilson like?' is the usual response.

And yet, returning to the UK after a few years in which I no longer invaded your TV set every week, I noticed a change. *Little Britain* ended in 2008 (or 2006, if you don't include the American version) and so there are plenty of younger folk – maybe those under the age of eighteen – who aren't as familiar with me.

But when I *do* get approached by people these days, it's pretty rare that anyone actually wants to talk about my work. What people really want to talk about . . . is fame. They want to know what it's like.

And so, in that spirit, I thought I'd make some observations – in no particular order – about being famous . . . (well, *my* level of famous, which I'd say is somewhere midway between Bruno Mars and Maureen from *Driving School*).

By the way – please note – this is not intended to be a whinge, a rant or a collection of boasts. It's just fame, as I have experienced it.

Here goes . . .

THE UNGRATEFUL CELEBRITY'S GUIDE TO BEING FAMOUS

1. Fame does not suddenly render you deaf or blind. You might think you have the best poker face, but I can see your shock/delight/disdain when you realise I am in the room. And I can *hear* you when you pass by me in the street and shout 'He's a lot shorter than I thought he'd be' or 'Oh no, I hate that bloke'.

2. When I first became famous people sometimes asked for an autograph. Now everyone has a phone with a camera on it. Sometimes I get asked for hundreds of photos a day and yet guess what? You might think you're being polite by not bothering me but I can see you sneaking that pic of me.

3. I definitely prefer it if you ask me for a photo as opposed to sneaking one.

4. No one knows how to work anyone else's camera phone. Or their own.

5. No one takes just one photo.

6. I won't think any less of you if you say you want a photo for yourself, but for some reason, I'd say at least three quarters of the people who

request a selfie tell me it's for someone else. A propos, people often ask me to pose for photos with their kids. I ask the kids if they know who I am and they shake their heads. Hence there are now hundreds of photos of me smiling with crying toddlers.

7. Many of the photos you see of stars arriving at an airport are taken seconds after the person has got off the flight, on their way to immigration. That's why people often look so tired and also why they sometimes argue with the photographers. While no member of the public is given access to that area (unless they are flying), snappers are. I assume the airport benefits financially from this. Certainly the airlines have staff that call up and tip off the press about who is on a flight. Restaurants, hotels, night clubs – there's a whole infrastructure of reliable sources who will earn extra revenue by letting journalists know your whereabouts. It's creepy.

8. Just because I'm famous doesn't mean I think I'm wonderful.

9. I am aware that people will surmise I am either lovely or horrible, based on a few seconds' evidence. I do try my hardest to be congenial, even when I am not in the best of moods. This makes me feel less guilty when I am having a really bad day and when – as my *Doctor Who* co-star Pearl Mackie put it so eloquently recently – 'I just don't have any chat left'.

During filming I incurred an injury on the set of *Doctor Who* that left me in permanent spasm for a few weeks. I found little relief from the pain and barely slept for the first couple of weeks but, schedules being what they are, I still had to leave the flat at 6.30 a.m. each day to go to work, hurtling through caves in second-century Aberdeen. Necking painkillers by the bucketload, I remained as bright and breezy as I could be. There were a lot of actors in these scenes and so, at the end of a long day, after four consecutive sleepless nights, instead of being taken back to my flat by one of our usual staff drivers, I was bundled into a minicab. No problem with that. Many people have to queue for the bus to get home. I'm lucky.

When I got in the car, the driver gasped. 'It's you! I know you! Yeah, they told me someone famous was getting in the car! So what are you filming here? And why don't I see you on TV anymore?' He then attempted to drive out the wrong way, and so the gate wouldn't open.

'That's the entrance,' I said. 'The exit is on the other side of the studio.'

'Oh, I've never been here before. What is this place anyway?' asked the driver.

Reader, I had no chat left. I was chatted out. I was Matt minus chat. I shouldn't have just opened the door, grabbed my bag and got out of the car without offering an explanation – but I did. That driver probably thinks I'm an arsehole. Actually, I probably am.

I lost it a couple of years ago too, when I took my friend's eleven-year-old son to see *Cats* at the London Palladium. During the interval I was ambushed and I felt bad for my friend's son, who sort of knows I'm a bit famous but doesn't really think of me in that way. He waited patiently as a line of people wanting selfies formed.

At the front of the line were two women, who'd had a drink or two I would say, both of whom wanted photos. One of the theatre staff helpfully took the camera phones from the women and they each got a photo, but that wasn't enough. They wanted more photos, some with just one of them and me, others with both of them and me, and then the same on the other phone, and then more photos because they checked to see if they'd come out and then one of the girls didn't like the pose she'd struck.

On and on it went, and the bell rang to let the audience know that it was time to start making our way back to our seats. The women had taken so long that everyone else in the queue had missed out on a photo. Straight after the show I was due to hotfoot it into a waiting cab to go and record a TV show, so I couldn't offer to pose for anyone afterwards. I apologised to the waiting crowd of people and we headed back towards our seats.

As we walked down the aisle of the auditorium, I noticed that the two women were dawdling in front of me. One still had her phone out and I realised that she was slyly filming herself in the foreground while framing me in the background, pointing back at me, showing me off like some kind of trophy. I felt this was unfair given that I had just posed endlessly for them both and I called her out on it.

She said, 'No, no, we weren't doing that.'

'Show me your phone then,' I replied.

She handed it to me. I looked and there it was, video footage and stills of the two girls, laughing and signalling at me.

So what? Why should I care?

Those are the two questions I can answer effortlessly as I type this, the responses being 'So what indeed' and 'I don't care. It's a bit rude but it really makes no difference to me'.

But in that moment I *did* care. It really bugged me that I had chatted with these women and willingly posed for umpteen photos at the expense of everyone else, and that they were still trying to sneak more.

'I'd really appreciate it if you would delete those pics,' I said.

The girl with the phone immediately agreed to, and started to press some buttons, but I now had the hump and I just didn't trust them. I looked over her shoulder and checked, imperiously. Yes, they had deleted the offending pictures, but I then started to delete the ones I had posed for too.

'Don't do *that!*' cried the other girl.

Too late. I'd already wiped the lot. The two girls stood there openmouthed as the lights started to go down and I scuttled off to my seat for the second act.

I spent the next hour sitting there conflicted. In one moment I felt that I had stood up for myself. Why should I be photographed without my permission, especially when I had given up several minutes of my time already for the same pushy people? The next moment I decided I had gone quite mad, and that I'd probably be reading about what happened on the *Daily Mail* website under the headline 'LITTLE SHIT'UN' – complete with a photo of the two girls holding a stack of *Little Britain* DVDs for the camera and looking sad.

I can't work out if this is a funny story or not, and whether I come out of it as a human being with limits, who just snapped, or whether you'd be entirely within your rights to think I'm a prick. I suspect that on that day, in that moment, those two women paid the price for all of the times people have sneaked up on me and stolen a photo without asking. It seems to happen everywhere. I've even had it in toilets, gym changing rooms or while asleep on a plane. The onus is always on the celeb to be bigger, to not react. Well, sod it. The more I think about it, they had it coming (and I'm also a bit of a prick).

10. The surprise of seeing a celebrity in real life is often coupled with an exclamation about the absurdity of seeing them in a specific place. That's right, not only have you spotted me, but you've done so in the Co-op in Fort William, or on the train to Stoke Poges, or in a cable car above Taronga Zoo or freezing my nuts off on the Brecon Beacons.

'What brings you *here*?' is usually the question.

'Well, everyone has to be somewhere.'

About twenty-five years ago Ashley Blaker and I were on the Tube on a Sunday morning, heading to Camden Market. I was a frequent visitor, scouring the stalls weekly for bootleg tapes of Queen concerts, the audio quality of which was invariably so poor it sounded like the band had dispensed with microphones and used walkie-talkies instead.

As we sat on the Northern Line train, passing through Golders Green, then Hampstead, then Belsize Park, we shared an unexpected moment that we still recall fondly today, with equal parts of joy and shame. The carriage doors opened and an elderly but sprightly and very glammed-up lady in a smart, thick lilac coat entered, escorted by a young gentleman. She sat opposite him, a couple of seats away from us, and chatted away, not seeking to draw attention to herself but not inhibited either. I didn't have to look at Ashley and he didn't have to look at me to know that we had simultaneously recognised the lady in the carriage. For this was Anna Wing, who some years before had played matriarch Lou Beale in *EastEnders*.

Our shock and delight at her unexpected presence, coupled with her cut-glass accent (rather than the Cockney tones we were used to hearing from her) sent Ashley and me into paroxysms of laughter. Trapped in the Tube carriage – as she was too – we wept, silently at first, our eyes desperately trained on the floor in the hope that we would be able to restore our dignity forthwith, or at least not be so obvious. We soon realised, however, that we were fighting a losing battle. We gave in and laughed, helplessly, and with some volume, barely a metre away from her. We shook. We rocked. We howled.

And she made no acknowledgement. There's grace for you.

I have since been on the receiving end of this type of behaviour. It happens a little less often to me, I suspect, than it might to some other poor celebs, as I am not attached to any one specific character and am known for being fairly ridiculous in the first place, but nonetheless, I have experienced it often enough to know that, despite not reacting to it at all, poor Anna Wing would unquestionably have been aware of our hysteria and quite possibly it might have embarrassed her almost as much as we embarrassed ourselves.

So I guess you could say I can't complain when it happens to me. I'm an icon. You're only human.

11. Sometimes people come up to me and say, 'They tell me you're famous. I actually don't know who you are'. To which I reply, 'Well, I don't know who you are either, so there you go.'

12. Because I'm a 'famous comedian', even when I say things that clearly aren't that funny, people often really laugh a lot. I wish it had been like that when I was working my way up, when some nights I couldn't get a laugh for love nor money, but I'm not complaining. Sometimes, though, when I am trying to be deadly serious, people laugh even more. And then sometimes, when I just *walk into a room*, people laugh. I haven't even done anything, but we catch each other's eye and that's enough. It's like having a superpower. Not as good a one as being able to shrink down to the size of an ant and then using your size to scurry under doors and help you solve mysteries, but still quite a good one.

13. You're never alone. When my dad was a teenager he skived off school for the day with some pals to watch a cricket match at Lord's. When the gang went back to school the next day, they were in big trouble. A couple of the teachers had been following the game on a TV

in the staff room when the camera happened to capture the band of reprobates – in school uniform – with their feet up, drinking and smoking. What rotten luck.

Nowadays, thanks to social media, somebody somewhere will post 'Just seen the fat one off *Little Britain* buying two sausage rolls at the Greggs in Leigh Delamere services' before I've even got back to the car. Consequently, if you're famous, you can't lie anymore. Your every bloody move is documented. It's positively Orwellian. Big Brother is watching me, and I don't even get an appearance fee. Still, at least I don't have to share a hot tub with George Galloway or Heavy D. BOOM!

14. Okay, this is something that happens a lot. A person will recognise me and come up to me and say hello, and we'll have a nice chat. Then a second person, watching this happen, will wait until the first person has gone and then sidle over and say, 'I bet it's really annoying when that happens, when people just come over and talk to you because you're famous.' As if they're not doing exactly that themselves.

15. If small talk could kill, all of your favourite celebrities would be lying dead on the ground. I meet hundreds of people in a week but we almost always end up talking about the same things. Don't get me wrong – I'm not ungrateful. I'm continually surprised and flattered that anybody wants to talk to me in the first place, and if all you really want to know is whether David Walliams is as funny in real life as he is on TV, that's fine. I will try and oblige. But if you bump into me by the turnstiles at the Emirates stadium or in the aisles of M&S in Cardiff, don't be afraid to talk about something else. In fact, be as random as you like: the benefits of reflexology, the Bay of Pigs invasion, the frightful gerrymandering of Lady Porter, whatever. Bring it on.

16. If I go to a restaurant once, and then go back two and a half years later, the waiter will say 'Diet Coke again, Mr Lucas?' You might say that's the sign of a good waiter. I say it's a bit weird. Oh, and yes, please. With a slice of lime. Not too much ice.

17. If I get the Tube, someone will usually say to me, 'Oh, I thought you'd be too famous to be on here', the inference being that as a

celebrity I must surely consider myself too rich and important to travel with the hoi polloi. If I'm sat in traffic in the back of a nice car with the window down, I'll hear a passer-by mutter, 'Oh, too up himself to get the Tube, I see'.

Flying is usually eventful. 'Thought you'd be in First Class,' says someone as I take my seat next to them on the plane. Guess what? Me too. I also thought they'd have invented hypersonic travel by now so I could nip over to Sydney for a Foster's and be home in time for *Wheel of Fortune*. I'll travel First Class if I've got enough air miles. Otherwise forget it. Walliams, on the other hand, has now sold so many children's books he can probably buy his own private jet, all decked out in pink, with a river inside it for him to swim up, but despite what you may read, most celebrities don't earn anything like what you might think.

Every so often there's a gleeful article in the tabloids about how some former star has fallen. It's usually someone who was in *Hollyoaks* who now does a bit of gardening, or a former children's TV presenter stacking the shelves at B&Q. We're all supposed to join in the derision, as if getting off your arse and working is somehow less admirable than sitting at home watching *Loose Women*. Bugger that. If this book doesn't sell and *Doctor Who* leaves me stranded on a far-away planet somewhere, don't be surprised if you see me at the Westfield in Stratford selling mobile phone cases. Those Orange Viscounts won't buy themselves.

18. There is smoke without fire. When you're famous, you get slandered and libelled relentlessly, and much of what is written about you has not the slightest kernel of truth in it, not even a grain. And you're expected to ignore it. Any other kind of response and you're considered weak and over-sensitive, or worse, guilty.

Most of the time, when you get libelled in a publication, it's best to shrug it off. Choose your battles. When it's more serious and you really do have to fight back, even if you get an apology and a contribution to your legal costs, you're still almost always out of pocket. I call it 'the fame tax'.

19. The vast majority of autograph hunters waiting at the stage door or behind the barrier at a film premiere are professional and will sell your signature immediately on eBay. They come equipped with marker pens and glossy 10 x 8 photos. I went through a stage where I would only sign the autograph if I could personally dedicate it to someone, because I thought it would be less use to a professional if it said 'Hello Sanjay' or 'Happy 36th wedding anniversary Sandy and Phil!' That was until I learned that the professionals have special tools to remove Sharpie ink.

Sometimes I just think 'Ah well, they've stood out there all night, it only takes a few seconds to sign, good luck to them'. Other times it bugs me that the professionals are out in force, because while some are polite and friendly, others can be aggressive and push real fans out of the way.

20. This one's specific to me, but people do sometimes come up to me and say 'Are you bovvered? Are you bovvered?' They are, of course, mistaking me for Catherine Tate – or rather, mistaking *Little Britain* teenage reprobate Vicky Pollard for Catherine's teenage reprobate Lauren. And in turn I know Catherine has folk saying, 'Yeah but no but' to her.

In response to the question, no, this doesn't bovver me particularly. It turns out almost every celebrity experiences this, including many who are a good deal more famous than I am. Mark Wahlberg, Matt Damon and Guy Pearce all get accused of being each other. Plenty of people talk to Rob Brydon thinking he's Anton du Beke. The only time it did freak me out was when, for a couple of months after the end of the second series of *Big Brother*, a few people thought I was that chap Bubble. And the main reason I didn't like it was because he was a Chelsea fan.

21. Yes, when you're famous you get invited to lots of shows for free. That's not a myth. But when it happens, be aware that you are there to endorse the show. You're expected to walk the red carpet (which for ladies, in particular, may require the purchase of a new dress and forking out for a stylist and make-up artist) and you'll be asked to pose for

photos with the cast, and with any other random celeb who happens to be on the carpet at the same time. Often a microphone will be shoved in your face, and even if you thought *Hamlet on Ice* was an insufferable pile of tosh, you'll be expected to rave on about how innovative it was. At the after-show party you'll be approached by gossip columnists looking for a scoop. I find it hard in those circumstances to relax and have a drink for fear of saying the wrong thing, or saying the right thing but still being misquoted.

22. Following on from the last point, if you're in a bar and someone offers to buy you a drink, that means you are sort of obliged to sit with them and have it. I actually like a chat with anyone, but if I'm in a bar I'm usually with someone already, so I tend to politely decline the offer. Another reason I say no is that I'm not really much of a drinker. Perhaps if pâtisseries were as entrenched in British culture as pubs are, and strangers sent éclairs or macaroons over to my table, I might not be quite so restrained.

23. Damon Albarn once said, 'Everyone accuses you of changing when you become famous, but as far as I'm concerned it's the people around you who change. I'm still the same.'

I can identify with that. If you ever read or hear someone say how they were 'dropped' by their friend or family member when they became famous, that might actually be because the friend or family member became a berk. I had a friend who worked in TV and who, at the height of *Little Britain*'s popularity, kept asking me to appear on whatever programme he was working on. I later heard that he would go to job interviews and make it clear that if he got the job, he'd be able to get me and other showbiz friends of his to contribute to the show. I felt a bit used. I think there might be some truth in what Damon said.

24. Despite what I assumed as a child, fame does not provide immunity to sadness or anxiety. Being a celebrity has its great sides, but if you see it as a solution to your problems, rather than a by-product of your achievements, you will be disappointed. Mostly it just means it takes you longer to get round Waitrose.

Fame is ridiculous, but it's the one thing I have that people seem to want most, generating more interest, more fascination, certainly more conversation than any other story I might be able to tell.

25. My favourite character in *Fame* was Bruno Martelli. I liked it when he played his synthesiser.

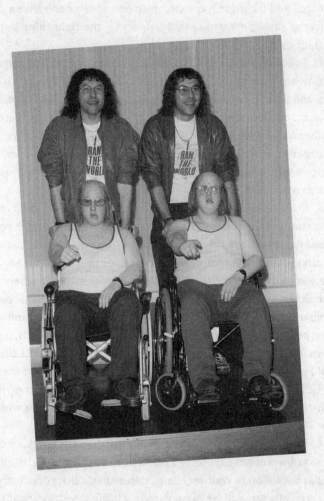

P – Prosopagnosia

So I've got this thing called prosopagnosia. I've never been officially diagnosed by a doctor or anything, but trust me, I've got it.

Prosopagnosia is also called 'face blindness' and is a cognitive disorder of perception where the ability to recognise familiar faces is impaired. Other aspects of visual processing – knowing what an object is, or being able to make a decision, for example – remain intact. (Thank you, Wikipedia, for helping me with this description, BTW.)

I'm not a vague person. I'm a stickler for detail, as anyone who's worked with me will testify. But when it comes to knowing *who anyone is*, I'm screwed, because I'm terrible at remembering faces. Useless.

Last year I was at a party. I tend to avoid parties – mainly because I get caught in embarrassing situations like these. I didn't know many people there, but I did recognise someone I had worked with a couple of years earlier. I was able to work out who he was because he'd been the cameraman on a film that was directed by the host of the party – so when he greeted me, my brain was able to figure out a link.

The cameraman then introduced me to his wife. She and I chatted for about twenty minutes. At that point the host of the party appeared next to me. I always know him, because he's very distinctive-looking – with long black hair and white eyebrows. I spent thirty seconds telling him what a lovely party it was, thanking him for the invitation, and then turned back to continue talking to the cameraman's wife. We spoke for a further five minutes, until she introduced herself. At which point I realised that I had actually been talking to two different people. Not only that, but when the original woman reappeared, I saw that the two women bore no physical similarity whatsoever.

At a party one could almost be forgiven for this kind of thing – you meet a lot of new people in a short space of time. But when you're working with people on a daily basis and still can't figure out who folk are, it's awkward.

These days I just apologise in advance, but for years I kept it to myself, because it's quite embarrassing to accidentally treat friends as strangers. The way I describe it is that it just takes me a lot longer to learn faces than most people. For some sufferers it's so extreme that they can't identify their own parents or even themselves. I don't have it as bad as all that. I can still function, and often people will be very forgiving, even before I tell them of my condition. 'Oh, you must meet tons of people,' they say, when I fail to recognise them. Yes, that's true too, but there are people I have worked with daily for the past six months, and who I often chat to, and I still wouldn't recognise them if I met them in the street.

In fact, I probably wouldn't recognise the street either. I'm useless with directions, but that is mainly because I am an idiot (see earlier chapter).

Howard and me with Bobby Moore & George Graham, Brent Cross Shopping Centre, 1989

Pompidou as Freddie

Q – Queen (and other Teenage Pursuits)

It was 1989. Having been spoilt on a rich early eighties diet of Madness, Duran Duran, Wham! and Elton, the fifteen-year-old me held no truck with Jive Bunny, New Kids on the Block or the inescapable offerings of Stock, Aitken and Waterman. Dance music was not to my taste – ditto hardcore hip-hop, heavy metal or bland R'n'B. It was time to find something else to listen to.

However, I was not a sexy skinny dude with long blond hair, blue eyes, a leather jacket and a cute girlfriend. I admired but couldn't identify with Nirvana, as my friends Alex and Nick did, while Jeremy banged his head to Metallica, which made my ears bleed. And everyone seemed to love Guns N' Roses. I didn't mind their songs, but that man's *voice*. Ugh. So nasal and whiny. No, thank you.

I needed to find my own music. I habitually scoured Watford market on a Saturday afternoon and Wembley market on a Sunday for LPs and cassettes. I found myself drawn to stars of the sixties and seventies – The Beatles, Elvis, Aretha, James Brown, Glen Campbell, Jackie Wilson, Marvin Gaye. My tastes were encouraged every week night by Randall Lee Rose, the deep-voiced American DJ who ruled Capital Gold and signed off every show by playing 'Sweet Dreams' (the Tommy McLain version) and Roy Rogers' 'Happy Trails'.

I loved The Proclaimers too. I'd seen them on the TV series *The Tube* and adored their raw mix of folk and soul, their harmonies and their strange accents. I'd put on one of their records and dance around my bedroom each day after school, crashing into the hi-fi and causing the needle to bounce off the vinyl. Like me, they looked unusual – so much so that they were often mistaken for a novelty act – but it was clear that behind the quirky presentation lay master songwriters. If you want proof, listen to 'Sunshine on Leith'. It's as beautiful a ballad as has ever been sung.

My *obsession*, however, was Queen. I adored their soaring melodies, Freddie's unrivalled vocals, the sound of Brian's home-made Red Special guitar, Roger's thumping beats and John's funky bass. I could and would bang on at length to anyone who happened to be passing about the differences between the versions of 'Seven Seas Of Rhye' that had appeared on their first two albums, the state-of-the-art lighting rig that the band toured with, the collectability of their Japanese laser disc – the list was endless.

In 1989 Freddie was still alive – but Queen weren't celebrated critically the way they are now. The music press sneered at them, damned them for playing Sun City in South Africa, made sly digs at Freddie's sexuality, said the band's lyrics meant nothing, said they should have quit after Live Aid. They didn't know what I knew, which was that Queen were quite clearly the greatest band in the world.

My bedroom wall was covered in Queen posters. I marvelled at Jeremy's mum and stepdad, who had been to see them at Wembley. My stepsister Barbra had a ticket to see them perform at Knebworth, but one of her friends let her down and she couldn't get there. I sat with her and we listened to the concert live on the radio. We didn't know at the time that the Knebworth show was to be their last.

I never got to see Queen live, but a few months after Freddie died there was a benefit concert at Wembley Stadium in aid of the newly founded Mercury Phoenix Trust and you can bet your bottom dollar bill I was there. Bowie and Annie Lennox sang 'Under Pressure', George Michael did 'Somebody To Love' and even Liza Minnelli performed 'We Are The Champions'.

I'd also been to Wembley a few times to see Arsenal play and, by the age of fourteen, was now regularly going to games at Highbury. Our parents were usually working, so Howard and me and my friend Darren would walk to Canons Park station, catch the bus to Edgware and get the Tube from there.

I was a Junior Gunner, which meant I could stand in the Family Enclosure, though it wasn't long before Darren and I opted to stand on the North Bank at Highbury with Howard and his friends. We'd arrive two hours before kick-off, as the turnstiles opened, and pick an optimum spot for ourselves. Then, five minutes before the match began, some giant lump would barge in front of us and we'd be jumping up and down throughout the match, barely able to see a thing.

One day in 1989 I saw an advert in the Arsenal programme which said that anyone under the age of sixteen could put their name down to be a ball boy. I sent in a letter and forgot all about it. A few months later I received a phone call telling me I would be working for the home games against Everton and Newcastle.

We met an hour before kick-off outside the famous Marble Halls. Bob Wilson, Arsenal's former goalie, said hello to us in the corridor and joked that if Arsenal were winning, we should take our time giving the ball back to the opposition. We got changed in one of the offices and I saw a large pile of tickets on the counter for the forthcoming match against Liverpool at Anfield. There was no hotter ticket in the country at that time and there were not many security cameras around either in those days. I remember thinking I could just swipe a couple for me and my brother and no one would probably notice.

I was thrilled to pull on the Arsenal tracksuit and walk out onto the pitch, standing on the halfway line while the players ran past. One or two patted my head for luck.

The second match – against Newcastle – took place on 15 April 1989. It was a day that would change British football forever. Some of the fans nearby had radios and during the first half somebody mentioned that someone had been killed in a crush up at Hillsborough.

I wasn't surprised. Only weeks earlier I had been in a couple of crushes in the North Bank and I genuinely thought I was going to die. They occurred towards the end of the match, when some fans made their way to the exit, while others remained in their path to watch the final seconds.

The year before, I had gone to Wembley to watch Arsenal lose unexpectedly to Luton Town in the Littlewoods Challenge Cup Final. Arsenal took the lead. The crowd celebrated wildly and I got pushed and pulled about so much that my flagstick went into my eye. We were then awarded a penalty. As Arsenal were already ahead and I was fearful of another crush, I was actually relieved when we didn't score.

On that day in April 1989, the full enormity of the tragedy in Sheffield wasn't yet known and at half-time, in the Players' Lounge, I had a Coke and still wanted to know the Tottenham score. Meanwhile Des Lynam was on *Grandstand* providing updates, turning paler by the second. That night I watched the news in horror and, back at Haberdashers' on the Monday, learned that two sisters from the girls' school – Sarah and Victoria Hicks – had perished at Hillsborough.

A few weeks later, when Arsenal beat the odds to clinch the league title at Anfield with virtually the last kick of the game, I was watching on TV in Edgware with Howard and his friends, but we got straight in the car and headed to Highbury, where a spontaneous street party broke out. A couple of days after that, Mum took me to see the victory parade. We cheered wildly as the players arrived on an open-top bus and joined in with Perry Groves as he led a chorus of 'Ooh, To Be a Gooner' from the Islington Town Hall balcony. Though the whole country had wanted

Liverpool to win that year, it was Arsenal's first title in eighteen seasons and we celebrated for months.

I continued going to Arsenal throughout my teenage years and beyond. I saw George Graham's steely team grind out 1–0 victories and witnessed Arsène Wenger's French revolution. In my twenties and thirties I fulfilled my dream of owning a season ticket. These days I live in the US, but I get up at silly o'clock to watch the matches live on telly, and when I'm back in London I go to as many games as possible.

I still love Arsenal. I get into arguments with strangers about Arsenal. I wear stupid Arsenal polo shirts and jumpers most days. I schedule work and book holidays around Arsenal fixtures. I think about Arsenal sometimes when I should be concentrating on helping the Doctor defeat those monsters that are trying to destroy the universe. My relationship with Arsenal has been a huge part of my life. At turns joyous, depressing, inspiring, exasperating. I could write a book about it. Maybe one day I will. But while football captivates many, it bores others rigid. One whole chapter about Arsenal would be too little for some readers and too much for the rest of you, so either forgive me or thank me for nipping back to Wembley – not as a spectator, but now – in 1990 – as a casual labourer, working there on weekends while studying at college.

The job was knackering, but at least it was varied. The foreman would hand the easiest jobs to his mates. The rest of us picked up a broom and set to work emptying bins and sweeping up horseshit. Yup, even me, your little gay dumpling. Sometimes the foreman had overbooked, and then he would send some of us home with no work, no money and no apology, chastising us for being late, even though we weren't.

Often we'd be employed on a match day. At 8 a.m. it was bearable. By 1 p.m., as the crowds began to arrive, the bins would fill with litter faster than we could empty them, and if the end of my shift coincided with the final whistle, it might take me two hours just to get onto a tube home.

I much preferred working the day *after* a big game – at least it was quiet. The key was to try and engineer a spot clearing up after the supporters of the winning team. There you were much more likely to find little gifts absent-mindedly left behind by jubilant, drunken fans: unopened cigarette packets, Sony Walkmans and, of course, money. One Sunday in 1991 I worked alone, personally cleaning every seat in the Olympic Gallery after Tottenham had won the FA Cup, and my irritation at the result (compounded by having seen Arsenal lose to Spurs in the semi-final) was in some way reduced by finding an extra £30 amongst the trash.

Despite the occasional unexpected cash bonus, I was keen to find another job and I soon did – this time working at Homerun Video Megastore in Harrow. I'd walked past the shop while it was being fitted and popped my head in speculatively, asking if they needed any weekend staff. It was a large shop, owned by an American who never graced us with his actual presence, but who was regarded by the management as some kind of a visionary, when clearly all he had done was just copy Blockbuster.

It was the first time I had worked at a computerised till with a barcode scanner. I amused myself no end one dull day by looking up the American owner's account and then renting out a selection of unlikely titles on it – *Pepé Le Pew*, *Carry On Abroad* and a *Mad Lizzie* workout tape.

Barcode scanners are the best. Who doesn't love the beep of a scanner? I used to know a guy called Biffo who worked at the Our Price in Watford, who told me that he once sat at the counter bored out of his tree repeatedly scanning a packet of Marlboro Lights and by Wednesday afternoon they were number 4 in the charts.

Anyway, for those of you old enough to remember going into a video shop, I'm pretty sure you were generally happy to be left alone to browse. If you wanted a particular film, you'd ask for it, yes? Well, the luxury of time and space was not afforded to the clientele of Homerun Video Megastore, because its employees were instructed to trail customers around the shop, haranguing them with questions, all of which had been helpfully printed out on a laminated card which we were to carry around with us at all times.

'Can I help you?' was the first one. Most people just said no. After much feedback the laminated card was reprinted, so that we were now to ask '*How* can I help you?' – to which most people replied 'I'm all right, actually'.

But we were still under orders to stalk anyone who came into the shop and interact with them. We had a huge catalogue of films, but there was one furious old man who would turn up early in the mornings, always in a terrible mood, perpetually frustrated with our selection: 'Where's the violent films? I want violent! I want *violent*!' I would try to help him, but my efforts were either met with 'That's a fifteen! I want an eighteen!' or 'That's a thriller! There's only one death. It's not violent! I want *violent*!'

Some of the other customers were more approachable. One middle-aged Asian man – who looked the spitting image of the Dalai Lama – would pop in week after week and engage me in long conversations about film. I loved that he seemed to share my passion for independent movies, rather than the mindless action flicks that took up most of the shelves.

One quiet Sunday we chatted as usual and then he said, 'I'll see you next week.'

'Oh, actually, it's my last day today,' I told him. 'I'm doing A levels and we've got our exams soon, so I need to focus on them.'

His face dropped. He seemed to leave the shop a broken man. I was momentarily baffled, but then became distracted by a kid being sick on the giant Sam the Spider slide in the play area.

A couple of hours later, the man who looked like the Dalai Lama returned. Trembling, he handed me a piece of paper with his phone number on it, took a deep breath, kissed me on the cheek and ran out. One of my colleagues saw this and burst out laughing. I was embarrassed for myself and felt sad for the man.

A few months afterwards I was sat on my own upstairs on the 340 bus from Harrow back to Stanmore, McDonald's takeaway bag on my lap, gazing out of the window, when I spotted the man. My heart sank. He looked up, saw me and then broke into a run towards the bus. He managed to get on just before the doors closed and then, dripping with sweat, headed up the stairs. He seemed so happy to see me, and despite the many empty seats available, joined me on mine, squeezing close and hemming me in.

'You didn't call.'

'Oh, um . . . I lost your number.'

He pulled out a piece of paper and a pen, wrote down his number again and this time his address too.

'How have you been?' he asked.

'Okay, thanks. I've got exams coming up soon.'

'I haven't been so good. I'm taking pills at the moment. For depression. They do help me in some ways, but they really piss me off because I can't get an erection anymore.'

Through his trousers he started to press down impatiently on his penis.

'Look, nothing. Useless. It's been months.'

I gulped and stared ahead, food getting cold in my lap.

'Come over sometime,' he said. 'To mine, yes? Please? Maybe you can . . . *help* me.'

He got off the bus. A few stops later so did I. I left my McNuggets on the seat. Didn't really fancy them anymore.

Ever since then, even though he's possibly one of the most virtuous men on the planet – and it was just someone who *looked* like him – every time I see the Dalai Lama on telly, I think 'Ugh, he touches his penis on the bus'.

Now we both know that I can't very well finish this chapter there, so allow me, if you will, to jump forward to 2011 . . .

. . . and the final week of my run in *Les Misérables*. Queen's manager Jim Beach threw a party in London for what would have been Freddie Mercury's sixty-fifth birthday, in aid of the Mercury Phoenix Trust. Roger Taylor, Brian May and their band performed some Queen numbers with guest performers, including Tom Chaplin from Keane, Mike Rutherford and Jeff Beck.

The theme of the party was 'Freddie for a Day'. Guests were encouraged to dress up as the man himself. I would have been jubilant just to have received an invite, but to my amazement I was asked to perform with the band. I hotfooted it from the Queen's Theatre (of course), still in my Monsieur Thénardier costume – and now sporting a Freddie-style moustache. Moments after I arrived I sang 'Good Old-Fashioned Lover Boy' onstage with Roger and Brian. I almost want to have kids just so I can tell them about it. It's weird because, several years later, I still can't quite comprehend it. It's too fantastical. It's too magical. But it happened.

In November 1991, two nights after Freddie died, we had a college trip to see a play in Hammersmith. My friend Claire and I made a detour to Freddie's home in Logan Place. 'Radio Gaga' was blasting from the house, but outside the mood was sombre. Fans lit candles and pinned notes to the front door. I wrote 'There Can Be Only One' – a reference to the movie *Highlander*, which Queen had provided the music for. I was tearful. For a closeted teen, the future seemed bleak and uncertain. I want to go back now and tell my young self that it not only gets better, but give it twenty years and you'll even get to be Freddie for a day.

I must be dreaming

R – Really Big Britain

David and I would write solidly for about six months, either at his place or mine. We'd start at 10 a.m. – or nine minutes past, given my time-keeping – drink copious amounts of peppermint tea, stop for an M&S microwaved lunch, or, if we were feeling like we needed to get out of the house, grab some noodles at Wagamama, and then write until about 4.30 or 5 p.m. We'd come up with three sketches a day, on average.

There would be periods of silence, periods of moping, periods of arguing over a word or comma, periods of being stumped on how to end a sketch. Every few weeks we'd gather with our producer Myfanwy and our script editor Mark Gatiss to read out the new stuff.

We rewrote and recast some of the sketches from the pilot and also relocated Marjorie back to the local church hall, as she had been in the radio show.

One set of characters that weren't in the radio show or the pilot emerged quite late on in the process . . . Lou and Andy.

David had played a very surreal character in our Paramount sketches in the mid-nineties that we called Cockney Film Star. He looked like Lou Reed and spoke with a funny lisp – though there were never any references in the sketches to Lou Reed.

In 2002 we did some *Rock Profile* sketches for Ralf Little's chat show on BBC Choice. We revisited Cockney Film Star – the way he looked and talked – but this time introduced him as Lou Reed, complete with references to his life and career.

Lodging with Lou was Andy Warhol – played by me, for some reason, as a childlike Scouser, the type of person who has to be looked after – and so dim that it was almost as if his great work was just a happy accident. There was an exchange between the two characters that went like this . . .

    LOU: What do you want for your lunch?
    ANDY: Chippy.
    LOU: That's fine, but if you have chips for your lunch then you can't have chips for your tea.
    ANDY: Yeah, I know.
    LOU: So what do you want for your tea?
    ANDY: Chippy.

And so on.

We thought it would be fun to develop the characters further for *Little Britain* and explore this strange relationship, but they weren't Lou Reed and Andy Warhol anymore – they didn't need to be – they were just Lou and Andy. David's character looked the same, though we wanted to make Andy appear a bit more real-looking.

I had worn a long wig with receding hair and a big pair of specs in Rhys Thomas's sitcom *Fun at the Funeral Parlour* and again while repeatedly and manically shouting the word 'Peanuts' on *Shooting Stars*. I loved how odd I looked, and thought the same combination would work nicely with Andy. The heavy prescription lenses magnified my eyes, which made me look more childlike, though it also meant I couldn't see very well.

We decided Andy was in a wheelchair and Lou was caring for him. The sketches followed a routine of Andy always wanting something in particular, Lou warning him that he wouldn't like it, Andy being resolute and then immediately regretting his choice.

They didn't read as particularly funny on the page, but we knew we had something and they quickly became the set of characters that David and I were most excited about. At the first reading, the four of us were crying with laughter. It was just so stupid, the lengths Andy went to in sticking to his guns – despite Lou always offering him a more sensible option.

After the hysteria had died down, Mark and Myfanwy both wondered if we were essentially just laughing at the expense of someone who was disabled. I said that him being in a wheelchair made him more dependent, but didn't mean that he was mentally disabled, and in my mind he never was – he was just someone who needed a bit of looking after. But Myfanwy felt strongly that, as much as we were all enjoying ourselves, it wasn't something that we'd be able to defend if people took offence.

I can't remember who suggested it. It might well have been Mark, actually, but we left that day having agreed that Andy could actually walk perfectly well, and that he was duping Lou. Suddenly this gave a whole new dimension to the sketches. Lou would leave some of the scenes before the end, and the viewers would see Andy up and about, doing ever more fantastical things.

Oddly, while it seemed clear *why* Andy might do this – laziness! – we never really spent too much time figuring out *how* this had come about. I've always liked the idea that Andy actually did have some kind of injury at some point, and that Lou had cared for him, but then he'd recovered and enjoyed the life of Riley so much that he'd neglected to mention he was now perfectly able.

When we filmed the sketch in the swimming pool – the most popular sketch we ever did – the plan was for Lou to exit to find some assistance and for Andy to jump off the diving board in his absence. We set the camera up and then I realised that Andy's behaviour would be even more shameless if Lou remained in the foreground, engrossed in conversation, blissfully unaware of what Andy was up to in the background. Pantomime, basically – 'He's behind you!'

It worked perfectly, with the happy coincidence of me even landing with a big splash at the exact moment that Lou explains that Andy has 'a fear of water'. Steve Furst, who joined us in the sketch, and with whom we worked several times over the years, nearly loses it at one point, but just manages to keep it together.

As soon as the director yelled 'Cut!', the crew applauded. Because it was all in one shot we were able to watch it back immediately. It had worked as we'd wanted it to, so we didn't do another take. I felt particularly proud of myself that I'd managed to jump from such a great height. A moment later, as the crew were packing up, the pool reopened to the public and a little boy who could not have been older than five casually sauntered off the same board. I felt a bit less smug.

Despite Andy not being disabled, Myfanwy steeled herself for the inevitable barrage of viewer complaints. We didn't receive any.

Little Britain premiered on BBC Three and within a couple of episodes I noticed that some newspapers were referring to it. A mention in Richard Littlejohn's column first, I think, then a cartoon in *The Sun* with Tony Blair saying 'No but yeah but . . .' This was a big surprise to me. I didn't think many people were watching the channel. In truth, they weren't – but those who were were watching us.

Vicky Pollard was the one character people seemed to talk and write about the most. Sometimes you get lucky and just do the right thing at the right time. I wouldn't call Sacha Baron Cohen lucky – I would call him the funniest man on the planet – but I would say that his timing with Ali G was also perfect. He expertly captured a social type that everyone was familiar with, but no one had pinpointed.

Everyone in Britain had seen someone like Vicky Pollard in their neighbourhood, but no one had nailed it. Catherine Tate did a pretty fantastic job with her character Lauren but, luckily for us, we got there first.

Reviews for the show were almost uniformly positive. Even Victor Lewis-Smith loved it. BBC Three had a big hit on their hands. By the time the series aired on BBC Two we were already a success. When the critics reviewed the first episode for its terrestrial transmission, they wrote about it warmly, having already got to know the characters over the course of the series.

The show received several awards and David and I went off to the BAFTAs, where we found ourselves nominated in competition with each other. We decided it was the first and last time such a situation was going to arise – at least on something we'd worked on together – and from that day onwards we were always nominated jointly.

The show won the first of three BAFTAs and we were the toast of the town.

By the way, I bet you every autobiography has a sentence like that at some point – 'and we were the toast of the town'. Well, now it's my turn. In fact, I'm going to say it again – 'and we were the toast of the town'!

We were up for lots of awards, invited to every opening night. David was in the papers every day, linked to any single female beauty you could think of. I was happier away from the red carpet, at home with Kevin. David would sometimes go to the premiere of a big movie while Kev and I would wait and catch it at the O2 Centre on Finchley Road on a Sunday, kicking our shoes off and wolfing down a giant bag of Haribo Starmix.

I lived with Kevin in West Hampstead then and, whereas before I had been stopped occasionally in the street, now everybody seemed to want to shake my hand. Our mailbag got busier and David and I took on an assistant, who helped with the many autograph requests that were coming through.

There was a new controller of BBC One – Lorraine Heggessey – who was a big fan of the show and had decided that, after it had screened on BBC Three, the second series should air on her channel. We got to work writing the second series, creating some new characters and retiring others to make way for them.

We gave Emily Howard a sidekick called Florence Rose – my mother's two middle names. This gave Emily the role of teacher, with Florence as her pupil. Emily was often exasperated by Florence, whose thick moustache, she felt, sometimes gave the game away.

David and I had watched a documentary made by Martin Parr which had featured two Women's Institute types who were judging a cake contest at a church fete. Despite the low stakes, they seemed to relish their power. I suggested we use them as a starting point and then we wrote a sketch in which, horrified, they would mark down various entrants upon discovering that they were a member of a minority.

As we wrote the second draft, David had an inspired idea – that one of the women was so disgusted on learning that she had sampled something made by someone black or Indian or gay – 'No more lesbian jam!' – that she would vomit uncontrollably.

When it came to filming the scenes, we knew that we wanted the vomit to be almost cartoon-like. We felt that this would be the only way to make it palatable – well, as palatable as it would ever be. The puke was made from porridge oats and vegetable soup. As we usually filmed in the hot summer (more daylight, less chance of rain), the heady cocktail, prepared in advance, was left sitting in large barrels, fermenting for hours. By the time it was finally used the smell was horrific. It was all we could do not to throw up for real.

Bitty was inspired by an experience David had recently had at a party where, to his surprise, someone was still breast-feeding their five-year-old. Taking what was already an extreme situation and making it even more so, we found it was a fun way to satirise the oddness of the upper classes with their seemingly impenetrable customs and rituals, as well as the meekness of the middle-class in-laws in their presence. We followed the story of Harvey's engagement, with Samantha Power playing his fiancée and Geraldine James as Harvey's mother. Samantha had appeared with us nearly a decade earlier on Paramount and had been a regular in the radio shows, so it was great to be working with her again.

I knew my mother would protest about the Bitty sketch – as she often did about the ruder stuff – so I made a point of watching her as she saw it for the first time, playing out on a big screen in front of the studio audience. When she told me off later, I said I had seen her laughing. 'You can't laugh and then complain,' I said.

The starting point for Bubbles de Vere came from *Rock Profile*, in which I'd given a pretty ropey impression of Dame Shirley Bassey. It was a fun performance, though – grand, flamboyant, exhibitionist and absurd. What elevated it in *Little Britain* was the appearance of the character.

David had always been more of a fan of prosthetics than me. He loved how they transformed him, whereas I would feel buried beneath the layers of latex, convinced I was being both hammy and wooden at the same time. Often when I watched someone on TV in prosthetics I found it distracting. However, we began to embrace them as the show went on, not least because we played so many characters and were keen to keep them looking distinctive.

The face and body make-up for Bubbles took six hours to apply, so the shoot days – already long – were hard on me and on Lisa Cavalli-Green, our amazing make-up designer. The outfit was heavy and restrictive and it is the nature of foam that as soon as you put it on it starts deteriorating, so I was perpetually followed around by a bunch of anxious make-up artists, constantly re-gluing flapping cheeks and torn breasts! I'd be tired and grumpy from the weight and the heat, and by the third day the suit had absorbed so much sweat that it gained ten pounds.

When it came to the second series, our director Steve Bendelack was making a movie, so Matt Lipsey took over. Myfanwy became pregnant with twins so we also needed to find a new producer. We struck gold with Geoff Posner, about as experienced a comedy director and producer as you will find. He has worked with everyone from Morecambe and Wise and The Two Ronnies through to Steve Coogan, Lenny Henry, Victoria Wood, French and Saunders, Harry Enfield and beyond.

When the second series premiered on BBC Three, we were gobsmacked to learn that 1.8 million people had tuned in to the first episode. That was more than had been watching at the same time on BBC Two. Channel Controller Stuart Murphy was delighted.

While the media charted our success and continued to write about us daily, there was a definite change of opinion among the critics who, across the board, slated the second series. I think this was partly a response to the fact that we were no longer a little comedy show – we had become a cultural phenomenon. Also the programme was repeated endlessly so it became over-familiar. But mainly, I think, it was because the second series was much cruder and bolder than the first. Even Dafydd's outfits went from the sort of stuff you could actually buy in Old Compton Street to crazy costumes that had to be specially made.

By the time the third series was transmitted, we were bigger than ever, scoring over twelve million viewers for our opening episode on BBC One. The critics no longer concealed their disdain – which was all the greater because of their powerlessness to reduce the size of the audience. The public had taken the show to their hearts.

It wasn't just the TV critics who poured their scorn on us. Headline-hungry columnists penned 'Am I The Only Person Who HATES *Little Britain*?' pieces, while a few pages later, the gossip columns led with photos of us doing mundane things – waiting for a cab or tying a shoelace.

The third series had an extra level of stress on top of that, as, behind the scenes, someone involved in the show was selling the schedule to one of the paparazzi. He knew exactly where we'd be, right down to which side of a building we'd be filming in front of. He also knew where we were being picked up from in the morning and dropped off in the evening.

During filming, he'd set up his camera right next to ours, as if he was part of the crew. It frustrated me because it meant that secrets from the show were being given away, or that images of characters appeared – shot while we were rehearsing – in which the make-up or costume was incomplete. The worst aspect, though, was that it made many of us paranoid about which trusted team member was leaking the information.

In the end we just had to let him film the rehearsal. Failure to do so meant he would have lingered distractingly next to the camera throughout filming and got his shots anyway. He showed his true class when he continued to snap us while we stood observing a minute's silence for those who had lost their lives in the 7 July bombings a few days earlier. After the silence was over our producer Geoff confronted him, and he replied, 'Don't start, Geoff. I had a friend in that.'

Looking back, I'm as certain as can be that I've figured out who it was who was giving away the schedule. I'll keep that to myself, though.

In one way – for me at least – the third series was easier. We had at last acquired a special cooling vest, which I could wear underneath the

Bubbles outfit, and which would have made Heath Robinson proud. It was a T-shirt with thin tubing sewn into it, which had a nozzle on the end that could be attached to a box with icy water in it. A car battery would power the water and make it pass through the tubing. The noise of the makeshift invention meant that it couldn't be used during a take, but during filming breaks it would be deployed frequently. It not only made me more comfortable, but it also meant that the make-up survived for longer as I didn't get so hot.

In the years since *Little Britain*, one of the things we've been accused of – and the same thing has happened with *Come Fly with Me* – is racism. I was unprepared for this. The conceit of both shows was a) to reflect contemporary British life and b) that the two of us played as many characters as possible, and as many different types as possible – fat, thin, tall, short, straight, gay, male, female, young, old. David and I saw playing different races simply as part of that. For instance, we never thought Marjorie was funny because a man was playing a woman.

There had been a time a few decades earlier when some white comics thought the very act of playing someone black was funny in itself, and then there was a time when that rightly fell by the wayside and hardly anybody played anything other than their own race. But we made *Little Britain* and *Come Fly with Me* in a small window of time when many considered it acceptable once more to play people of all colours.

When Vic and Bob played Otis Redding and Marvin Gaye, they darkened their skin. Harry Enfield did the same when he played Nelson Mandela. Chris Morris did it in *The Day Today*. Eddie Murphy played an old white Jewish man in *Coming to America* and Lenny Henry played Steve Martin. It was a different era.

I understand the response that some modern audiences have to this aspect of our work. Of course I wouldn't have turned up in *Coronation Street* playing someone of another race, but within the world of our show, where we wanted to reflect the multi-culture of Britain – and in the context of what our contemporaries of all races were doing or had

Little Me

recently done – it didn't feel aggressive or divisive and I don't remember it being taken that way either, at the time.

Britain felt very very different – even seven years ago – to the way it feels now, in this jittery post-Brexit referendum era. Ditto the US, with Donald Trump and the rise of the Alt-Right. Racial tensions existed, of course, but they hadn't risen to the surface the way they have done of late. Labour were in government. We didn't see those horrendous YouTube clips of drunken racists abusing immigrants on the bus that seem to have become the norm these days. And we didn't have newspapers giving column inches to nasty opportunists like Nigel Farage and Katie Hopkins, spouting their repulsive anti-Muslim polemic.

There is one caveat to this, however – Ting Tong, the Thai ladyboy. I thought we got the tone of those sketches wrong.

There had been a few documentaries on TV about Thai brides and the downtrodden men who went abroad to find them. Often the marriages didn't work, with unions taking place too quickly and expectations on both sides unmet.

David and I had seen these shows and when we arrived after a few weeks off to begin work writing the third series, we discovered we had both come up with the same idea – to use the Western Man/Thai Bride relationship as the basis for a set of sketches.

Somewhere along the way, however, we ended up producing something that was too rudimentary and insensitive. We hadn't worked hard enough to create an interesting character in Ting Tong. My performance was crude and simplistic and hard to defend. I have a feeling that if we hadn't spent all the time and money on those prosthetics we might have reviewed those sketches and cut them out of the show.

We can't change the past. But we can change the future. One of the things I'm asked often is whether we might do more *Little Britain* or *Come Fly with Me*.

If we did, then I wouldn't play Precious now, or Taaj. As it happens, in the case of Precious, I think we pretty much did the joke anyway, so although it was some people's favourite, I'm not sure what else we'd have done with her. Taaj, on the other hand, has lots of life in him. I'd be very happy for me and David to bring Taaj back and have an Asian actor play him.

An accusation levelled at us at the time, which I think was made an issue by people needing to fill column inches rather than being a genuine concern, was 'class tourism'. The argument that we were posh boys specifically belittling working-class characters in our shows doesn't hold up for me. Yes, Vicky and Lou and Andy are working class, but Marjorie and Carol Beer are resolutely middle class, and we had plenty of upper-class idiots in our show too, like Sir Bernard and the characters in the Bitty sketches.

It only took one journalist to accuse us of 'class tourism' before every other interviewer asked us to defend ourselves against the charges. I had no idea how to respond, because to me it was such a manufactured concern. David pointed out more stridently that a ban on people writing about anyone other than those from their own social class would mean we'd never have had Shakespeare, Dickens, Mozart etc., so where does it end?

Little Britain had its fans and its dissenters, but even after the press turned on it, it remained the highest-rating TV comedy in the UK.

It was time to take it on the road.

S – Southend, Sydney and Sunset Boulevard

It was hard to believe that it had been eight years since David and I had done our last live show. Back then, in 1997, I had figured we would effectively be a live act, especially given how rude our material was, but in fact, because of *Rock Profile* and *Little Britain*, we had done very little live work together since.

We had a wildly enthusiastic response from the audience in April 2004 when we performed a handful of sketches – Lou & Andy, Vicky Pollard, the Prime Minister & Sebastian, and Dafydd – at a benefit for the Teenage Cancer Trust at the Royal Albert Hall. It was *Little Britain*'s first live outing. Alan Partridge, Jimmy Carr and Ricky Gervais were all on the bill that night too. I really felt we'd arrived.

Little Britain Live sold out within two hours of going on sale – over 250,000 tickets – before a single word had been written. Phil McIntyre produced the show, which was to open in the autumn of 2005. We met various potential directors and chose Jeremy Sams, who had been responsible for a recent production of *Noises Off* in the West End and on Broadway. I had seen it and could not remember an audience laughing so much at anything before or since. Jeremy understood perfectly the pace we needed to hit, and was generous too, coming up with great gags which we'd throw in. We couldn't have wished for a better director.

Despite knowing that we'd have tons of costume and make-up changes, David and I were keen to be onstage together as much as possible. We felt that was what the audience wanted to see.

Jeremy helped us put it all together and figure out the right order for the scenes. He also conceived a fantastic set where whole rooms could slide on and offstage with ease. It looked high-tech and computerised, but in actual fact was completely mechanical, with stagehands in the wings manically placing furniture on tracks and pulling levers. Behind us was a huge screen, with projected backdrops. After each sketch Tom Baker's voiceover would play and the projection would take the audience on a point-of-view journey across Britain to the next destination.

Backstage there was organised chaos. The make-up and costume changes took place immediately behind the projected screen. I'd arrive and within seconds Jeremy Rent would become Marjorie Dawes. Sometimes we'd have to wear three costumes, one on top of the other, as there was only time to rip one off, not pull one on. We'd just have to stand still, arms out, while three or four costume and make-up assistants would transform us, while a sound guy fixed the microphone. It was like a Formula One pit stop.

The show began in Portsmouth, the same town where we'd stormed it eight years earlier with *Sir Bernard's Grand Tour*. We were very nervous, as we'd only had four days of technical rehearsals – one of the toughest weeks of my working life. There wasn't enough time and the show was beginning to feel over-ambitious. Props didn't work, parts of the set hadn't arrived, costume and make-up changes were taking too long and the projected footage was still being created.

Opening night. We went for an early Chinese meal nearby, too nervous to eat much, then returned to the theatre. Expectations were high and several of the newspapers had sent reviewers. There was to be no West End or Broadway-style preview period. We had a few technical problems that night, but we got away with it. The reviews – for the first time in a couple of years – were great.

Over the next eighteen months we performed the show over 250 times, playing to over 800,000 people. It went into the *Guinness Book of Records* as the biggest comedy tour of all time. When we came to London we played the Hammersmith Apollo, and ended up doing more nights there than any other comedy act in its history.

The strangest thing of all, though, was that we became the first British comedy tour to play arenas.

Rob Newman and David Baddiel had done a night at Wembley Arena some years earlier to celebrate the end of their tour. Our producers Phil and Paul had suggested we do an arena show in Manchester 'just as an experiment'. It was added on to the end of the first touring block, just before we broke for Christmas on 20 December 2005. We were very tired by then, as it was our ninth night performing in a row. During the days we would modify the show, even writing new stuff, and David, extraordinarily, would also train for his sensational swim across the English Channel.

At the interval David and I came offstage utterly despondent.

'No one's laughing,' we said. 'It's a disaster.'

Phil and Paul were jubilant, however. 'What? It's a triumph!'

We were baffled. We hadn't been able to hear the audience the way we'd done in the smaller theatres – but in the vast auditorium it had been a completely different story, with the crowd in hysterics.

And that's how we ended up doing over forty arena dates.

Suddenly we had to factor in big screens and cameras. It changed our timing – partly because it was taking a lot longer for the sound of the audience laughing to reach us (we added special microphones in the audience, relaying the laughter to us, via speakers on the stage) and partly because the audience were now primarily watching the screens. It meant we were doing a sort of hybrid of a live show and a TV show. Each of us needed to be onscreen at the time of a joke, or it didn't get as big a laugh. I would have to wait to see the red light in the distance, out of the corner of my eye, denoting which camera was showing on the big screen at that moment and adjust my timing accordingly.

But it worked. Although we hadn't been on a stage for a long time, our years of live experience paid off. Many people were expecting a cash-in, but actually I think the stage show was better than the TV show in many ways.

Joining us on tour were Paul Putner and Samantha Power, and we'd find a local girl in each city to do a brief walk-on. That was it – apart from the poor folk who were dragged out of the crowd!

David did his audience participation bit in the first half, as children's entertainer Des Kaye – 'Wicky Woo!' During a game of 'Hide the Sausage' he would almost always wrestle the trousers off some poor lad. You could never get away with that today. In fact he didn't always get away with it then. Sometimes David would get a clout for his troubles and I'd see him in the wings afterwards, nursing a sore ear.

In the second half, in an age before 'fat-shaming' was considered the antisocial activity it is today, Marjorie would head into the audience to find someone willing to go through the very public ordeal of a FatFighters weigh-in. I learned quickly that it was often better to find a man, as the audience – and I – would feel guilty laughing at a woman in the same way.

When the show came to London, Tony Head appeared as the PM, much to the audience's delight. He was our little surprise, which helped lift the show as it reached a climax. Ruth Jones guested too, as Myfanwy.

Some months earlier we'd made a special episode of *Little Britain* for Comic Relief – with guest appearances by George Michael, Robbie Williams and Sir Elton John. In a meeting I wondered aloud whether the BBC might permit us to sell the episode on DVD in shops ahead of its transmission on Red Nose Day. Within days HMV and Sainsbury's had agreed to sell the DVD exclusively. In just a couple of weeks we sold over 600,000 copies and raised an additional £2 million for the charity.

During the London leg of the *Little Britain* tour, we decided to do a special night in aid of Comic Relief. Some clangs coming up. Ready? Okay, here we go . . . Peter Kay, Russell Brand, Jonathan Ross, Dawn French, Peter Serafinowicz, Patsy Kensit and Kate Thornton all joined in – and poor Jeremy Edwards lost his trousers and nearly his underpants, thanks to Des Kaye – but the highlight for me was the appearance of the real Dennis Waterman.

We were nervous enough during the day, rehearsing so many people. It was a big ask of everybody. When Dennis arrived, we wondered how he'd be with us, given that we'd heard people did our bizarre high-pitched impression of him everywhere he went. I think he could see that we were a bit apprehensive – like a pair of naughty schoolboys – but he was delightful. When he appeared onstage during our sketch, it took a moment for the audience to figure out what was happening. He then got the biggest, most deserved cheer of the night. As he took centre stage and broke into 'I Could Be So Good For You', with full backing track, the audience went wild. David and I clapped and sang along behind him. My friend Alex Godfrey observed – correctly – that he'd never seen such a big grin on my face. I can confirm that it was and probably will always be the happiest moment of my career.

During rehearsals for the Comic Relief gig, David had been very stressed. We tended to react differently to pressure. He would brood, while I'd go and eat my body weight in chocolate. If we had differences, we'd usually either think 'I'll let that one go' or deal with it there and then, before it became an issue. I've heard stories of people throttling each other or walking out on tour, but we really only had two proper arguments in the whole eighteen months' period, both before the show.

One was in Oxford when I was getting a rash on my face because we had to kiss passionately (as Judy and Maggie) and he had stopped shaving every day. He took exception to the notion that I had said it was 'painful' rather than 'uncomfortable' – and we were suddenly hurling obscenities at each other. Another time we bickered in Canberra over nothing – we were near the end of the tour by then and were probably just fed up with each other. On both occasions we sorted it out within an hour, hugged and did the show. That was as dramatic as we got. I think it helped that we travelled separately, which meant we had our own space. We were supposed to have separate dressing rooms too, but if there was enough space we actually preferred to share. That way we could talk about how the show was going and figure out if we wanted to add or change anything.

We found that audiences were warmer and more enthusiastic the further away we were from London. The only place we found impenetrable was Brighton. We had a few shows there and at a couple of them the audience seemed almost inconvenienced by our presence, as if they'd been expecting someone else and we'd stumbled in by mistake.

When I got the tour schedule through, I had kept an eye out for one venue in particular: I had a score to settle. On 5 February 2006, over ten years after I was booed off in the early hours, I returned to the Edinburgh Playhouse. Compared to the enormous arenas we had somehow found ourselves playing, what had once felt like an imposing place now felt nice and cosy. We had a great show. Even better, Craig and Charlie Reid – aka The Proclaimers – came along with their families and their manager Kenny. I would clang 500 clangs!

We had quite a few special visitors to our show, mainly in London. Sir Elton John and Kylie Minogue came; and one night we kept Kate Moss and Pete Doherty waiting in the bar because we were busy chatting to Sir Paul McCartney. David said afterwards that he had had a voice in his head throughout the show, which he could hear after every single line – 'I wonder what Paul McCartney thought of *that* joke. I wonder what Paul McCartney thought of *that* joke. I wonder what Paul McCartney thought of *that* joke.'

I haven't bothered with the clangs, because I don't know if any of the people I just mentioned are that big a deal.

We really enjoyed our residency in London. The show was finely honed by then and also the Hammersmith Apollo is great for comedy. It's big enough for it to feel like an event, but small enough for it to feel intimate.

Every night at Hammersmith we had friends and family in, many of whom we'd barely seen as we'd been on the road for a year. Joe, a younger cousin of mine, who was studying at Haberdashers' at the time, came along and told me afterwards that one of my old school teachers had seen the show a few days earlier.

'Oh, she should have come backstage and said hello!' I cried.

'I told her that, but she said she thought it was a bit rude.'

'It wouldn't have been rude at all,' I replied. 'I'd love to have seen her.'

'No – she said the show was rude.'

The day after we finished in London, Kevin and I had our civil partnership ceremony and then, a few weeks later, *Little Britain Live* headed off to Australia.

My oldest friend Jeremy and his wife Lauren had emigrated there the year before, and Kevin and I were very happy to be able to spend time with them. I also got to appear in *Kath & Kim* as Sharon's half-sister Karen. Kevin and I had met Jane Turner, Gina Riley and Gina's husband Rick a couple of years earlier in London and had become good friends.

David and I found it bizarre that we were so famous in a country we'd never visited before. The thing that struck me most about Australia was that it felt closer to home than Paris, despite the geographical distance. The Australian tour was a sell-out and we ended up playing to over 100,000 people.

We also met up a couple of times with Billy Crystal, who was touring his '700 Sundays' show around Australia at the same time. Kevin and I had seen it on Broadway a couple of years earlier. I thought it was the greatest comedy show I'd ever seen and I bombarded Billy with questions. I'm not sure what he made of our show – it had become increasingly vulgar as the tour went on – but he was very polite!

We were also making a documentary about our Australian visit, and so we caught up with Dame Edna Everage. Barry Humphries had been a huge influence on both of us. We'd met him a few times before and always knew we were in the presence of greatness.

We were treated royally by the Australians and it remains one of my favourite places in the world. We went to watch a *Little Britain* tribute drag show; we launched the Mardi Gras (with me in character as Dafydd); and we paid a visit to perhaps the most famous road in Australia – certainly the most famous in Erinsborough – Ramsay Street. I had watched *Neighbours* as a kid and so we jumped at the chance to lurk in the background at the Scarlet Bar as Lou and Andy, alongside Harold Bishop, Paul Robinson, Toadfish and co.

Apart from our brief squabble in Canberra, David and I had a wonderful time in Australia. The only thing that truly upset us was that one of the audience members went backstage after the show one night and stole the Dennis Waterman wig! Aside from the fact that it cost several thousand pounds to make, it meant that the make-up team had to hastily improvise with another wig for the rest of the tour and the character didn't look quite as he should. The person who stole the wig then got in contact, saying they would return it if they could have dinner with us, but we didn't really fancy it, funnily enough.

It wasn't the first time something had gone missing backstage. Years earlier, during the *Shooting Stars* tour, my pink romper suit had been pinched by some drunken staff who worked for the sponsorship company. I had flipped out – it was only two weeks after my father had died – and threatened to destroy the large sponsorship logo that sat on the stage. The suit was returned. Another time Paul Putner and Tim Atack had their wallets pinched from the dressing room during a preview of our show at the Battersea Arts Centre. When the wig went missing, it wasn't the cost or the inconvenience that freaked me out – both of those could be dealt with, ultimately. It was the sense that someone – anyone – could walk into our dressing room. Even when we recorded our *Little Britain* radio shows, I would bring my bag onstage with me!

The tour finished in Perth. David, Kevin and I were rushed out of the venue and off to the airport, where we flew through the night to Tokyo, barely grabbing a wink of sleep. *Little Britain* was being released on TV and DVD in Japan and we had agreed to go on a promotional tour. We were fascinated by Tokyo, but we were exhausted from the tour and the lack of sleep. I had caught a cold on the plane and spent the day blowing my nose while talking to journalists, only discovering later that this is frowned upon in Japanese company.

We appeared on various TV shows there, including *Waratte iitomo!*, with the iconic Tamori. The thing that amused us the most was seeing so many people walking around Tokyo wearing those little surgical face masks. I wanted to walk out on *Waratte iitomo!* wearing one, but was discouraged by our publicist.

Little Britain seemed to be reaching its natural end, but it was to have one last hurrah.

During the tour I had received an email from Will Young (I think I'd better 'Clang' right now), who had seen the show, asking if he could pass my details on to his manager Simon Fuller.

Simon had created *Pop Idol* and *So You Think You Can Dance* and managed the Spice Girls, David and Victoria Beckham and Annie Lennox amongst others. We had never met him before, but he flew to see us on tour in Birmingham and told us that he had taken the liberty of talking to HBO's head honcho Chris Albrecht about *Little Britain*. He said that Chris was interested in us making a version for America.

David and I were flown with our agents to LA. We had a brief meeting at the Peninsula Hotel in Beverly Hills with Simon and a pair of genial guys called David and Larry. They were veterans in the industry, managed Billy Crystal, Robin Williams and various others, and would be executive producers on the show.

We went to HBO, met with Chris Albrecht and left half an hour later with our own US TV series. We hadn't even got ourselves an American agent at that point. Meetings with all of the big agencies followed and we signed with the biggest, CAA. We were then serenaded by various movie studios and signed a deal with Dreamworks – before we'd even had an idea for a film!

The Americans seemed to be impressed with our ratings, our merchandise sales and the amount of tickets we'd sold on tour. In a world before Netflix, AMC and Amazon, there was nothing to rival HBO. They were the only place to be – unless we'd wanted to try and make a network show, which felt like a whole other world to us. So much of what we did was adult – you couldn't have Bubbles or Dafydd or Bitty on mainstream American TV, the advertisers would have been in uproar.

We agreed that we would take some of our original sketches and Americanise the characters. For instance, Dafydd would become Latino, and the only gay in his border town of Laredo, Texas. We completed this process and had begun to write some brand new characters when word reached us that there was now a new head of HBO – Mike Lombardo – and he wanted us to feature the characters in their original British form.

Little Britain USA would be set and filmed entirely in the US so we had to figure out a reason and context to allow our most popular characters to be in America. Although our shows had already played to a small audience on BBC America, this new show would effectively work as series one for HBO viewers who had never seen us before, and series four for our existing audience in the UK and around the world.

To inspire us, we went with David and Larry and our producer Stephanie on a short research tour around some American cities. Branson, Missouri, was definitely the strangest – like a Christian gambling-free Las Vegas, where the Osmonds and Andy Williams did nightly shows. In Chicago we went to Wrigley Field to see a baseball game. We had a great time the next day in rural Illinois at the Sandwich Fair – a huge, old-fashioned, typically American event with shows, parades and competitions.

We returned to LA to write. Our show runner was Michael Patrick Jann, who had been a part of an American sketch group called The State. After we read each sketch aloud, Michael would often say it was 'quite good'. This felt like faint praise to us and we were sad that he didn't think much of our efforts. It wasn't until years later that I learned that the Americans use the phrase 'quite good' the way the British say 'very good!' Sorry if we appeared ungrateful, Michael!

We filmed on location in Wilmington, a seaside town in North Carolina. In the summer humidity, we baked in our hot costumes. When we weren't filming or learning lines, we had dialect rehearsals, so we could make a respectable stab at the American accent.

The studio scenes were shot in LA and were directed by David Schwimmer, who was one of the best studio directors I've ever worked with. Full of great ideas, the only annoying thing was that he wasn't playing all the parts himself, as he's clearly one of the funniest people in the world.

It was a fresh challenge filming Marjorie in front of an audience and we had special guests, including Sarah Chalke and a very game Rosie O'Donnell. Rosie had been a big champion of the show and she did a great job of standing up to Marjorie.

One of the Emily Howard sketches included an appearance by Sting, who we happened to meet on a flight a few months earlier. He was going to be in LA while we were filming, as The Police had re-formed and were playing the Hollywood Bowl. He suggested we head to the concert and watch the sound check, and then we could meet him immediately after to discuss the sketch we were all filming the following day.

I sat at the Hollywood Bowl, a few rows back, Walliams on my left, Schwimmer on my right, watching The Police rehearse. Also onstage during the sound check, dancing away, were a few people who'd donated money to charity and been invited to meet the band in return. After each number Sting would complain he had a sore throat and ask if anybody else wanted to sing for a bit. One or two of the charity donors took the mic for a few seconds before sheepishly handing it back to the singer.

After yet one more appeal from Sting, Schwimmer nudged me. 'You can sing. Go on.'

'Noooooooo,' I replied.

'Well, now's your moment. In thirty seconds' time it'll be too late,' said Ross out of *Friends*.

I walked up to the stage. There were four of us – The Police, and yours truly.

'Oh, hello, Matt,' said Sting. 'What do you want to sing?'

I hadn't realised there'd be a choice. It was like karaoke, with the words on a discreet little screen at the foot of the stage.

'Um, "Every Little Thing She Does Is Magic", please.'

I'd never sung it before, but as luck would have it, it just happened to be in my key. I was able to really belt it. Afterwards Mr Sting told me I was really good. I mean, he'd have probably said that anyway, but still.

And that is how I came to sing lead vocals on 'Every Little Thing She Does Is Magic' at the Hollywood Bowl, with The Police, and Sting on backing vocals.

It wasn't filmed. But it happened. You'll just have to take my word for it.

I've had a few odd moments like that. I once sang backing vocals on 'Ain't No Pleasing You' with Chas & Dave on a TV show – which might not sound like much to you, but I bloody love Chas & Dave – and I say that even as a fervent Arsenal fan.

Also I got to share vocals with Peter Kay and The Proclaimers for Comic Relief on 'I'm Gonna Be (500 Miles)' – which went to number one for three weeks. (Still waiting for that gold disc, by the way.)

And . . . I once sang with Queen, of course.

Back to 2008. As we were making *Little Britain USA* I got the sense that the new guard at HBO would probably not have commissioned it – but, having inherited it, they were stuck with it! Suddenly, in the context of what the channel was doing – the big new series was *True Blood* – our programme felt old-fashioned. A big bone of contention was the laughter track. During the edit, Mike Lombardo asked if we could try removing it, to make the show feel more contemporary and pacey.

We didn't like to be obstructive, but we felt we had to say no. When it came to the footage we'd shot on location, we could indeed lose the laughter as requested, but because the studio audience had been so lively and chortled throughout, we knew we wouldn't be able to remove their laughter from the sketches we'd shot in front of them without sitting in a booth and re-dubbing virtually every single line of dialogue.

Besides, the scenes we filmed in front of an audience were shot and lit very differently to the location footage. When you go on the road you tend to film with just one camera. It's much more intimate. In the studio you tend to do big set-piece sketches. Everything is lit more brightly. The action is covered by five cameras at the same time, all of which are much further away, and there is much less movement from them. Consequently the performances are bigger. The timing, too, is affected by how the audience responds. We had set out to make – and had made – a big broad sketch show. We felt that re-voicing sketches full of dialogue and cutting out the laughter track would not have addressed HBO's concerns.

Despite their misgivings, I thought we'd done a decent job. There were lots of fun new characters in the series, like the little girl Ellie-Grace and her mother, and two butch gym buddies with micro-penises. HBO might have felt the laughter was intrusive – but it was real.

The majority of American reviewers were generally pretty positive about the show. The UK press, however – now gleefully charting our 'downfall' – summarised the notices by quoting only the bad ones! The *Daily Star* went one step further. It ran an article, picked up by lots of other news outlets, quoting members of various outraged and offended gay rights groups, apparently disgusted and grief-stricken by the Dafydd sketches.

I was confused and disappointed. The show had not yet aired – in fact, preview copies hadn't even been distributed to critics – so I couldn't fathom how they could have seen any footage. Furthermore, I really didn't think there was anything homophobic in the show.

David suggested we get our lawyers onto it and they put a detective on the case. We learned that not only were the quotes entirely fictional, but so were the individuals and the organisations quoted. We sued the *Daily Star*, who ran an apology. We gave the proceeds to local gay rights charities – ones that actually existed!

Despite these obstacles, HBO told us that they would like a second series. We began writing and had penned three episodes' worth of sketches when they had a change of heart. They said they wanted to relaunch the show. They still wanted another series, but first they would like a ninety-minute special. We said we were reluctant to do ninety minutes of solid sketches. Could we at least do two forty-five minute specials? They said no, it had to be ninety minutes. We didn't fancy it, so that was that.

Ha – look at us with our big ideas, turning down a feature-length HBO special.

The film we developed with Dreamworks – and Ben Stiller's company Red Hour – was to be called 'Diva Las Vegas'. We worked closely with an Englishman based in LA called Will Davies, who had written lots of comedies including *Twins* and *How to Train Your Dragon*. We figured out the plot together and added gags to Will's script. The story featured some of the *Little Britain* characters and lots of new ones in a big-budget, madcap comedy. Had the HBO show been a smash, maybe 'Diva Las Vegas' might have been made. It's certainly a funny script, albeit in a town with piles of funny scripts sitting on shelves gathering dust.

Dust? Anybody? No?

People had told us that *Little Britain* wouldn't work in the US without us in it. Though I'm sure they said the same thing to Ricky Gervais and Stephen Merchant. They made the right choices when it came to the American version of *The Office* and, having thought about it since, I think we should have tried to do a deal to remake the show, using our concepts and scripts as a basis, and then recast it. I'd love to have seen – would still love to see, in fact – 'This is America', starring two or three homegrown comedians, with a voiceover by James Earl Jones or Morgan Freeman.

It's not easy for me to look back on *Little Britain USA*. The events of 2008 were overshadowed by the breakdown in my relationship with Kevin. David was supportive as it became clear that Kevin had become consumed by drug addiction. When I wasn't on set – and even when I was – I was focused on trying to save not only our relationship but his life. There is much that I could say about that period and what followed, but, as I explained in the Preface, some things must remain private.

David and I returned to the UK. We wanted to re-orientate the material we had written and produce a final series of *Little Britain* for the BBC, but there was a new controller of BBC One – Jay Hunt – and she felt that the show had had its day. We offered to show her the scripts, but she said she thought it was time for us to do something else. So if you want to know why we stopped making *Little Britain* – well, it wasn't our choice and there's at least half a series' worth still lurking on our hard drives somewhere!

I will admit we were a little surprised, but we didn't mope. Jay Hunt remained keen to keep us at the BBC, so we set to work trying to think of what to do next. David suggested we do a big new sketch show – something with all of the things that we couldn't do in *Little Britain*, like monologues and parodies, something more family-orientated that could play on a Saturday night. While it was a good idea, I wasn't sure that we should follow *Little Britain* immediately with another sketch show.

Instead we decided to answer the critics who accused us of just trotting out the same jokes week in week out by developing a series that would be something completely different each time. We created six new scenarios. One of them revolved around an airport. As we started to write, it became clear that it had a lot more life in it than just half an hour. We asked Jay if we could do a whole series of it and luckily for us she said yes.

5/29/2008   12:04

T – The TARDIS

'Are you excited?' asked one of the runners as he led me down the corridor.

What a strange question, I thought. Am I twelve years old? Is this my first job in television?

It was the autumn of 2015 and I was anything but excited. I was anxious.

The orange duffel coat I was asked to try on seemed broad to me. I mean, obviously it had to be broad to fit me, but . . . you know what I mean.

In a large, nondescript room at BBC Roath Lock studios in Cardiff maybe fifty people were gathered for a read-through of the *Doctor Who* Christmas Special.

Once or twice over the years I had had an availability check for *Doctor Who*. I had always been unavailable.

Scratch that. I had always *told* them I was unavailable. I had resolved never to appear in the show. Why on earth had I said yes now?

Let's go back and forth, travel through time like the Doctor. And I'll do my best to explain.

A month earlier I had been asked to put myself 'on camera' for the role of Bottom in Russell T. Davies's BBC adaptation of *A Midsummer Night's Dream*. I'd not had much experience with Shakespeare. In 2000 I was cast to play Thersites in a production of *Troilus and Cressida*. The director wrote to us a couple of weeks before rehearsals began and suggested we read *The Iliad*, Chaucer's *Troilus and Criseyde* and a deeply scary memoir about Bosnia just to get us into the mood. A talented troupe of actors and one of Britain's hottest up-and-coming directors contrived to put on a mess of a production that baffled and bored anyone who came to see it in equal measure. We toured the country, playing to tiny audiences in enormous theatres and even though the production was not nearly good enough, the director somehow managed to wangle us a three-week run at the Old Vic. We were shredded by the critics. I remember sitting on the Tube on the way to the theatre, as people around me read copies of the *London Evening Standard* in which I was (rightly) slated. As the run came to a close, I was so dispirited I seriously questioned whether it might be time to quit performing altogether and try something else.

In the summer of 2015 I'd worked hard for a day or two on the *Midsummer Night's Dream* scenes, by myself, at my home in LA. I had three friends staying, but I gave them my apologies and sent them out on excursions while I holed myself away in my office, trying to work out how to play Shakespeare without anyone there to direct me.

Eventually the time came to record myself. I can't say it was any good, but I can say I gave it my all as I performed in front of my webcam (wahey!) and emailed the scenes off.

A couple of weeks later, I learned that I hadn't got the job. I allowed myself to be disappointed, but also remembered that there are many more experienced Shakespearean actors than me, so maybe it just wasn't meant to be.

Shortly after that, though, I was offered a small guest role in the *Doctor Who* Christmas Special by the same casting director. Without even reading the script, I thought that perhaps I should say yes because that would make me feel better about not getting the other job. I also thought that *maybe* I would be ready to step back into the TARDIS.

It had been around eight years since I had last been in it. Eight years since Kevin had left and taken the TARDIS with him. The *actual* TARDIS, that is.

When *Little Britain* went big, I wasn't really sure what to do with the spoils. I'd not had any experience of that kind of life. I bought a house with too many floors. I had my own box at Arsenal, where our dog Milo would sit on the seat next to me. And I bought a TARDIS from the BBC . . .

It was the one that had been used on the Christopher Eccleston series and David Tennant's first series too. The production team needed to build a slightly bigger one so I took this one off their hands for a low five-figure sum.

I bought it for Kevin. I had enjoyed *Doctor Who* as a kid, tuning in to the adventures of Tom Baker, Peter Davison and Colin Baker, but Kevin was a true Whovian, a devoted fan. When Russell T. Davies brought the show back after a hiatus that felt like a lifetime, Kevin's excitement was so great that I arranged for us to travel to Wales and visit the set. That night we went to the episode launch screening and then, to cap it off, managed to cadge a lift back to London with Captain Jack himself, John Barrowman. I'd never seen Kevin so happy.

And so the TARDIS was delivered to our house in Marylebone in pieces and installed in the basement. We even had a hole cut into the basement ceiling to make room for the light on top. Inside the police box Kevin put up some fairy lights. Visitors would have photos taken inside it. It was loved and cared for.

The gift had been so well received that for his next birthday I somehow managed to talk the BBC into letting me buy a Dalek. This was more expensive, but I thought it would make a great addition to the TARDIS. The Dalek arrived but we couldn't get it through the doors of the house. There was talk of cutting it vertically in half to get it in, but there was no guarantee that it could be successfully put back together again. Within minutes it went back to Wales, never to be seen again.

When Kevin left me in 2008, after nearly six years together, he took the TARDIS with him and, to my knowledge, installed it in his new home in Edinburgh. I'm afraid I don't know where it is now. I heard that it might have been donated by his family after his death to a primary school somewhere.

Sitting in that read-through of 'The Husbands of River Song', I looked around at the sea of friendly faces. I was excited to be working with Alex Kingston, Greg Davies and, of course, Peter Capaldi, who I had met briefly the year before when we did a scene together in the film *Paddington*.

As always happens at the beginning of a read-through, a chain started around the room, with each person introducing themselves and stating their job on the show. When it reached me, I surprised even myself by saying 'I'm Matt Lucas and I play the Doctor'. There was a brief gasp, during which the occupants of the room turned as one to see if Peter was chuckling. He was. Everyone else then burst into laughter.

I didn't have all that much to do in the episode and, as the other actors read their parts, I scanned the room. As well as the cast there were lots of production staff. And I started to imagine an alternative reality in which Kevin was alive and well and had got himself a dream job, perhaps in the publicity department or on *Doctor Who Magazine*. I pictured him, thirty-eight now, less hair, listening to the actors, laughing at the script. We were still not together in this version, but there would be a polite, coy exchange afterwards, maybe an arrangement to have a cuppa while I was in Cardiff and then slowly we would allow ourselves to fall in love all over again. By the end of the read-through I was feeling a profound, almost new sense of loss. It was as I had feared it would be, maybe even worse.

Since his death I have somehow survived on this earth, partly by carving out new pathways. I avoid the songs, the places, the loves and the life that we shared, because it is often too painful to experience it without him.

I had always told myself that going on *Doctor Who* would bring too many feelings to the surface. It turned out I was right. So I was upset, not only because I was feeling his loss acutely, but because it was self-induced. I could and should have said no to the role.

Don't get me wrong, by the way. At no point, on no day, in no hour or minute do I ever *not* think of him. How could I not? We two were one. When Kevin died, half of me died with him. Those who know me will tell you that I have changed immeasurably and irrevocably. I have lost. I am lost. Sometimes I dream about him. He always emerges, having only pretended to have left. My joy at seeing him again is tempered by a sense of betrayal, as I ask him why he went away.

Then I wake up and realise he is gone. Again.

After four and a half years together, I proposed to Kevin. We had a civil partnership ceremony. My mother was tentatively pleased, I would say. My brother Howard was opposed to a formal union, saying immediately that he 'didn't agree with that sort of thing'. On the day of the ceremony he came along 'to help with security' and lingered outside the room, poking his head in, while we said our vows. Afterwards at the reception he stood up and spoke. It wasn't planned, but he gave the most beautiful speech I have ever heard. He talked about how it had been hard for him to come to terms with my sexuality, hard even for him to be there today, but that he had looked around the room and seen how happy I was – how happy we all were – and realised that he was happy too. He welcomed Kevin to the family, with love.

He was right. I was so happy. Kevin either was too – and then wasn't – or already wasn't. I will never really know. Eighteen months later, he left me for someone else while in rehab, and less than eighteen months after that, he killed himself.

The facts do not tell the whole story. Nor will I, as I have explained already. But I will say this: Kevin and I never stopped loving each other. We wanted to be together. He suffered from a drug addiction that I knew nothing about for a long, long time, and when I did we fought it the best way we knew how. At first that meant being together and then it meant being apart. I lived in hope that he would find a way to manage his addiction. I dreamed of getting back together with him and he wanted to get back with me. It wasn't to be. Some people don't have the armour.

Yes, this is a chapter about *Doctor Who* – and it is also a chapter about grief. About walking the tightrope and not looking down.

When Kevin died, one of our friends contacted me. He too had lost a former partner in similar circumstances. Like ours it was a relationship that had collapsed under the strain of the battle. He told me that he felt guilty until he realised that it was a narcissistic response to think that he could have changed something that even the addict himself could not. I will always be indebted to him for his words of wisdom.

Everyone's grief is different. On the night Kevin died, as I lay in bed, reporters repeatedly rang my doorbell. A swarm of paparazzi sat opposite my front door chattering away and stayed for a week. I didn't leave the house during that time. The press wrote that I was on suicide watch. It wasn't true. I spent much of the next year battling the papers, getting inaccuracies corrected.

I've no idea how to mourn. I mean, I know what to do for the first couple of weeks, when visitors come to the house and there's a funeral to think about. After that I have plenty of experience, but have gleaned little wisdom. When my father died, I spent the next three years smoking pot. Once Kevin was gone I refused all drink (and had long since given up cannabis). Instead, I downloaded Grindr and went on an empty sexual rampage that would have put Casanova to shame.

In the background – almost as a footnote – David and I made *Come Fly with Me*. I haven't written much about the show in this book – though I know it's one of our most popular works – because I barely remember a thing about it. I guess it's locked away somewhere or perhaps I was too busy drowning to take anything else in. I viewed some clips from it while I was writing this to try and remind myself. It's like watching someone else.

Isn't that strange, not to have a relationship with my own work? I think it's also because my working relationship with David was breaking down too. I'm not here to settle scores and I don't have any anger. Actually, in some of my darkest hours, the writing saved me. We laughed and laughed. It was the safest place to be.

The preparation for and filming of *Come Fly with Me*, however, had been tough on both of us. Throughout our relationship David and I would often find ourselves at loggerheads during rehearsals and shooting, though each series we did would be enough of a success that – perhaps like childbirth – we would both forget about the pain and begin the whole process again. However, I no longer had the capability to either absorb or deflect anyone else's anxiety. I just had to get out of the way of it.

Even when David and I were in sync – which we were for much of the time – I still struggled to remain in London, living and working as I had done before Kevin's death. It felt dishonest, as if I was pretending that everything was as it had been, when in reality my world had collapsed. I saw Kevin everywhere. All roads led back to the same place.

So in 2012 I moved to America, to the warmth of the Californian sun. Slowly – very slowly – things started to get a little easier – or at least more manageable – as I set about rebuilding my life.

I grieve Kevin's loss every day. It's a grief that does not go. It consumes me. Eight years on, it's embedded in me now. Irrevocable. Part of the fabric. And yet on a rare day when I realise that I haven't actually thought about him for an hour or two, *then* I feel the guilt. Damned if I do, damned if I don't.

I would still love to have kids one day – if I was in a settled relationship – but I have convinced myself that the grief has become such an inseparable part of me now that it'll be in the genes. Even if I never mentioned Kevin again, it would still be passed on.

I said yes to *Doctor Who* – yes to the TARDIS – because I realised I hadn't ever really been away from it. I'm going to mourn and love Kevin all day, every day for the rest of my life. I could be on a plane, a train, a boat. I could be in the most luxurious hotel or watching the greatest band perform. I could be hiking, swimming, playing with the dogs and he'll still be with me.

So I might just as well go and chase after some monsters in space, I suppose.

After the read-through, when we came to film the episode, I told myself to just get on with it, for these few weeks at least. And, in truth, I had a blast.

Doug Mackinnon, the director, was emphatic that I should play Nardole in a big, silly way. This was, after all, a Christmas Special.

While I was filming, news reached me that the person who was earmarked to play Bottom in *A Midsummer Night's Dream* was no longer able to do it. Shortly after wrapping on *Doctor Who*, I returned to the same studio in Cardiff and worked with the same crew to tackle Shakespeare once more.

Of course Shakespeare wrote plays, not films. Usually when you rehearse a play you have a book in your hand for a couple of weeks and lots of time to rehearse. I've never known that kind of luxury – or anything approaching it – on a film or TV set. We had to think on our feet, make quick decisions and commit to them.

My co-stars were a fun bunch. I was chuffed to be acting alongside Bernard Cribbins, whose work I had loved since I was a kid. I was kept very entertained by Javone Prince and Fisayo Akinade teaching Elaine Paige how to be a human beatbox. Richard Wilson and I became close and even went to Vegas together afterwards. The film was warmly received and, to my surprise, I had the best reviews of my career.

After the *Doctor Who* Christmas Special was broadcast, I mentioned to the show runner Steven Moffat that I would be happy to return at any point. He called my bluff and ordered me back. I was in early talks to appear in a sitcom pilot in America, but I curtailed them and flew to the UK. Initially it was going to be for three episodes, but then it grew and grew until I was in the whole series and another Christmas Special too.

The news that I was returning to the show was not greeted with joy in all quarters. Some fans were baffled. Others were fuming. Why was such a minor character being revived? They were also concerned because in 'The Husbands of River Song' Nardole had been rather over-the-top. How would this cartoonish performance affect the series?

Well, the writing changed, for a start. *Doctor Who* Christmas Specials are always pleasantly ridiculous. The scripts for the series now showed more sides to the character and I reasoned that it might be a smart move to calm down the performance too.

It was a gruelling shoot, from June 2016 to April 2017. The entrance to Roath Lock studios is as insalubrious as you can imagine. Drive through the gate and you'll pass a row of skips, groaning with scrap, and a small, rotting boat. Stop at the rusty trailers and then head inside to the chilly studio. There you will find magic happening, albeit on a BBC budget. Lunch is half an hour. You buy your own.

On camera I like to improvise. Once we had a few takes of the scripted version in the can, I would be allowed to riff a little, offering stuff up, looking at other options. It never offended me if it wasn't used, though often it was – 'Some of my best friends are Blueish' was a line I just threw in.

I loved working with the Doctor's companion Bill, aka Pearl Mackie, who gave such an effortlessly natural, contemporary, warm performance, and who was playful and fun away from the cameras too. She worked the longest hours. The prettier you are, the earlier your make-up call. With me, it only took twenty minutes. I'm already fat and bald!

I much admired Peter's work, of course. Often, between set-ups, while Pearl and I goofed around, he would take himself away, sitting in the corner at a desk or sometimes even on the TARDIS set, revising the numerous lengthy speeches that the Doctor had to deliver. On a day when he had fewer lines, he could clown around like the rest of us. Saving the world is hard work. You need a break sometimes.

In the gaps in filming I did my best to be insufferably jolly. Whenever runners Lauren, Rhun or Chris asked me if I needed anything, I'd regularly demand something impossible, or at the very least, pointless.

'Four barrels of unpasteurised rice milk, please.'

'Hilary Swank's autobiography, if you wouldn't mind.'

'Eleven bottles of Dettol and a peanut. Now!'

The crew were the best I've ever worked with, and the nicest. It's a long shoot and we became like a family. *Doctor Who* punches above its weight. The flashy American shows it competes with shoot in swanky studios with money to burn – but no challenge was too great for us. On those freezing, soaking outdoor night shoots we drank watery tea, swapped jokes, wolfed down soggy sandwiches and then got on with the business of making the best sci-fi show on the box.

Even the fans – for the most part – came round to what I was doing and enjoyed the lightness Nardole brought to the dark world of the show. One or two bombarded me with abuse on Twitter (while still following me, of course), but on the whole I was heartened by the response.

I'd love to return as Nardole one day and riff with the next Doctor. That orange duffel coat came to fit me rather well in the end, keeping me warm on those chilly Cardiff days. In the meantime I imagine he's triumphed over those Mondasian Cybermen, found his way back to Darillium for a bit, and has his feet up somewhere, munching on a Jaffa Cake and playing with a toy elephant.

Les Mis at the Queens
Theatre, London, 2011

U – Upstage

Well, we've got a TARDIS so we might as well use it, to travel back in time again. It's the summer of 1988. The fourteen-year-old me is at that school drama noticeboard again, this time reading about auditions for a role in a West End play, no less.

The piece in question was Catherine Cookson's *The Fifteen Streets* – a soapy potboiler, based on a book by Britain's then bestselling author. Set amidst the poverty of the dockyard slums of Tyneside at the turn of the century, the play revolved around two fighting brothers and their heartbroken mother. It had toured the UK and somehow found its way to London's Playhouse Theatre. Tickets were still available at all prices.

In those days, if you were between the ages of fourteen and sixteen, you could only work as an actor for eighty days a year. The children in the cast had worked nearly all of their eligible days so it was time to recast.

Open auditions took place on a scorching Saturday morning at Wimbledon Theatre, on the stage, behind the curtain. Queuing outside beforehand, I sized up the others and exchanged small talk, making sure to let everyone know that they were up against a veteran of the theatre, thanks to my barnstorming performance as Accrington Stanley the previous year.

We were brought in in small groups and were required to shout and chant in Geordie accents. I had seen *Auf Wiedersehen, Pet* and did my best Jimmy Nail impression, which was pitiful, I'm sure, but, at fourteen years old, my energy and enthusiasm somehow earned me a recall later that afternoon.

I killed time for a few hours and then got the bus back to the theatre, shaking with nerves. On the way my heart sank as I felt a familiar sensation. Throughout that summer, without any warning, I had succumbed to sudden, unexplained gushing nosebleeds. Sure enough it wasn't long before my hilarious 'Miami Mice' T-shirt (Mickey as Don Johnson) was streaked with blood. I didn't have time to get myself clean so I must have looked a sight at the second audition, but somehow I was offered a part in the play as a 'children's extra'.

Fame and riches lay in wait, I told myself jubilantly. Then came the reveal that we were not going to get paid *as such* because we were not Equity card-holders and didn't have solo lines, but that we would receive thirty pounds for expenses per week each. There were some grumbles, but I didn't care. Thirty pounds a week was better than nothing, especially as my mum said I could keep it all for myself.

It was agreed with my parents that one of them would collect me from the show every night, but that I would make my own way to the theatre each day. I was used to walking down the road to get the school coach, but this was a new experience. I would head to Stanmore station, get the Tube all the way to Charing Cross, and then walk down Villiers Street to the Playhouse Theatre.

I found it scary and exciting to be out on my own. It had been drummed into me not to talk to strangers, but sometimes people would just begin a conversation. I was on the Tube when one young guy noticed my Arsenal scarf and chatted to me about football. After half an hour he suddenly complained that there were a lot of Jews around at football matches these days and asked if I was a Jew. I shook my head. I think he could tell that I was lying and there was a pause and then he changed the subject.

There were maybe eight boys and two girls joining the cast of the play. In rehearsals it became clear that the boys were cut from two different types of cloth – middle-class namby-pamby swots like me and the rough, fearless Cockney kids, who, despite having voluntarily auditioned like the rest of us, seemed to think acting was for cissies. The agenda for them was to ridicule the poor director during rehearsals and muck about as much as possible.

We quickly learned our parts, which consisted of walking on and off a lot, and delivering simple playground chants that had been written especially for the piece, like . . .

> John O'Brien kissed mad Nancy
> Gave her money, tickled her fancy.
> We know Nancy is quite mad
> But John O'Brien is the dad.

We then joined the existing cast for more rehearsals. I was thrilled to be working with professional actors. I scoured the theatre programme and familiarised myself with the cast and their credits. One of the actors, Ian Tucker, had been the original Gavroche in *Les Misérables* and it was his voice you could hear on the cast album. Another, Patrick Holt, then seventy-six, had been a leading man in lots of Rank pictures in the fifties and kindly indulged me with stories about his career. I'm sure I was a nuisance, spending as much time with the adults as possible when I ought to have been sat quietly in my dressing room, but I knew I wanted a career as an actor and I couldn't miss the chance to learn as much about the profession as possible.

I also befriended Betty, an elderly no-nonsense Scot who sat in a tiny kiosk at the stage door. She'd worked at the Playhouse for years, knew everyone and everything that went on there. She smoked like a chimney and consequently had a voice so deep that whenever she answered the phone you would hear her berating whoever was on the other end for calling her 'sir'.

The dramatic high point of the play was a brutal onstage fight between the two rival brothers. They pushed, pulled, slammed and hurled each other all over the place. It seemed inconceivable to me that they didn't get hurt, but one of the actors told me that there had been an hour of rehearsal for every second of the fight. Nothing was left to chance. It was precisely choreographed. I saw it from close up every night and to this day I've never seen anything as visceral and intense.

In other parts of the show, many of us were more relaxed. There was a lengthy scene that took place on market day, with stalls all over the stage. The principal cast members were at the front of the stage delivering their lines, while the rest of us swanned around in the background. It's not uncommon for some actors to play pranks and games to keep themselves from being bored as the run goes on and at this point one of the cast had taken to surreptitiously balancing small props on the shoulders of other actors. I could often be found hiding at the back of the stage, doubled over in hysterics at the sight of one of the other actors discovering an entire slice of bread on their shoulder.

Our cast had only been in the show for a handful of performances when we were suddenly given our notice. The show was to close at the end of the month. I was disappointed but immediately philosophical. I wasn't a professional actor and yet in the space of a year I had performed at the Edinburgh Festival and in the West End. It was the stuff of dreams.

And now, every few years, I like to return to the stage.

I had a great time originating the role of Leigh Bowery in Boy George's musical *Taboo* in 2002, but my favourite experience came some years later in *Les Misérables*. I adored the show as a child and listened to the tape in the car repeatedly with my mum. I went to see it for my thirteenth birthday and several times more over the years.

When David and I were on our *Little Britain Live* tour, we heard that the producer of *Les Mis*, Cameron Mackintosh, was in the audience. He came backstage afterwards and – in a brave move for him considering he had just heard me attempt to sing in the show's finale – took me at face value when I told him I'd love to play the innkeeper Thénardier one day. Over the next few years there were sporadic conversations about the possibility. Because of my schedule with David, the idea of going into the show in London wasn't realistic at that time, but there was talk of a big one-off concert to celebrate its twentieth anniversary in Hyde Park or even at Wembley Stadium.

First, however, I had to go to Cameron's office in Bedford Square and sing for him. He seemed happy enough with what he heard. I also mentioned that I would love to play Javert one day, but he quickly nipped that one in the bud!

Sometime later I learned that there was to be a twenty-fifth anniversary concert at the O2 in London. I was to be the only person onstage who had not yet been in the show. Cameron was very keen for me to appear for a few weeks in the London production – as Alfie Boe and Nick Jonas would do – but I was busy with David, writing and filming *Come Fly with Me*.

I was, however, able to spend three days working on the stage at the Queen's Theatre with the musical director, who taught me my part. I then had another rehearsal at the Welsh Centre in London, where we sometimes rehearsed *Little Britain* and later on had *Doctor Who* script read-throughs. There I met Jenny Galloway (who was playing Madame Thénardier) and Alfie Boe for the first time. I had seen Jenny's performance on TV in the tenth anniversary show, but I only knew Alfie Boe from a brief appearance in an episode of *The Apprentice*, when he sang at an ice skating rink!

I was expecting a grand, towering, stuck-up tenor – but instead, waiting patiently in the corner in jeans and T-shirt, was this quiet, unassuming, humble man. And what a voice! I had never heard

Valjean performed in a purely operatic style before. When he sang 'Who Am I?' at the piano that day, it was clear that he was going to reinvent the role.

Come Fly with Me wrapped on the Friday night and the following morning I arrived at the O2 in Greenwich for my first rehearsal with the cast of the concert. The week that followed was one of the most exciting of my life, as the show came together.

Whenever I wasn't rehearsing, I would sit and watch the others. I was tense and nervous because we only had a week before we were going to be onstage at the O2, but also because two days after the concert would be the first anniversary of Kevin's death. On the second day of rehearsals, when the students sang 'Do You Hear The People Sing?' I broke down in tears. I don't think anyone saw, other than Emily, my assistant. Kevin and I had been to see *Les Misérables* together and he'd shared my love of it. I was heartbroken that he wouldn't be there with me.

On the Friday afternoon we assembled for the first time with the full orchestra. The sound was magical. It started to hit me that, in forty-eight hours' time, I would be onstage in *Les Misérables* – not in my bedroom singing it in front of the mirror, but at the O2 in front of nearly 20,000 people.

On the Saturday night, as we were rehearsing on the stage, Cameron decided that the wigs and make-up looked too theatrical on the big screens. He scrapped the lot. On the Sunday morning, during the dress rehearsal, he decided that the parts of the show that were being performed on the balcony at the back didn't feel connected to the rest of the performance. Much of what had been rehearsed was hastily discarded.

Tickets had sold out so quickly for the evening performance that Cameron had added a matinee in the afternoon. Those who were unable to come along could go to a local cinema and watch the evening show beamed live.

The matinee was a bit of a mess. Because of Cameron's changes we were still rehearsing until a few moments before the doors opened. He thought that I would – or should – receive a big round of applause on my entrance and so he called for four additional bars of intro music as I came on, to cover this.

We rehearsed it once hurriedly amidst a number of other changes and then I went to get into costume and make-up, but as soon as I walked out in front of the audience, I immediately panicked and reverted back to what I had been practising all week. If you know the show, then just imagine me singing the 'My band of soaks, my den of dissolutes' segment to *the wrong music*. It was excruciating and there was no way of communicating with the conductor or the orchestra without stopping – which I didn't dare do.

As I sang the right words to the wrong tune in front of the audience – including the poor writers of the piece Alain Boublil, Claude-Michel Schönberg and Herbert Kretzmer – I hurriedly tried to calculate what the ongoing consequences might be of this error. Would I now be four bars ahead *for the entirety* of 'Master Of The House'? Would the whole show now be out of sync?!

I reached the end of the ballsed-up intro and waited – and the orchestra caught up with me. I took a deep breath and launched into the song.

> Welcome, monsieur, sit yourself down
> And meet the best innkeeper in town . . .

I was back where I was supposed to be. Phew. But I had freaked myself out and struggled to focus for the remainder of the song. Now suffering stage fright, I fluffed a few words here and there, but smiled my best smile and I like to tell myself that no one will ever know. Oh, hang on, I've just told you. Well, anyway, please don't mention it to anyone else. Thank you.

When I spoke with Alfie at the interval he too was kicking himself over a missed cue or two. It seems a few of us had been a bit wobbly. Between the two shows I apologised to Alain and Claude-Michel (not least because they had initially tried to cut the intro to the song for the concert and I had begged them not to) and resolved not to let nerves get the better of me in the evening show.

I managed to keep my head and I'm proud of how it turned out that night. I'm also relieved that that is the performance that people have watched on TV and DVD and not the one from the afternoon!

Alfie Boe stole the show. His rendition of 'Bring Him Home' brought the house down. The audience applauded for several minutes. Backstage we watched the screens in awe and pride.

The experience was so enjoyable, so rewarding, truly the realisation of a dream that, when I heard that Alfie Boe was going back into the West End production, I just knew I had to join him. Alfie and I had become close. He'd even been staying at my house for a while. We'd had so much fun singing together in my kitchen, I was not going to miss the chance to hear him at full blast every night.

I later learned that, because Alfie and I are both quite short, the rest of the cast had to be too. Craig Mather, Liam Tamne, Hadley Fraser – none of us are giants. We called ourselves 'Les Minirables'. In the West End Madame Thénardier was played by Katy Secombe – daughter of Harry – and we instantly had a great chemistry. In fact I still have many friends from the West End run.

One of the joys of playing Thénardier is that, because he doesn't appear in the first forty-five minutes of the show, whoever plays him is also in the chorus for the opening scenes. That meant that I was a convict singing 'Look Down' and the podgiest wretch you'll ever see belting out 'At The End Of The Day', joining the others at the back of the stage and edging forward in that iconic stagger. I worked in the factory and in the fields, and joined the other villagers in scorn when naughty Valjean swiped that candlestick.

The way *Les Misérables* is staged – in the original London production, with the revolving set – is that, unless you are in the spotlight, you're pretty much in shadow. Once I spent the whole of the show chastising myself because I'd got the giggles during 'At The End Of The Day', but when I went to see the show again recently I was reminded that you can't really see anyone's faces anyway. I always gave my best onstage, but – knowing that most of us were barely visible at times – I could be mischievous too, as I had been nearly twenty-five years earlier in *The Fifteen Streets*. Oddly enough, when making comedy with David, we hardly ever mucked about – it was too serious a business – and yet here we all were, in this musical tragedy, with everyone dying everywhere, having the time of our lives.

One night I decided to paint a large black moustache on my face and thick, dark eyebrows. I looked like one of the Super Mario Bros. I went on in the factory scene as normal and the absurdity of my appearance reduced the rest of the cast to tears. However, one of the principals remained alone onstage singing and was understandably distracted by the raucous laughter in the wings. I got a big bollocking and apologised profusely to everyone, especially the performer who had been directly affected. What no one knew was that that morning had been my very last at the house in Marylebone where I'd lived with Kevin. It had been sold, so a few hours earlier I had said goodbye to it, grabbed a case, walked out the door and checked into a hotel. I was emotionally drained and had painted the moustache on in the evening in an attempt to cheer myself up.

After that, I did my best to behave, but it wasn't long before I was fooling around again. In the factory scene I was in a line of workers queuing up to receive a sou for a day's work. I usually liked to entertain the others (and poor Carl Mullaney, who had the onstage job of paying us) by either refusing to accept the coin or grabbing the whole pile and making off with it. One night I handed out coins backstage to everyone else in the factory beforehand and we all paid a stunned Carl instead.

In *Les Misérables*, whoever is playing Thénardier shares a dressing room with the actor playing Javert. I was lucky enough to be with Hadley Fraser, one of the few people I have ever met who can claim to be even sillier than me. We'd often challenge each other when it came to the bows to see who could do the grandest, the longest, the shortest or the lowest. Gradually the challenges became more esoteric and oblique – who could do the most gracious, the least grateful, the angriest, the haughtiest. At the end of one matinee I scampered around backstage handing out multiple packets of Fizz Wiz. That afternoon we took our bows with frothing mouths.

Some of the cast liked to join in my antics, while others were naturally more serious (okay then, *professional*), but there's a theatrical tradition that all of the actors and even the crew muck about a bit on the final matinee of their run. Usually there's a note given at the company warm-up session an hour before the show that there is still a paying audience out there and that everyone *must* behave, but that soon gets forgotten. The unwritten rule is that, as long as the audience doesn't know what's going on and the show isn't affected, you can pretty much do what you like.

I set myself a challenge in my final matinee to discreetly eat as many bananas as possible onstage during the show. I planned carefully how and where to secrete them, and while Valjean was being given his yellow ticket of leave and the rest of the convicts were bashing rocks with their picks, I reasoned that *my character* had earned a tea break. I sat down on the stage and tucked into my first banana. The fact that there were almost certainly no bananas in France during that period wasn't going to stop me. Throughout the performance I produced banana after banana and, because of the way the show is lit, none of the audience members were any the wiser. Well, I *say* that – one or two might have spotted me chomping on one alongside Madame Thénardier when we popped up through the trap-door during 'One Day More'.

Due to other work commitments I left the show before the rest of the cast and I was very touched that they all made such a fuss of me on my final weekend. Alfie Boe gave a speech onstage in front of the audience. Afterwards a party was thrown and I was presented with a book that the rest of the cast had put together. Alongside some lovely messages there were photos of the cast and crew – each sporting a large black moustache in my honour.

One of my remaining ambitions is to perform on Broadway. Cameron asked me on a couple of occasions to join the production of *Les*

Misérables there. Maybe I was crazy to say no, but when it came to it, I had such a wonderful time in London doing it, with the most brilliant, talented, warm group of people, that I figured I should probably quit while I was ahead. Maybe one day I'll change my mind and do the role again somewhere – I do love that show – but for now I am happy to cherish the memories.

V – Various Other Things I've Been In

In the interests of housekeeping and making sure everything is in order before I go, the purpose of this chapter is to talk about various other things I've been in.

Yes. We're approaching the end now. How will you cope when I'm gone? Will you sit in the corner of the room, rocking silently, waiting for me to pen a sequel to this opus? Or will you just move coolly on to the next sleb? Will you buy John Barrowman's tome, in which he reveals why he sounds all Canadian when he does *Loose Women* and like a Govanhill tough guy when he's on *Scotland Today*, or Katie Price's latest book, in which she finally explains the difference between Katie Price and Jordan? (Spoiler: Jordan wears slightly cheaper foundation.)

Anyway, aside from when I was in the audience on *Jim'll Fix It* and in the coffee shop on *Saturday Superstore* (I asked Owen Paul a question), my first TV appearance was in *Minder*.

Don't believe me? Okay then, check my IMDb page.

Actually, don't – you won't find it on there.

I was in *Minder* but I wasn't credited or paid. In fact, I'll go one step further. I wasn't even supposed to be there. One day my friend Nick came into college and told me that his grandfather – who was a bookmaker – had heard that George Cole and co. were going to be filming some scenes on a race day at Hackney Wick. Nick and I both loved *Minder* and took the afternoon off lessons to go and have a gander.

On the way there we talked about the likelihood of meeting Arthur Daley himself (small, we decided, but worth a try). This then developed into a challenge – not just to talk to the actors but to share the screen with them.

We turned up at the track and, sure enough, we found out where production was shooting. We casually mingled with some of the background artistes – or 'extras', as they used to be called – and joined them in the line-up. As we waited we talked to Gary Webster (who had recently replaced Dennis Waterman in the show) about Arsenal. We also chatted to some of the other background artistes, one of whom we had spotted in a Kellogg's Fruit 'n Fibre advert and another whom Nick had recognised from one of the *Indiana Jones* movies. One elderly man kept himself apart from the group. He was ill-tempered and extremely anxious in case his face appeared on camera. He told us that he would never get 'proper acting work' if he became known as an extra. The others told us he was deluding himself.

No one in the production team seemed to notice that these two seventeen-year-old boys had suddenly appeared, and so we helped ourselves to tea and biscuits and simply dotted ourselves along the filming route. Although we never summoned up the courage to speak to George Cole, as the camera tracks along, you can see the two of us walking behind him. Check out the screenshot. We're keeping straight faces, but inside we're jubilant.

My first proper TV acting job was in 1994 and was a line in *The Imaginatively Titled Punt & Dennis Show*. On the day, Steve Punt had a lot of dialogue and kept himself to himself, while Hugh Dennis just had the punchline in the sketch and was relaxed and larking about. The thing I remember most is that there was a joke in the scene about 'Big Ron' Tarr, a non-speaking background artiste who, over time, had become one of *EastEnders*' most popular and recognisable characters. On the day we filmed, Ron himself wasn't available, so instead a 'Big Ron' lookalike was hired to do the job. To my surprise, he told us this wasn't his first booking. It has always struck me as about the most niche job there could be.

My second TV acting gig later that year was on the second series of *The Smell of Reeves and Mortimer*. I was beyond thrilled to be working with my heroes at last. I'd been to a couple of recordings from the first series and Bob had hinted to me that I might be asked to appear if the show returned.

Before we shot in the studio, we went on location. I had been to plenty of studio recordings where they would have several cameras all covering the same action from different angles, but I was surprised to learn on location that just one camera was used, and then moved and the lighting changed, before the whole scene was filmed over and over again. I was struck by how long the process seemed to take.

In youth theatre I had become accustomed to discussing details and nuances with the director following each rehearsal and performance. Little analysis or discussion took place here. After each take I would look round to the director or Vic or Bob and ask 'Was that okay?' They seemed surprised by the question and would give a distracted nod. I learned that, in general, a film or TV director will only tell you to change something if they think it isn't working. They rarely engage at length with the subtleties of your performance, as time is tight and they have so many different things to focus on as they look at the monitor.

Continuity was another concept that I had not considered beforehand. There was a lady – the script supervisor – whose job it was to make sure you stood in the same place and moved your hands in the same way on each take. Unprepared for this, I had made all sorts of instinctive choices – hands in my pockets on this line, then hands out of my pockets, then pointing, then hands back in my pockets, the arms folded, then on my hips etc. – all of which I then had to remember on top of my lines. I learned quickly that it was far simpler to keep my hands by my sides and stay in one place for the whole scene.

Actually, should you be remotely interested, here are some other things I have learned while filming over the years.

Eating onscreen – which sounds fun – is less fun on the eleventh take. I was delighted when we wrote that Marjorie Dawes, visiting her mum in hospital, tucked into a box of Cadbury Milk Tray (free chocolate on the BBC – result!), but it soon became sickly and it was nigh on impossible to talk properly with a mouthful of gooey chocolate caramel. A spittoon was hastily improvised.

Sitting down is *always* preferable, especially if you're doing one of those scenes that takes two days to film. I was very jealous of the actors in *The Royle Family* on that comfy sofa. If you do have to do something physically demanding, then at least be strategic and don't expend all of your energy in rehearsals.

There's nothing worse than trying to remember your lines during a take. We're all human and we all blank sometimes – particularly as we get older (eek!) – but knowing the lines properly in advance allows you to get on with acting.

Large stuck-on moustaches are *very* itchy, especially where the long hairs at the top go up your nose. Small moustaches are bearable. Beards that go from ear to ear look great but as soon as you start talking, they need to be repeatedly re-stuck with cold, stinky glue that doesn't work very effectively and is then suddenly a total bugger to get off at the end of the day. If you don't remove it properly, you can wake up in the middle of the night, as I have done many times, with the pillow stuck to your cheek.

Sometimes you try on some shoes in advance. They look perfect and the costume designer is in ecstasy. They're a bit tight and they pinch your toes a little, but it's only for a few days, right? NO! You'll hate them by 9 a.m., hate the costume designer by 10 a.m. and hate yourself by 11 a.m. You'll be in a mood all day, kicking them off at any opportunity. 'You won't see my feet in this shot, will you? Can I go without? Just in this shot?'

The director makes the creative decisions and the producer does the hiring and firing, but really everything on set is run by the First, or rather the First Assistant Director. This is the person who organises the filming schedule and then hollers from dawn to dusk like a sergeant major. They'll tell you which scene we're about to film and which angle we're shooting it from. They'll call the actors on to set. They'll order the costume and make-up departments over for 'checks' – which occur immediately before each take. There are quiet ones and there are loud ones, who scream and shout. They constantly harry – 'Come on, people, we need to keep moving'. They can be brash and infuriating and then show great sensitivity. I am in constant awe of all of them. It is the ultimate multi-tasking job and definitely the most demanding role on any set.

You might feel like a diva when you ask for a cup of tea and sit on your arse while some poor girl on work experience called Tabitha scampers off in the rain to get it for you, but actually if you did get up and get it for yourself, and then the First AD called for you and you weren't there, there would be a post-mortem. Budgets – and therefore schedules – are always tighter than you'd anticipate. Ditto, if it seems like you're being called in, rushed to make-up, squeezed into costume and then made to sit around for hours doing nothing, it's because no one wants to be responsible for you not being there in the eventuality that you are suddenly needed. It might unexpectedly hail or an actor might be taken ill or some other act of God might occur – and then you could be called upon earlier than planned. What can NEVER happen on a set . . . EVER . . . is nothing at all.

Whatever you're filming, I can guarantee you will either be too hot or too cold. British shows tend to shoot in the summer (apart from *Doctor Who* – as I write this, I'm about to spend three days in the forest and it's minus 4 degrees). As Ashley Blaker once said to me, this country is too cold, apart from that one week of the year when it's too hot.

You can't throw a sickie – if you're ill, you're expected to go in and film regardless. Too much money has been invested and the schedule is too packed for an actor to have the flu. You'd have to have been already dead for several weeks, with a doctor's letter to prove it, before you're allowed to stay in bed for even one day and recover.

Crews can spend hours lighting a shot of a dandelion in the morning. Tape measures come out, tracks are laid, we film for a couple of hours and then the director decides to switch the dandelion for a buttercup and we start all over again. Then, towards the end of the day, some bright spark realises that we've still got a whole scene to do before the sun sets. This is what is commonly referred to as the 'kick, bollock, scramble hour', in which you film seven pages in forty-five minutes. Director Ben Wheatley once told an interviewer that the process of filming was 'Hollywood in the morning, *Hollyoaks* in the afternoon'.

And lastly, when you're not on camera, you're quite possibly still on mic. I daren't think of how many times I've forgotten this. Yes, the producer is a berk but you definitely don't want him to know that's what you think!

Right, lecture over. What else have I been in?

Well, I was in a lovely BBC film of *The Wind in the Willows* in 2006. Less lovely was the fact that I wore padding and thick, heavy costumes in the 40-degree heat of a Romanian summer. My prosthetic make-up melted off continually.

The food at the studio consisted of out-of-date army rations (honestly), so I survived on a diet of salad and sweets. Filming hours were long and for some reason we were staying an hour away from set. On the way there, the streets were lined with stray dogs and cats – both dead and alive. I saw one puppy cross the road and get sliced in half six feet in front of me, an image too horrific to forget.

I grew so exhausted during the shoot that I began sleep-walking at night. The first time, I woke up with the lights on, in the bathroom, naked, peeing at the wall, with no knowledge of how I had got there.

The second time I woke up, again naked, trying and thankfully failing to open the front door.

And yet I loved the job and had a blast filming with the other actors. Mark Gatiss and Lee Ingleby, like me, delighted in the company of Bob Hoskins, who played Badger and was permanently but very entertainingly irascible. As mischievous as actors can be, there is also a sense that you have to try to behave on set, because you don't want to get a reputation for being difficult. Bob had reached an age and level where he wasn't worried about anything like that anymore. If he thought anything was taking too long, he'd simply bellow 'SHALL WE GET A FUCKING MOVE ON?!' at the top of his voice and within seconds we'd be shooting again. We loved it.

Because of the cost of flying out actors from the UK, a lot of the smaller roles in the film were taken by local actors, whose voices would be re-dubbed at a later date. Many of them spoke little or no English and had learned their lines phonetically. They'd deliver their dialogue almost quizzically, with the strangest, most random intonations and then stare blankly at me. As the shoot wore on – and high on sugar – I found myself becoming more and more helpless with laughter when appearing alongside them. I longed for it and dreaded it. Rachel Talalay, one of the most brilliant directors I have ever worked with, was sympathetic and understood the absurdity of the situation. How she managed to cut around my crazed performance, I'll never know. When one actor carefully pronounced the 'b' in 'doubt', I collapsed on the floor in stitches, the camera still rolling. I was embarrassed and apologetic – those poor actors – but then as soon as the First shouted 'Action!', the same thing would happen again.

The worst instance of 'corpsing' I have ever experienced was onstage in *Prick Up Your Ears*, a play about Joe Orton and Kenneth Halliwell. A woman in the third row had a laugh that sounded like a wild animal and every time she cackled, so did half the audience – not at the action onstage but at the noises she was making.

Eventually the laughter spread to the stage itself. There were three of us in the play and we now found ourselves chortling along, until the show stopped several times, for two or three minutes at a time, while the whole room just roared.

At one point, on maybe the second or third outbreak, with the play again having simply collapsed, I stepped forward and said, 'Ladies and gentlemen, I'm terribly sorry but a hyena seems to have escaped from the zoo.'

The audience applauded and it was my vain hope that by truly acknowledging the hysteria in the room we might all – cast and audience – somehow draw it to an end. No such luck – we simply couldn't find a way to get past it. As we played out the brutal, bloody death scene at the play's close, the audience continued to titter. If the director had been in that night he would have rightly been apoplectic. But he wasn't. And there was no one to take control.

Afterwards, the mood backstage was in stark contrast. The reality of what had just happened began to sink in. An audience had come to see a West End play and instead they had seen a mess. A shambles. A debacle. We felt ashamed at our amateurish behaviour. The other two actors in the play expressed fury at me for having stepped out of character with my gag, but I countered that the play had already fallen apart by then and more likely they were angry with themselves for laughing so much.

You could argue that I was in the wrong for my actions. I don't know the correct thing to do in that situation. Despite my youth theatre experience, I have never trained formally as an actor, I didn't go to drama school and took the stand-up route instead. I still feel like I'm learning on the job and I'm always surprised when anyone casts me in anything, to be honest.

One of the biggest surprises of my career was when I found myself in a giant Disney movie. Having eagerly awaited the arrival of any and every new Disney film as a kid, I didn't dare imagine that one day I'd be in one myself. I wish I could tell you stories of how I had to go through thirty-eight auditions and sleep with someone very powerful but the truth is that one day I simply got a call to go and meet Tim Burton, who was about to direct a big-budget, 3D live-action *Alice in Wonderland*.

As I arrived at his office in Belsize Park, he was sat at his desk doodling Tweedledum and Tweedledee. To my surprise there was no audition. He just told me a little about the movie and said he hoped I'd be up for playing both the Tweedles. I then went off to the US to film *Little Britain USA*, straight from that to Hungary to do a series for Comedy Central called *Kröd Mändoon and the Flaming Sword of Fire* and then, forty-eight hours later, head spinning, I was at Culver City Studios on set with Helena Bonham Carter, Mia Wasikowska and Anne Hathaway.

I think we gave up on the clangs, didn't we?

On my first day I was introduced to Richard 'Dick' Zanuck, one of the producers of the film and a Hollywood legend. My trailer was huge and like a lovely log cabin. I'd never seen anything like it. Dick took one look at it and to my surprise promptly sent it away for something even bigger. During the shoot I would grill him on his career. For someone so successful – he had produced monster hits like *Jaws*, *Cocoon* and *Driving Miss Daisy* – he was incredibly gracious and always had time for me.

All of my scenes were shot on green screen and I wore a not-too-flattering green leotard with so much padding round the middle that I looked like an apple on legs. Because I was playing both Tweedles, it was suggested that I might have another actor around, who could stand in for whichever Tweedle I wasn't playing at that particular time. The producers found a very smart, talented actor called Ethan Cohn, who impressed them so much that they went on to give him a role in the movie as one of the Queen's courtiers. For parts of the film the Tweedles are a good deal taller than Alice. Ethan and I learned to walk on stilts so that we were at the right eyeline for Mia. Special tall chairs were built for us so we could rest between takes without having to take the stilts off.

Ahead of filming, Tim Burton asked me to write a page or two about how I saw the Tweedles, and then we sat in his trailer and talked it through. Because they fought in such a juvenile way I wanted to play them as kids and he seemed to like that. I loved working with him because he would always let me do one or two takes before giving me any notes. I've worked in the past with directors who are so prescriptive – before I've had a chance to even try anything – and I find that can shut me down creatively. Tim was the opposite.

I was on the movie for about ten weeks. Most of the time – as anyone who has played a supporting role on a huge movie will tell you – I did nothing. That is to say, I got picked up at 6 a.m. from my suite at the Sunset Marquis Hotel where Disney had put me up, was driven to set, got dressed and had make-up and breakfast. By then it was about 7.45 a.m. One of the runners would knock on my trailer door and give me a five-minute warning. Very occasionally I would find myself on set five minutes later. However, more often than not I guess I was there 'just in case', which meant I would then lie on the sofa watching TV for a few hours, have a nap, wake up, have lunch (whatever I fancied, because I had a driver who would go and get it), get another five-minute warning, watch some more TV, have another nap and then, around 6 p.m., get driven back to the hotel.

It sounds glorious – and it sort of is – but my mind doesn't respond well to inactivity. There's only so much local American TV news you can watch. I wasn't used to it. I had just come off *Little Britain* where, even if I wasn't in the scene, I had co-written it and would be pacing by the monitors, scrutinising the action and bothering David by suggesting changes.

And so on *Alice* I took to wandering around the set, keeping myself occupied. It goes against protocol, but I would occasionally even go and see if any other actors were at a loose end as well. One day I knocked on Johnny Depp's door. Similarly twiddling his thumbs, he was watching YouTube videos of people falling over and chuckling to himself. I joined him and we whiled away a most pleasant afternoon.

Sometimes I would go and chat with the make-up artists. Johnny had his own make-up trailer, but the rest of the cast shared one. There was a bank of three workstations where Mia and Anne and I would sit, and then one separate workstation at the end, on a slightly raised level behind a thin screen, where there was more space. Here Helena would have her prosthetic Red Queen make-up applied each day.

One afternoon, again bored out of my tree, I went to chat with the make-up artists as usual, and was being particularly silly, riffing away, doing lots of loud, crazy voices. People were either heartily entertained or simply being polite, but I was in full flow.

The following morning, while being made up, I was talking to the make-up designer about a film she had worked on previously, starring Dustin Hoffman. I spoke in awe of him. She then casually told me that he had popped into that very trailer the day before so she could cut his hair.

'When?!' I asked. 'Oh, I wish I could have met him.'

'When you were doing all your voices, Matt,' she said.

At that point I realised that one of the greatest actors on the planet had come in for a short back and sides and had been subjected throughout to the mad, indulgent rantings of a fat British idiot (see chapter I).

Actually, some months later I did meet the great man himself at a friend's house in the Hollywood Hills. The friend is also famous, but that's enough clangs for now. Anyway, Dustin was eating a corn on the cob and it accidentally fell off his plate and into the pool. As we talked he found one of those little nets and fished it out. Seconds later the cob fell into the pool again and he had to fish it out again. I accept that there is no great dramatic thrust to this particular showbiz anecdote, but you've got Dustin Hoffman, George Dawes, a swimming pool and a slippery corn cob. If that's not enough for you, I suspect you'll never be happy.

I hope, by the way, that Dustin Hoffman doesn't mind me retelling that half-anecdote. I'm quite sure that the image in your mind now of him rescuing a cob from a pool with a net in no way detracts from your memory of him in such classic films as *Papillon* and *Marathon Man*.

Eighteen months after we finished shooting, *Alice in Wonderland* was released. *Avatar* had recently been the first breakout hit in the new wave of 3D movies (where, finally, you didn't have to wear the flimsy paper glasses with one green and one red eye). An audience hungry for more 3D flocked to see Tim Burton's film and it surpassed all box-office expectations.

My next Hollywood role was in *Bridesmaids* – another surprise smasheroonie. Having been a big fan of *Freaks and Geeks*, it was a thrill to be working with its creator Paul Feig, who was directing. The producer was Judd Apatow, responsible for launching the film careers of a generation of comedians.

I met with Paul in LA while on a brief publicity junket for *Alice in Wonderland*. Paul knows more about British comedy than most British people I've met. I was flattered by his knowledge of and enthusiasm for my and David's work. He was keen for me to be in the movie and I was keen too, though I was about to film *Come Fly with Me* back in the UK and the two shoots were scheduled for the same time.

I spoke with David and it was agreed that I could go to LA to film *Bridesmaids*, as long as I was away for no longer than a week. On my return I would head straight into rehearsals for *Come Fly with Me*. So *Bridesmaids* is the thing I am best known for in America and yet I was only on it for three and a half days.

Playing my sister was Rebel Wilson. Although we'd never met before, we instantly became bosom buddies, confidantes and – eventually – real-life roommates. I was blown away by Rebel's confidence on camera. She owned every scene she was in. Away from the cameras she was down-to-earth and unassuming. It felt like I'd known her my whole life.

I was surprised by the amount of improvisation we did. A lot of the lines were made up as the cameras rolled. Kristen Wiig – the star of the movie and one of the writers – was very generous in allowing us to do our own thing. I love her performance in the movie. The aeroplane scene is a masterclass.

My third American film – and my first lead role – was Jonas Åkerlund's quirky black comedy *Small Apartments*. I played Franklin Franklin, an oddball who may or may not have killed his landlord. As a Brit playing an American in an American film, I did as much work as I could on the accent. I had a dialect coach who I worked with every day for two weeks before the shoot and who joined me on set, sharing my trailer. I also made the decision to stay in dialect for most of the time, starting from when I left the house each morning until the moment the First AD yelled 'That's a wrap' each night. That meant, much to their amusement, that whenever my mum or my friends or my British agent phoned me, I would talk to them in my best Southern Californian drawl. To clarify, I stayed in dialect but not in character. I am not insane.

Despite being a low-budget indie movie, the cast was a veritable clang-a-thon of classy actors – Billy Crystal, James Marsden, Rosie Perez, James Caan, Juno Temple and more. Also appearing was Drago himself, the action hero Dolph Lundgren. Never in my life did I ever think I would be present to hear the two words 'Action, Dolph!'

Johnny Knoxville also appeared. I love *Jackass* and was delighted to find out that Johnny is the most charming, self-effacing guy you could meet. Like me, he was used to doing much lighter stuff. The pair of us – both out of our comfort zones – bonded and remain friends.

Although it was not a huge blockbuster, *Small Apartments* has become a late-night cult favourite and also garnered some acclaim on its release from the critics. Despite my worst fears, not one of the American reviewers made any comment at all about my accent, which either means it was so good they didn't notice or so bad they didn't actually realise it was supposed to be American in the first place.

Back in the world of television I made a series in 2014 for the BBC called *Pompidou*.

Ah, dear Pompy.

When I was setting up my new company John Stanley Productions, named after my late father, Ashley Blaker re-introduced me to Julian Dutton, who I'd been on the bill with a few times on the comedy circuit in the early nineties. Julian wanted to make a silent sketch show. The three of us worked together to create a bunch of characters and premises, but one of them – Pompidou – soon felt more complete and inspired than the others, so we ditched them and made the show just about him.

Pompidou was a doddering old aristocrat who had fallen on hard times. He'd been forced to move out of his crumbling stately pile and into a run-down caravan. His efforts to get rich quick again – or rather, just keep his head above water – formed the basis of the show.

Some episodes involved some of Julian and Ashley's work, others I wrote alone. Also – Dennis Waterman-style – I wrote the feemtoon. All of the music, in fact. And co-directed. I took on a lot, maybe too much.

My performance was inspired to some extent by Sir Bernard Chumley, but there were echoes of Jon Pertwee as Worzel Gummidge in there and – in the way Pompidou spoke gibberish – Pingu.

The magnificent Alex Macqueen – who I had appeared with in *The Wind in the Willows* and *Kröd Mändoon* – came onboard as Hove, Pompidou's long-suffering butler. Completing the trio was Marion, Pompidou's elegant Afghan hound.

I wish I could tell you that *Pompidou* ran for series after series and was loved all around the world, but, with a few exceptions, it was dismissed by the critics and left audiences – who were used to my more adult comedy – baffled. It was, however, adored by kids. And that's good enough for me.

Of all the shows I've done, *Pompidou* is by far my favourite. It's a very different type of programme – innocent, ambitious, anarchic – and it takes you an episode or two to get into it, but I really think it's worth the investment.

I harbour genuine ambitions of making a second series or maybe even a film one day. If I never get the opportunity to do so, then I remain both philosophical and thankful, because there are not many people who get to write and star in their own TV series. I've been lucky enough to have done quite a few.

Pompidou was the best.

W – What are the Scores, George Dawes?

I've talked about some of the highs and lows of my life in comedy, but before we say goodbye I want to go back to where – in some ways – that comedy journey really began.

In 1995 I heard a whisper from our mutual friend Dorian Crook that Vic and Bob were turning their one-off quiz show *Shooting Stars* into a full series. They had recorded an episode in 1993 as part of a special 'At Home with Vic & Bob' night on BBC Two, welcoming them to the channel and introducing them to new viewers who might not yet be familiar with their work.

It was Reeves and Mortimer's take on a panel game show, but the questions were usually ridiculous, designed either to trip up the guests, or bring out a different side to them or just to mystify them. Vic and Bob delighted in selecting an unlikely mix of celebrities to compete, often a mélange of traditional showbiz types, daytime TV stars and the coolest indie singers.

As in their previous work, there were several motifs and running jokes. Questions for one round appeared on a giant bird – 'The Dove from Above' – which guests were asked to beckon down. Another round involved panellists having to guess which song Vic was singing, though his renditions – in the style of a hammered club singer – were joyously incoherent. The final game saw one of the winning team involved in a physical challenge – for instance, how long could a guest stay inside a barrel while Vic and Bob bashed it repeatedly, or how many tomatoes could someone lob at a giant moving photo of Judy Finnigan.

Jonathan Ross and Danny Baker had been team captains in the original show. Ulrika Jonsson, the TV-AM weather-girl-turned-presenter of ITV's *Gladiators* – who had been one of the guests in the pilot – had now been promoted to team captain. The other team captain was to be Mark Lamarr, a spiky, bequiffed stand-up who had co-hosted *The Word* on Channel 4. I had never met either of them, but Mark's reputation as a fearless compère preceded him.

I've mentioned already that I appeared in a few sketches in the second series of *The Smell of Reeves and Mortimer* the year before. My favourite had been a *Masterchef* parody that saw Vic flying about the studio on wires as Loyd Grossman with an enormous, bulbous, papier-mâché forehead that was glued on and was so heavy that someone had to hold his head up between takes. Bob's make-up was also extraordinary. He had a tiny nose stuck on about halfway down his real nose, and then the tip of his real nose was obscured by a moustache. I played Quentin Mint, a sozzled toff in a top hat. Quentin proudly lifted the silver cloche to reveal his dish – a man's arse. David Walliams turned up shaken for our usual writing session a few days after the sketch had screened, saying it had given him a terrible nightmare.

During the series recordings I got to know Vic a bit better. While Bob was street-smart about the industry, knew much about the workings of television and would later direct shows, Vic – or Jim, as I was allowed to call him – had a quieter, more childlike quality to him. Away from the set I would sometimes stay at his home in Kent and learned that, while he and Bob might well have been the greatest comics of their era, Jim was far more interested in art, music and animals. He was a warm, generous host and I loved spending time with him. It felt like a real escape from the pressures of university and the circuit.

Vic and Bob told me that they wanted me to be a regular in *Shooting Stars*. I was to be the scorekeeper, who they'd come to at the end of each round. I assumed I would be doing it as Sir Bernard, but they told me they wanted to call me George Dawes and that I would be dressed as a baby. At just twenty-one, I still had a fanciful notion that it was only a matter of time before the RSC were going to snap me up – and I didn't much fancy wearing a nappy every week on national television. Instead I suggested a blue romper suit. It came and it was pink. That's compromise, I suppose.

As a kid I had tried my hand at a couple of musical instruments. At seven I'd had piano lessons with Vivienne, who lived in the house opposite. I would go to see her on a Saturday morning and was given a little Bontempi organ for my birthday to practise on, but rarely did, and found reading music tricky, preferring to play by ear. I wanted to pass all the grades but I didn't want to put in the work. Also I was bothered by the fact that my lesson coincided with the weekly broadcast of the anarchic TV show *Tiswas*, which everyone would talk about at school. One Saturday morning, I came downstairs ready for my lesson and my parents told me they had cancelled it – and all future lessons – because I hadn't been practising. I was really disappointed, not just because I wasn't going to be able to play the piano like my friend Jeremy, but because it was my own fault. Looking back, it's one of my greatest regrets.

My brother learned the trumpet, briefly, and then the trumpet was passed to me and I had a few lessons, lugging the case on a little trolley up the road to primary school, but – despite puffing my cheeks and pursing my lips beautifully – I found it hard to actually make the noise you're supposed to make, so that was over pretty quickly too.

My friend Mark Weston had a drum kit and whenever I went to his house he'd let me play on it, showing me how to hold the sticks, where to hit the skins, and teaching me various different drumbeats. At secondary school I took up lessons and really enjoyed them, partly because my instructor, a Geordie called Jim Beryl, was smart and funny and felt like a friend as much as a teacher, and partly because the lessons were scheduled during the school day. Sometimes, in the middle of Double Chemistry, I would put my hand up – 'Sorry, sir, I've got my drum lesson' – and the teacher would be obliged to release me. As I left the room smiling, I felt the glares of my jealous classmates burn into me like CIF_3.

See what I did there? I used a chemistry metaphor. Obviously that will be the only chemistry metaphor in this book. I was *dreadful* at chemistry. In my final exam I achieved a mark of 14 per cent. I was actually furious – not because I'd failed but because I'd had a bet with Howard that I would score fewer marks than he had done in his final exam. He got 12 per cent. I was aiming for 10 per cent. I had started cracking gags on the paper. Here's one that I remember . . .

Q – Give an example of how kerotene is used in industry.

A – No idea. In fact I've not heard of kerotene before but I *do* know that it's used as an example in this exam paper. Will that do?

Objectively I should have scored lower than Howard, but whoever was marking the paper had started awarding me points based on how funny he thought my answers were. When I got my paper back, I was so disappointed at scoring higher than my brother that I complained to the teacher, who wasn't amused and gave me a detention. Thoroughly deserved.

Aaaaanyway, I was no Roger Taylor, but Grandma Margot bought me a drum kit for my bar mitzvah and I continued to play. I must have mentioned it to Vic and Bob at some point, because they decided it might be nice for me to be seated at a drum kit on *Shooting Stars*.

We rehearsed the first episode in London, with the drum kit set up, and I met Ulrika and Mark for the first time. Members of the crew stood in for the guests. At the end of each round Vic and Bob would throw to me for the scores. I discovered then that I wasn't going to be given lines to say by Vic and Bob. I was to figure that stuff out for myself. I wasn't really sure how to broach it. I tried to be a bit dry and witty, but I sounded like I was doing a third-rate impression of the then-ubiquitous Angus Deayton.

Also, because of space restrictions, I was going to be in another studio entirely, watching on monitors. The camera was going to come to me and I would then appear on a screen – but then it was decided close to recording that there was just enough room for me in the studio with the others after all.

On a shooting day we would rehearse the show a couple of times – once without the team captains, and then again with them, though they wouldn't hear the questions until the actual recording. In the minutes leading up to the show, as the audience filed in, I'd sit in the green room downstairs with the others, all dressed in their natty suits while I sported a giant onesie (long before Justin Bieber and Harry Styles made them fashionable, I might add), puffing on a Marlboro Light. As we waited in the wings to go on, Bob developed a ritual of coming over and telling me, 'You look a twat, Matt,' and we'd both laugh, though I think he laughed a little more than I did.

I'd watch the opening of the show from the side of the studio floor, nervous as hell, and then Vic and Bob would introduce me.

'There's someone missing, Vic. It's the man with the scores, it's Georgie Dawes!'

Vic and Bob would sing, 'He's a baby!' over Led Zeppelin's 'Black Dog' and I'd run on, waving manically at the camera before taking my seat at the drums.

The quiz would begin and I really wasn't sure what to do when the camera came to me, other than give the scores, so I mainly just did my best 'angry baby' impression and shrieked. The audience was understandably uninterested in my contribution – and I don't blame them. Everyone else on the show was funny – or at least famous. I was just a bald man shouting.

After three or four episodes of this I was desperate to expand my repertoire and make a bit more of an impact, but I was starting to realise that it was useless trying to prepare anything in advance. The show went off on such strange flights of fancy and I never had the slightest idea of the kind of exchange I would be following.

Also, I hadn't really got a handle on who George Dawes was as a character. Jokes about just being a baby felt a bit one-note and weren't really sustainable. Halfway through one of the tapings, having not yet received a laugh, I decided to be a bit bolder. I decided to just open my mouth and see what came out.

'What are the scores, George Dawes?'

The camera came to me. Instead of just yelling or going straight to the scores as usual, I spoke quietly down the lens. 'Soooo . . . you want to know the scores then, you fat cow?'

Now, this is, in and of itself, perhaps vaguely amusing. But it was greeted with hysteria from audience, guests, hosts and crew alike.

And I am quite sure it was greeted with that response because it *seemed* as if I was about to say 'fat cunt'. That's my reading of it.

Regardless, from that moment on, the audience was mine. Anything and everything I did was greeted with laughter.

As we did more shows I became more confident, though in that first series in particular some recordings were tougher than others – not just for me, but for everyone. It wasn't like anything else on TV and I think many members of the audience had arrived expecting to see something like Noel's *Telly Addicts*.

One of the things that was unavoidable, but which would handicap me, I felt, was the fact that there were only five cameras on the floor – a close-up on either Vic or Bob, their two-shot, a camera on Ulrika's team, another on Mark's team and a big wide shot of the studio – which meant that I didn't have my own camera, so whenever Vic and Bob threw to me, I had to wait for one of the cameras to turn around and find the right position. Then I would get a cue to speak. I would then wait for a runner wearing a headset to hurriedly write down the score – as dictated to them by someone in the gallery – and hold it up on a sheet of paper for me to read. Not wearing my glasses, I would squint to read it, and then I'd have to think of something funny to say. Whatever momentum there might have been had usually dissipated by then.

The recordings became more and more ambitious. There were stunts and special effects. Sometimes the director would decide it was easier to just record all of my direct pieces to camera in one block at the very end of the evening. The guests would often say goodbye to the audience and even Vic and Bob might wander off. Many of the crowd, having been sitting in the studio for several hours, without food or being allowed a toilet break, took this as their cue to leave. So the next time you're watching one of those early episodes of *Shooting Stars* on Challenge, spare a thought for poor George, struggling through his bits in a rapidly emptying studio.

Despite being a bag of nerves most of the time, it was an amazing experience. I had the best seat in the house, watching Vic and Bob – my idols-turned-mentors – at their peak, up close, as they went from being cult comics to the biggest, most-loved double act on television. I especially loved watching them rehearse, as they built and modified their routines throughout the day.

I also got to meet a bunch of celebrities. I was beginning to discover the music of Pulp, who had just released the extraordinary 'Common People' that very week and I was excited to meet Jarvis Cocker. With his natty suits, thick black specs and dry Northern wit, he fitted perfectly into Vic and Bob's world.

John Peel, who I was also a fan of, seemed to be regretting appearing on the show. He was selected to take part in the final challenge, which saw him dressed as a baby in a pram, and he grumbled throughout. I couldn't tell if it was an act or not.

Little and Large and Hale and Pace – two double acts I had watched avidly on TV while I was growing up and whose routines I quoted back to them – were warm and friendly and knew how to play along.

Chris Rea was brilliant on the show, I thought, and was the first guest who made the decision to come on with a persona – in his case, totally deadpan and apparently mystified by goings on. He was the perfect foil that week to Vic and Bob's madness. After the episode went out, people kept asking me 'Was he *really* like that?' No – he was a delight. He loved every minute. He was just playing.

I had a bit in my stand-up act, in which I changed the words of a popular Madonna song from 'Erotic, erotic, put your hands all over my body' to 'Bill Oddie, Bill Oddie, put your hands all over my body'. When the man himself appeared on the show, I sang it at the end of a round.

Oddie groaned loudly. 'Oh, I've heard that a million times!' – and there was a moment of unease. I apologised profusely in the next recording break and then asked the producer if we could cut the gag out. At the time I thought it was a shame that he hadn't enjoyed it, but I can see his point – for me it was just a gag, for him it probably would have meant viewers of the show yelling it at him wherever he went.

As the series recording drew to an end, I rather grandly told the producers I would be killing off George Dawes and trying a different character out next series. In truth I really wanted to do Sir Bernard on the show. I was so much more assured as him, so much funnier. I had big TV ambitions for the character and wanted the audience to get to know him too. In retrospect it was very presumptuous of me to do that. It was naive, certainly, as there was no guarantee – if there was a second series – that Vic and Bob would even want me back. I'd had a few good moments, but it wasn't clear cut that I'd be staying. At twenty-one, I hadn't learned humility yet!

I was still at university when we made that first series of *Shooting Stars*. As in my previous double life a couple of years earlier, when I'd played the stand-up circuit while working at Chelsea Sportsland, I would hang up my romper suit and head back to Bristol after recordings. The following morning I'd be at a seminar furiously taking down notes, or sat at my desk in my bedroom trying in vain to stay on top of my coursework.

I'd assumed the comedy thing was something I would do as a hobby, and then I could turn professional once I had completed my degree. Things had clearly taken off much earlier than I'd anticipated. In my second year at university I appeared in both *The Smell of Reeves and*

Mortimer and *Shooting Stars* and was at the stage where I could have gigged every night of the week if I'd wanted to.

I spoke of little else but my comedy career and my new life. I'm quite sure I alienated the others on my Theatre, Film and Television course – many of whom had similar ambitions of their own – and I rarely socialised with my housemates anymore. Most weekends I was away performing somewhere, but on the rare occasion I wasn't, I could be found in my bedroom, desperately trying to catch up on my studies. In truth I was running on empty – trying to squeeze too much in. I became (unreasonably) resentful of the increasing demands of the degree – which would have been substantial but manageable if I didn't also effectively have a full-time job writing and performing comedy.

And then one day my tutor told me that he was giving me the lead role in a play. I thanked him, but in truth I was mortified. I was already weeks behind on my coursework and I had a diary full of bookings. How on earth was I going to fit this in too? Oh, the irony! Ten years earlier at Habs I would have done anything for a part in . . . well . . . anything. Now I had somehow been cast in something against my will – and there was nothing I could do about it.

My course wasn't actually a vocational one – it was a university degree that was built around theories and analysis of film, TV and theatre. Many of those who graduated became writers, teachers, directors and producers. For the most part I found lectures impenetrable and even when we studied something fun and light, everyone did their best to find the most sinister hidden agenda. On our course, my favourite film *Singin' in the Rain* became an insidious piece of misogynist propaganda, designed to keep women in their place and reinforce the wealth and power of the ruling patriarchy – that sort of thing.

We acted only occasionally, and usually in devised pieces. A typically bewildering lunchtime performance saw my friends Claire and Lucy hurling raw meat across the room. Another abstract show, apparently inspired by the recent death of River Phoenix, featured a group of topless male students from the year above groping each other frenetically in silence.

However, we were now to put on a production as part of our course, so I couldn't get out of it. My role was that of Mercy in an English medieval morality play called *Mankind* – notable because it dates back to *c.* 1470 and is thought by some to be the earliest surviving play in the English language.

Our tutor, who specialised in Medieval Studies, was incredibly excited that we were putting on the show. It was, he said, hardly ever performed, so our production was of global cultural significance. He had invited academics from all over the UK and would be filming the show too.

My already overflowing diary – packed with lectures, gigs, coursework, *Shooting Stars* and the writing of my first Edinburgh show with David – was now also jam-packed with rehearsals for the play, but the biggest challenge of all was learning the lines. They were written in verse and there were so many of them that I had to cancel several gigs while I stayed in my room for weeks and crammed them in.

Here's how it starts . . .

> The very founder and beginner of our first creation
> Among us sinful wretches he oweth to be magnified,
> That for our disobedience he hath none indignation
> To send his own son to be torn and crucified.
> Our obsequious service to him should be applied,
> Where he was lord of all and made all thing of nought,
> For the sinful sinner to have him revived,
> And for his redemption, set his own son at nought.
>
> It may be said and verified, mankind was dear bought.
> By the piteous death of Jhesu he had his remedy.
> He was purged of his default that wretchedly had wrought
> By his glorious passion, that blessed lavatory.
> O sovereigns, I beseech you your conditions to rectify
> And with humility and reverence to have a remotion
> To this blessed prince that our nature doth glorify.

And that's just the beginning. There's *loads* more. It goes on and on and on.

To my annoyance I had to stop smoking weed. It played havoc with my memory. I spent the entirety of the rehearsal period in a state of panic, wondering how on earth I was going to remember all these lines. In the end I just had to get on with it. The play was a success and we were all word-perfect. I was relieved and surprised to have got through it, and hoped there might be a moment's pause to catch my breath, but the demands of the course continued to increase.

While battling away at my Amstrad word processor one night, trying and failing to make headway on my thesis on DV8 Physical Theatre Company's *Dead Dreams of Monochrome Men*, I realised something had to give.

I arranged for an appointment with the head of the Drama Department and requested a year out from the degree – and, to my surprise, my wish was granted. The idea was that I would be able to accept the TV and radio work I was being offered and then come back to take my final year.

Who was I trying to kid?

David and I went to the Edinburgh Festival a few months later, in the summer of 1995. It was abundantly clear there was something special happening when the two of us were onstage together. Off the back of the show we were offered our own series on the newly formed Paramount TV channel. We were on our way.

My 'year off' had barely begun before I wrote to the university and explained that, while I wanted to return and finish my course as agreed, I didn't feel I could *guarantee* it. I received a genial and gracious response. They understood that I had to follow my dream.

My mother and grandmother were devastated. My parents had not been to university, but they had worked incredibly hard to get me and my brother through private school and beyond. My father worked all hours and I rarely saw him. My mum had two, sometimes three jobs. They had made sacrifices and provided unerring love and support, and

here was I, stepping away from university just one year from gradua-
tion. My parents had always supported my dreams of being an actor, but
we all knew how precarious a profession it could be. A degree would
allow me to teach between jobs. Now I would have nothing.

Mum and Grandma made it their mission to stop me leaving the
course. There was no other topic of conversation. They couldn't understand how I could be so reckless.

Amidst all the drama my father quietly took me aside and told me
that he thought I was making the right choice. He said that I wouldn't
be able to guarantee that I'd have the same work opportunities a year
down the line. 'The course is a means to an end. Maybe you're already
at the end. You have to do this and you have to do it now.'

Mum and Grandma were furious with him for supporting my plan of
action. I was grateful for his understanding. I can say, though, that even
without it, I had already made up my mind.

Shooting Stars went out on BBC Two in the autumn of 1995. Vic and
Bob had a devoted fan base but they hadn't yet breached the mainstream. This show would change that.

The previews in the press were mixed, so my hopes were not high. I
was largely ignored, apart from a line in *The Observer*, which dismissed
me as a 'baby fetishist'. I didn't even know such a thing existed, though
I would soon receive plenty of weird and wonderful letters from people
who did, and who assumed I was one too, going into detail about their
'adult baby' lives.

Once the series began, however, the media fell in love with it. The
broadsheets celebrated its surrealism, originality and subversiveness,
while the tabloids loved Ulrika and her evolution from homely
weather girl to the ultimate 'ladette' – funny, sexy and able to down
a pint in seconds.

The public just took it for what it was. They liked the slapstick, the
silliness, the celebs and the catchphrases.

The night after the first show aired I went to have a drink with friends
at the Good Mixer pub. As I was on the upward escalator at Camden

Town Tube station, a man on the downward escalator pointed at me –
'TV! Saw you on TV!'

And so it began.

It was quiet at first, occasional. And then after a while I was stopped
pretty much wherever I went by people telling me they loved the show
and wanting to know what Ulrika was like in real life.

My mum, on the other hand, was bewildered by the whole thing and
was still disappointed that I wasn't doing something a bit weightier.
Now back from Bristol, I was living full-time at home again. I tried to
avoid watching the show with her because I'd constantly be looking over
and seeing a confused expression on her face.

'Do people actually *like* this?' she would enquire, genuinely
bamboozled.

Mum has always been upfront in telling me what she thinks of my
work – good or bad. After all, I'm still her little boy.

In fact, I remember in the run-up to the broadcast of the first episode
of *Shooting Stars*, I would talk about little else. It was all still very new to
me. One day I was re-enacting a gag I'd done at one of the recordings,
and she cut me off halfway through.

'Yeah, never mind *Shooting Stars*. You go and tidy your room.'

I was quite a messy kid, in fairness.

Shooting Stars came back for a second series. It had been a moderate
success, rather than a big hit, but in those days – believe it or not – you
didn't have to be an instant smash to get a second series. Shows were
allowed to find their feet.

This time the BBC decided to commission a much longer run. With
so many episodes – and a weekly repeat on the Sunday – we were able
to build an audience properly. Also we no longer had to record more
than one episode a night, which meant that Vic and Bob could be more
ambitious. Props, special effects, songs – all of those things took time to
get right, and now we had even more.

I had watched the first series go out and been underwhelmed by my
own contributions. Setting aside the novelty of 'There's a man on
national TV dressed as a baby', I didn't think I was very funny. Yet Vic

and Bob had faith in me and were keen for me to revive the character. I decided I needed to push myself a little more. I started to ask for different outfits and props. I still didn't often write gags in advance, but I did start to keep a little piece of paper on the drum kit, that would say something like . . .

Posh
Scouse
Bristol
Stutter
Pakistani
Geordie
Nasal
Scottish
New Jersey

. . . basically just reminding myself of dialects and voices that I could do.

Sometimes I just played around with language, coming up with rhymes like 'One of the main issues is the misuse of disused tissues' or mispronouncing words: 'marmalade' became 'mar-malla-dee'. It was more funny-peculiar than funny-haha but the audience didn't seem to mind. If something went especially well, I'd try and think of a sequel to the joke to slip into a later episode.

I found that the audience particularly enjoyed it when I adopted an aggressive Cockney persona, and I used it to interact with some of the guests. A recent ex-member of Take That, who had turned up to the recording rather merry, got a scolding from George for his troubles . . .

'Robbie Williams, you filthy cow! Sort your life out and start making *changes*!'

I was also cheeky to Griff Rhys Jones, asking him if he had seen *Pretty Woman*, and when he answered yes I replied, 'So what? So have I. It's been on telly four times. It was in cinemas. It's been on video for years. You think you're some kind of big shot?'

One week Bob suggested that I might like to shake things up a bit. He said maybe I should play George's mum or dad. 'You could call yourself Marjorie Dawes,' he added, in a reference to the children's rhyme 'See Saw Margery Daw'.

The make-up department found a nice wig and from then on, Marjorie would make occasional appearances in the show. Like George, she was prone to sudden crazed outbursts, but on the whole she was mild-mannered in comparison.

The voice was inspired by my own mother's, and I thought that it might be fun if Marjorie was always on a diet, as women of a certain age always seemed to be. I came up with the idea that she could even be dispensing advice. She mentioned the new 'Half the Calories' diet . . .

'Take a bit of cake and cut it in half and it's only half the calories. And because it's only half the calories, you can have twice as much.'

In that second series, *Shooting Stars* got weirder and wilder, bigger and barmier. And now, each time I was introduced, I would get a huge cheer from the audience. I didn't expect that at all. Vic, Bob, Ulrika and Mark were the stars. I had presumed my bits were merely tolerated.

No longer was the audience filing out while I was doing my retakes. They stayed and lapped up every moment. If I had to do a bit again I would often change the line, keeping the audience fresh.

After the second series aired, Vic, Bob, Mark, Ulrika and I went on a nationwide tour, playing to 90,000 people over forty dates.

The first half of the show featured three musical impersonators – the type you see on *Stars in Their Eyes*. It was usually Elton John, Freddie Mercury and either Rod Stewart or Neil Diamond. The audience, expecting something subversive, waited patiently for Vic and Bob to wander on halfway through with the punchline, but it never happened. By the time the actual *Shooting Stars* part of the show began, the audience was often quite grumpy.

On the opening night in Manchester there were some technical problems, which meant that the audience watched the sound-alikes and then waited nearly an hour for the main event. The lights dimmed and then came up again, and then dimmed again. There was an unexpected pause, while we waited for the go-ahead to start the show. The audience, who had been cheering, fell silent, and one really loud lone Cockney voice screamed, 'Twenty-five quid for this? You thieving CUNTS!'

Everyone heard it. There was silence for two seconds. The curtain went up, out came Vic and Bob, and all was forgiven.

The show was a bit of a shambles, to be honest, but a lovable shambles. Local celebrities were hired. Sometimes we lucked out and the audience got added value, like when Paul Heaton appeared in his hometown of Hull or Ben Elton joined us in Cambridge. Other times the audience was stumped by the booking of a local radio weatherman or a lower division reserve-team footballer.

We went around the country in a large tour bus, driven by a friendly Scouser called Dave. No matter where we stopped for lunch, he always ordered soup. 'It's very hard to get soup wrong,' he reasoned.

Vic and Ulrika seemed to be in the papers every day and we had press following us around, though they didn't bother much with me. After the show each night I was usually the first to leave the bar, heading to my room for a joint in front of the TV.

One day an offer came in – a big multinational company wanted to fly us all out first class to Singapore, to do a private *Shooting Stars* show. The only snag was that the audience would be made up of employees, and the CEO and his cronies would be the guests. There was £200k on the table, and Vic and Bob said we could split it five ways. My jaw dropped. I was in, most definitely. The idea of being paid £40,000 for anything was unheard of, let alone one night's work, and this was twenty years ago!

Mark Lamarr was the first to pooh-pooh the idea. 'I think we've all earned enough out of this show,' he said. The others seemed to agree. And that was that. It was never mentioned again. I had earned a fraction of what the others were on and it was an eye-opener to learn that anyone could turn down money like that.

My youthful ideological approach to earning money – 'I will never sell out, I am an artist' – had already been tested when I was offered a small fortune for George Dawes to be the new face of Walkers Crisps. I approved the scripts, was measured up for a new romper suit – and then received a call. Someone high up at Pepsi (who owned Walkers) had remembered that actually he hated my bits in *Shooting Stars*. The campaign was scrapped. A few weeks later a new advert for Walkers appeared, starring Paul Gascoigne and Gary Lineker. I can only assume it was a big success, because twenty years later Gary is still eating crisps and getting paid for it.

I soon got offered another advert, though, and I became the Cadbury's Creme Egg man for the next three years. The money allowed me to put a hefty deposit down on a flat in West Hampstead. My mum, who had worried so much about my career choice, was delighted.

We recorded a third series of *Shooting Stars* in 1997 and after that it felt like the right time to put it to bed. Vic and Bob were so creative, so full of ideas, it made sense that they wanted to explore other avenues. Before we all went our separate ways, the original team got together for one last time. Our live tour at the end of 1996 had been a big success, but had never reached London. Now our promoter Phil McIntyre – who David and I would work with years later on *Little Britain Live* – had booked us into the Hammersmith Apollo, on a double bill with a stage version of *The Fast Show*.

Shooting Stars was the highest-rating show on BBC Two, often getting as many as seven million viewers a week, but Vic and Bob decided that we should do the first half and *The Fast Show* should do the second. If pressed, I would suggest that this was so they could get to the bar earlier.

Our opening night at Hammersmith was a disaster. It had been over a year since we had done the tour and we were very under-rehearsed. The audience shuffled around restlessly and I was upset because I didn't think any of us were focused or committed enough. *Shooting Stars* might have looked like a muck-about, but the reality was that it required lots of planning. At Hammersmith nobody seemed to be steering the ship. We didn't even have a director. The reviews were damning and I didn't disagree with any of them.

The Fast Show, on the other hand, did one of the best live comedy shows I've ever seen. It was magnificently staged, full of invention and originality, and really broke new ground in terms of transferring a TV show to stage. They'd also spent a ton of money on it. It looked expensive. The audience loved it.

In the course of the run, we – literally – got our act together. Finally we delivered a funny hour and played to big laughs, but we were always the starter and *The Fast Show* was the main course. One week John Thomson had filming commitments and Bob and I stepped in to cover for him. I was chuffed to be performing with Paul Whitehouse, Charlie Higson and co. I had to take a custard pie in the face from Paul each night and couldn't have been happier.

On the last night of the record-breaking Hammersmith run (only to be broken years later by *Little Britain*) there was a big party, with ice sculptures and lots of celebs. And that was the end of *Shooting Stars*.

Or so I thought.

Four years later I was booked to appear in an episode of Vic and Bob's reboot of *Randall & Hopkirk (Deceased)*. It had been a while since we'd worked together and I mentioned that I was missing doing *Shooting Stars* and that there was still nothing like it on television. If they ever wanted to do it again, I was in.

And it happened. Mark didn't return, but Ulrika did, and Will Self and Johnny Vegas made up the teams. It was lovely being back behind the kit. I improvised as I had before, but this time I started adding songs to my repertoire.

Sometimes they were covers, but always with a twist. Using Google Translate, I sang *The Flintstones* theme tune in dodgy German and the *Happy Days* theme in a kind of French.

But it was the original songs that really resonated with viewers. One of my favourites involved a baked potato puppet. The audience wasn't expecting it to move – it looked very much like a real baked potato – so when it started singing back to me, they were in fits.

I remember Bob telling me the secret to writing a good comic song is to cut it in half, and then cut it in half again. Mine rarely exceeded a minute, and sometimes they were only forty seconds long. The time constraints forced me to focus on what I really wanted to say in the song.

Another time I had written a fun piece of big band music and set myself the task of shouting 'Peanuts!' as loudly as possible, at various intervals. It was inspired by the peanut sellers at Highbury in the eighties, who'd walk the terraces during the game. I'd always buy a bag for 30p. Once you'd cracked the shells and spat out the bitter skins, there were only about a dozen nuts there. I don't even like peanuts that much, but I'd always buy a bag.

I digress.

On the night of the 'Peanuts' song, I found that I couldn't stop laughing. I was a terrible giggler at the best of times, but on this occasion I was just helpless. It was mainly because I looked so perfectly odd, with my long-haired, receding wig and big glasses. Vic and Bob, too, were in hysterics, as was the audience. Usually, if I erupted into laughter, we'd do the sequence again, but on that night I knew – no matter how many times I tried – I'd never get through it with a straight face. We did one take and that's what you saw.

Another time I couldn't get it together was when we filmed a spoof 'Geordie Jumpers' commercial. There are countless outtakes. However, the ultimate scene of me out of control, was when Bob and I did a sketch on location.

The sketch – if you can call it that – involved me buying a caravan from Bob. In another sketch that we'd shot a few days earlier, I had been called upon to shake my head so fast that my cheeks wobbled. I'd never been asked to do this before and was delighted to discover that I was a natural. When it came to the caravan sketch, there wasn't really a script – just the idea that I would wobble my cheeks after each line.

There's a rehearsal that unfortunately wasn't filmed, in which Bob and I ended up on the floor, laughing so much we were unable to get up. The footage that viewers did eventually see was the only vaguely usable take, but even that involved a copious helping of hysteria.

We did two series of *Shooting Stars* with Will and Johnny and they had a warmer feel to them than the original shows. We were now a little older, and less concerned with the Britpop scene and being hip.

Will Self, despite his po-faced onscreen persona, is one of the warmest, most self-effacing people you will ever meet. Johnny Vegas, another big cuddly ball of loveliness, brought an amazing new dimension to the show. Audiences adored him, and I would sit in awe, watching him improvise, painting a picture of a man teetering on the brink. He would go off on his own journey, often adding about an hour to each recording, but I didn't mind too much. Again, I had the best seat in the house.

As ever we had some weird and wonderful guests. Vic told me we were on the verge of getting Art Garfunkel, but it fell through at the last minute. Mo Mowlam appeared, and – as the recording came to an end – so did Michael Aspel, presenting her with a *This Is Your Life* book. We also had Larry Hagman, who said it was the strangest show he'd ever been in, which is saying something when you consider that his brother died in *Dallas* and then turned up in the shower as if nothing had happened a year later.

I only ever struggled with one booking and that was 'Mad' Frankie Fraser. I was really upset when I arrived at the BBC, looked at the call sheet and saw he was coming on the show that day. I don't know how much of what was written about him was true, but ostensibly his celebrity arose from his life as a gangland torturer who had spent forty-two years in prison.

A few hours later the guests arrived and in walked Frankie, now a frail little old man, who couldn't have been friendlier to me. I got on with the show and we even had a couple of funny moments on it together, but I still think it was an error of judgement inviting a violent criminal on the programme. I'm sure many viewers were equally bemused.

For those two series, we would record in the studio next to *Top of the Pops*, which had recently moved to Television Centre after years at Elstree. I would get changed in my dressing room and then head down the corridors in my big pink romper suit – but now I had to run the gauntlet of hundreds of pubescent girls, all queuing to see their favourite bands perform. They would howl at the sight of me and I would have to pretend that I wasn't in any way embarrassed.

The most exquisitely cringe-inducing memory of being spotted in the romper suit came one night after a tough recording, when I hadn't received many laughs. Walking back past the *Top of the Pops* studio, a lone girl – made up to the nines – caught sight of me.

'Looks attractive,' she said, rolling her eyes.

'Well, actually,' I replied indignantly, 'I work here. This is . . . what I wear to work.'

The girl snorted with laughter.

I then caught sight of a familiar face – a tall male model who I had chatted up a few months earlier in Heaven nightclub. We had spent much of the evening in a corner of the club kissing. I had been quite smitten and we had swapped numbers, but when it came to meeting up for a proper date, he 'ghosted' me, as I believe the young people of today refer to it. I hadn't seen hide nor hair of him since.

He now had a job on *Top of the Pops* and was escorting a cool-looking indie band to the green room. He stopped, looked at me, and then at the girl, who was in hysterics, and stifled a laugh. As he walked off, I heard him say, 'Yeah, you get some weird types round here'. The band sniggered, while I slunk back to my dressing room in silence.

After series four and five of *Shooting Stars*, the BBC decided that it had run its course . . . but then they brought it back yet again a few years later.

Shooting Stars ran for eight series in total. I did the first six. I was going to do the seventh series, but it was shooting just a few months after Kev had died. I just couldn't do it, I couldn't get myself together. I was replaced as scorekeeper by the brilliant Angelos Epithemiou. There were no hard feelings on my part. I even snuck in one time during rehearsals to say hello.

In the spring of 2017, eight years after we had last worked together, an email appeared in my inbox from Lisa Clark, Vic and Bob's producer. They were bringing back *Big Night Out* and were wondering if I might be free to join them in some sketches. On a scorching day in May we hugged and reminisced, then got dressed up and just mucked about. First I was Rag'n'Bone Man, then I was an assortment of different oddballs. As ever, a huge collection of wigs and moustaches had been laid out. We chose what we wanted to wear and what we wanted to say, in the moment. Despite boasting to the crew that I don't corpse anymore, I laughed my head off throughout and we had to do several takes. It was like no time had passed at all. I loved every minute.

It has been a pleasure and a privilege to work with and for Vic and Bob. I don't know if the words 'important' and 'comedy' should ever go together, but if they do, then Vic and Bob really are the most important comedians of their generation. They're certainly my favourites. I owe them everything.

Well, I was going to finish there but my stepfather has *insisted* I end this chapter by informing you that in 2017, over twenty years after leaving empty-handed, I returned to Bristol University to receive an honorary degree.

It was a joyous day. I loved getting dressed up and beneath the giant cap there was already a big grin on my silly face. In my address I admonished the great institution for what had clearly been a grave administrative error . . .

'Today you bring the entire university honours system into question, by celebrating a charlatan, who left university a year early, in 1995 – when most of this year's graduates were still in nappies – so he could wear a romper suit of his own, appear in some Cadbury Creme Egg adverts and then do a sketch show with his friend.

'And this afternoon I stand here before you in receipt of this great tribute.

'You fools. You've honoured the wrong one. Walliams'll be fuming. He hasn't got one of these and he's swum more channels than there are on a Sky Plus box.'

And so it was that I left the university that day a Doctor of Letters.

Of sorts. As it happens, the university does request that I do not actually put any letters after my name. Well, I'm afraid there's no chance of me honouring that. I'm putting everything after my name. In fact while I'm at it, I might even make myself a Sir, like David Beckham. And I shall insist on being called Doctor Lucas from now on. I'm even going to open up my own general practice in Fishponds, so if you do have anything troubling you, just book an appointment with Carol in reception.

Doctor Matt (probably the most ridiculous photo in the whole book)

X – Xenophobia

I'm not particularly xenophobic. If anything, I probably prefer foreign people to British ones. I just couldn't think of anything else for the letter X. Sorry.

Y – Yankee Doodle

I fell in love with America long before I ever went there. The images I saw in the movies and on TV made me sure that that's where I wanted to be one day.

America was confident, loud, brash and busy. Americans were colourful and quick-witted. They had authority. And America was always open – unlike suburban Stanmore, where the shops closed at 5 p.m.

America got everything before we did – TV shows, films, music, gadgets. It set the trends. If any of my friends were lucky enough to go on a family holiday to the States, I would press them for details on their return. Where did they visit? How did the people talk? What adverts did they have on TV?

Disneyland was the ultimate destination. I loved Mickey Mouse. Not as a fan, you understand, but as a friend.

'Next year in Jerusalem,' we said at Passover, but I always added 'or Disneyland'.

I finally made it to the US in 1998, shortly before I turned twenty-five, spending a week in San Francisco. I returned there the following year and went to Miami, Vegas and LA.

While I was in LA my British agent managed to set up a few meetings for me with some American TV executives. Young and inexperienced, I really wasn't sure how to pitch myself, so I tried to be funny. I met my match at NBC with a fast-talking, high-ranking producer who asked me what my ambition was.

'To have a doll of myself in shops that people can buy,' I joked, but he seemed to take me at face value.

Over the next decade I went to the States at every opportunity, often to New York with Kevin to see the shows on Broadway. We talked about getting an apartment in Manhattan one day. We went to Disneyworld too. All gays love Disney. It's part of the deal.

But it was California that would become my home, after his death. A new start. My aim was not to hit it big over there, just to rebuild. The fact that I could work there was a bonus. The weather, the tranquillity and the relative anonymity were the deciding factors.

And so here I am, in the sun. Well, in the shade, mainly. I'm so pale I have to make sure I don't get burnt. Billy Connolly once said, 'I'm blue. It takes me a week to get white.' I can identify with that.

I've made some lovely friends here. Many of them are from the UK too. We have sing-songs around the piano. I can play chords. Sometimes, when no one is around, I sing 'The Baked Potato Song' for my own amusement.

Every couple of weeks I walk up the street and see a comedy show at Largo at the Coronet. It's a terrific venue where the greatest comedians – Larry David, Sarah Silverman, Bill Burr, Patton Oswalt – try out their new material. Twenty years after I quit the circuit, I toy with the idea of dipping my toe back in, just popping up at small clubs around the city. I think I might be ready to perform as myself at last.

I do my best to be a bit healthier. I eat sensibly and go for long walks with my dogs, swim, hike a couple of times a week. When I'm back in Britain, all that collapses, of course.

And every few months I come back to London, to see family and friends, to work, and to catch a couple of Arsenal matches.

I've no idea what the future holds. I love America and I love Britain. I don't love Trump or Brexit.

Maybe I'll work with Walliams again one day; maybe I won't. I'm aware that people would like us to reunite. I respect that. I know we made magic together and that such a relationship is a rare thing indeed. I also wonder if it might be best left where it was.

Since I can remember I have worked and worked and worked. It might be time to slow down a little. I still haven't seen *Game of Thrones*. I'm thinking of taking a month off just to catch up on that.

But then again I really really want to write a musical. I've got four different ideas bouncing around in my head, vying for attention, and some tunes which are driving me mad.

Z – Zzzzzzz

Are you still awake? Probably not.

When I was a kid and I had a friend to stay over, I was always the last to fall asleep. I would be chatting away, barely noticing that the other person's responses were becoming shorter and less frequent. I'd be prattling on about something or other for quite a while before I realised that the friend had already drifted off and I was on my own.

I've often found sleep elusive. There is too much on my mind, usually. But I have bad habits too. Eating late and reading nonsense online until the small hours. Sometimes my filming schedule allows for a later start the next day, but I then become so excited at the prospect of a lie-in that I can't sleep. I'm an idiot, remember? And on the rare occasion I do nod off for a full eight hours – or even more – I wake up in a panic. Have I slept too much? Will I now not be able to sleep tonight?

Much of this book was written late at night. I was filming full-time on *Doctor Who* as I was writing it. I'd get back to the flat in Cardiff around 7.30 p.m., have a bath, something to eat, look at my lines and then get stuck in. The peace and the solitude allowed me to focus.

When I told people I had a memoir coming out, some of them asked me who was going to be writing it. For better or for worse, I've written every word. It's been hard working out how much to share. I have a sneaking feeling I might have said too much. Well, it's done now.

Thank you for joining me. Let's keep in touch.

Night night.

Matt x

Acknowledgements

First, thanks to you for reading it (or at least buying it). Or finding it, borrowing it or stealing it.

And then thanks to Jamie Byng for letting me write this book, to my editor Simon Thorogood for bountiful help and wisdom, to Andy Gotts for making me look a right nosh in the cover photo, to John Ainsworth for producing the audiobook and to everyone at Canongate.

Thanks to my assistant Emily Greaves, who I've already thanked at the beginning of the book and now I'm thanking her again.

Thanks to my agent Melanie Rockcliffe, Dylan Hearn and everyone at Troika Talent for nearly twenty years of supreme patience. You're the best. Also thanks to Gary Farrow, Kevin McLaughlin and to Richard Weitz, Karina Manashil, Meredith Wechter and everyone at WME.

Thanks to Peter Capaldi, Pearl Mackie and the amazing crew of *Doctor Who* for putting up with me while I wrote this book, and thanks to the many wonderful people I've been lucky enough to have worked with – and who have supported me – over the years, including (in no particular order) Edgar Wright, Chris Niel, Samira Higham, Saurabh Kakkar, Ivor Dembina, David Arnold, Blur, Jay Hunt, Charlie Hanson, Joe Cole, Adam Tandy, David Foxxe, Rhys Thomas, Sacha Baron Cohen, Stuart Murphy, Russell T. Davies, Jon Plowman, Kevan Frost, Robert Popper, Mark Freeland, Paul Kaye, Gub Neal, Lucy Armitage, Ulrika Jonsson, Paul Jackson, Ian Stone, Jane Root, Lorraine Heggessey, Danny Cohen, Harry Hill, Julian Dutton, Ivor Benjamin, Will Self, Mark Gatiss, Samara Bay, Lee Ingleby, Bob Hoskins, Peter Kay, Craig and Charlie Reid, Daniel Kramer, Kenny MacDonald, David Schwimmer, Peter Knight, Brad Johnson, Gareth Carrivick, Charu Bala Chokshi, Richard

Wilson, Johnny Vegas, Steve Hamilton Shaw, Cosmo Williams, Geoffrey Perkins, Ronnie Corbett, Jack Dee, Katy Secombe, Kevin Anderson, Paul Feig, Judd Apatow, Steve Furst, Joanne Condon, Leelo Ross, Phil McIntyre, Paul Roberts, Jeremy Sams, Jimmy Darmody, Jason Heyman, Michael Patrick Jann, Peter Principato, Jonas Akerlund, Rachel Talalay, Chris Millis, Steven Moffat, Cameron Mackintosh, Lisa Clark, Tim Burton, Bitter Ruin, Tom Baker, Dan McGrath, Anthony Head, Ruth Jones, Jean Ainslie and Samantha Power. Apologies to anyone I foolishly left out and also apologies to Gary Barlow, Barry Gibb, Steps – basically everyone we lampooned in *Rock Profile* – and very special apologies to Dennis Waterman, who deserved far better.

Special thanks to Vic Reeves, Bob Mortimer, Myfanwy Moore and Geoff Posner.

Even specialler thanks to David Walliams (without whom I would have been less than half as funny).

Thanks to my teachers Michael Cook, Janet Harrison and Liam Buckley.

Thanks to my dear friends, especially (but not only) Alex, Nick and Jenny, Ashley and Gemma, Ben and Nathan, Rebel, Florian, Benjamin the softball king, Roger, Vinh, Alex and Joe, Robert and Rosie, Ignacio, Jamie, Jeremy and Lauren, Ian, Kyle, Mike, Lukas, Craig and Rosie, Sarah, Tom, Pedro, Putner, Laurence, Belinda, Dorian, Kenny and Caroline, Nathan, Nickey, Tomas, Sultana and Steve, Robert and Mike, Dean and Tamara, Alfie and Sarah, JCM, Alex Macqueen, Georgia, Rikki and Monika, Rachel, Jonjo, Dom, Paul and Laurie, Alicia, Eli, Jordi, Scott and Barbara, Don and Gail, Ben and Emma, Chris, Lynn and John, Jan, Edna, David, Paul and Raimund, Darren, Andrew, Mark and Jason, Ross and Rob and anyone else who knows me.

Thank you to Mum, Ralph, Howard, Dad and Andie, Barbra, Darren, Robert, Dalia and Wendy and all my lovely family.

Up the Arsenal

And finally, thank you, Milo, and thank you, Hob.

I love you Pippi xxxx

Image Credits

While every effort has been made to contact copyright-holders of illustrations, the author and publishers would be grateful for information about any illustrations where they have been unable to trace them, and would be glad to make amendments to further editions.

Index

advertisements 296–7
Aherne, Caroline 51
Ainslie, Jean 161
Akinade, Fisayo 252
Albarn, Damon 55, 203
Albrecht, Chris 237
Alice in Wonderland 274–7
alopecia 14–24
America 64–5, 143–5, 237–8, 240–2, 305–7
Apatow, Judd 278
Arsenal FC 181, 209–11
Atack, Tim 52, 53, 82
Australia 235–6
Aztec Club 46–7

Baddiel, David 133, 231
BAFTAs 220–1
Baker, Danny 282
Baker, Tom 160–1, 230
baldness 14–24
bar mitzvah 150, 151–3
Barlow, Gary 158
Baron Cohen, Sacha 133, 220
Barrymore, Michael 52
BBC One 221, 224

BBC Three 166–70, 220
BBC Two 158–9, 170–1
Beach, Jim 214
Bendelack, Steve 223
Big Night Out 302
Bitty (character) 222
Björk 157
Blaker, Ashley 50, 133, 198–9
  and *Little Britain* 139, 160, 165
  and *Pompidou* 279, 280
Bloch, Andrew 4, 5, 7
Blur 54–5
Boe, Alfie 259–60, 261, 262, 264
Bonham Carter, Helena 275, 276
Boublil, Alain 261–2
Bovril 65–6
Bowery, Leigh 258
Boy George 158, 258
Bradbury, Jason 26, 29, 80–1
Brand, Russell 232
Bridesmaids 144, 193, 277–8
Bristol University 50, 52, 100–2, 163–4, 288–92, 302
Bros 192
Brydon, Rob 90

bullying 136–9
Burton, Tim 274–5

Caan, James 279
Capaldi, Peter 74, 248, 253
Cavalli-Green, Lisa 223
celebrities 189–204
Chalke, Sarah 238
Chas & Dave 239–40
cheese 61–2
Chelsea FC 28, 37–41
chips 66–7
chocolate 73–5
Chuck, Charlie 52
Chumley, Sir Bernard
    (character) 27, 28–30, 31,
    36, 52
Clark, Lisa 301–2
class 227
Cocker, Jarvis 287
Cohn, Ethan 275
Cole, George 268
Come Fly with Me 141–2, 225,
    250–1
Comedy Café 29–30, 50–1
comedy circuit 25–7, 29–34,
    35–50, 43–4
Comedy Club (TV show) 50,
    51
Comedy Store 33, 37, 41
Comic Relief 232–3, 240
coming out 89–90, 99–100,
    101–10
Craig, Dean 133

Craig, Kenny 165
Cresswell, Addison 53
Cribbins, Bernard 252
crisps 70–2
Crook, Dorian 35, 52, 81
Crystal, Billy 47, 235, 279

Davies, Greg 248
Davies, Russell T. 246, 247
Davies, Will 241
Dawes, Marjorie (character) 161,
    168, 238
De Vere, Bubbles
    (character) 222–3, 225
Dean, Letitia 159
Dembina, Ivor 25–6
Dennis, Hugh 269
Depp, Johnny 276
Dobson, Anita 157
Doctor Who 74, 195, 245–9,
    252–4
Doherty, Pete 234
Dreamworks 237, 241–2
Dutton, Julian 279, 280

Eclair, Jenny 48
Edinburgh Fringe Festival 10–12,
    52–4, 81, 84–5
Edwards, Barry 3–4, 5, 6, 10
Edwards, Buster 192
Edwards, Jeremy 232
Elton, Ben 296
Enfield, Harry 27, 163

fame 189–204
family life 179–87
Fast Show, The 297, 298
Feig, Paul 277, 278
Fifteen Streets, The 255–8
filming 270–2
food 57–75
Fraser, Hadley 262, 263–4
Fraser, 'Mad' Frankie 300
French, Dawn 232
fruity chews 63
Fuller, Simon 237

G-A-Y 110
Galloway, Jenny 259
Gatiss, Mark 217, 219, 273
gay marriage 111–12
Gill, Jackie 191
Goodhew, Duncan 18–19
grief 250, 251

Haberdashers' Aske's Boys'
    School 3–10, 11, 58, 95–6,
    119–23, 128–33, 136–40
  and Jews 150–1
Hagman, Larry 300
Hale and Pace 287
Hall, Steve 133
Halliwell, Geri 158
Hardee, Malcolm 44, 45
Hathaway, Anne 275, 276
HBO 237–8, 240–1
Head, Tony 169, 232
Heaton, Paul 296

Heaven 107–9, 110, 112–15
Hebrew lessons 149–50
Heggessey, Lorraine 221
Higson, Charlie 298
Hill, Harry 43, 52
Hillsborough disaster 210
Hirst, Damien 54
Hislop, Ian 163
Hoffman, Dustin 277
Holt, Patrick 257
Homerun Video
    Megastore 212–14
homosexuality 31, 89–117,
    162–3
Hoskins, Bob 273
Howard, Emily (character) 161,
    162, 221, 239
Humphries, Barry 235
Hunt, Jay 242, 243

ice cream 63–4
Imaginatively Titled Punt &
    Dennis Show, The 268–9
Ingleby, Lee 273
Israel 149

James, Alex 54, 55
James, Geraldine 222
Jann, Michael Patrick 238
Japan 236
Jason (character) 161, 163
Jewish comedy circuit 49–50
Jewish Free School (JFS) 119,
    120–1

Jewishness 147–53
John, Sir Elton 232, 234
Jonas, Nick 259
Jones, Ruth 232
Jonsson, Ulrika 282, 284, 292,
        295, 296, 298

Kath & Kim 235
Kay, Peter 232, 240
Kaye, Paul 163
Kensit, Patsy 232
Kingston, Alex 248
Knoxville, Johnny 279

Lamarr, Mark 52, 282, 284, 295, 296
Law, Jude 11
League of Gentlemen, The 156,
        159, 168
Les Misérables 258–65
Linehan, Graham 167–8
Lipsey, Matt 223
Little, Chris 133
Little and Large 287
Little Britain 139, 159–71, 193,
        217–27
Little Britain Live 229–36
Little Britain USA 237–9, 240–1,
        242
Lobatto, Diana (mother) 124,
        179, 182–3, 185
    and baldness 14, 16, 21, 22, 23
    and homosexuality 94–5,
        106–7
    and *Shooting Stars* 293

Lock, Sean 52
Lombardo, Mike 237, 240
Lou and Andy
        (characters) 217–20
Lucas, Andie (stepmother)
        125, 127, 183–4
Lucas, Howard (brother) 8, 20–1,
        27, 105–6, 152, 153
    and family life 179–80, 184,
        185–6
Lucas, John (father) 179, 182–3,
        184–5, 186–7
    and baldness 14, 16, 22
    and prison 123–8
Lundgren, Dolph 279

McCartney, Sir Paul 234
McCooney, Ray 166
McGee, Kevin 2, 154, 187, 221,
        235, 242, 249–50, 251
    and *Doctor Who* 247–9
McIntyre, Phil 229, 297
McKellen, Sir Ian 93, 103
Mackie, Pearl 195, 253
Mackinnon, Doug 252
Mackintosh, Cameron 259,
        260–1, 264–5
Macqueen, Alex 280
Mandelson, Peter 165
Mankind 290–1
Marsden, James 279
matzo ball soup 72–3
May, Brian 157, 214, 215
Mazer, Dan 133

Mercury, Freddie 98–9, 184, 208, 209, 214–15
Michael, George 158, 232
Middle of the Book song 172–7
Midsummer Night's Dream, A 246, 252
Minder 267–8
Minogue, Kylie 234
Moffat, Steven 252
Moir, Jim *see* Reeves, Vic
Moore, Myfanwy 157, 167–8, 217, 219, 220
Mortimer, Bob 34–5, 36–7, 43, 50–1, 157, 269
  and *Big Night Out* 302
  and *Shooting Stars* 281–3, 284–5, 287, 292, 293–4, 295, 297
Moss, Kate 234
Mowlam, Mo 300
Murphy, Stuart 166–7, 170, 223
music 207–8

Nabarro, Dean 133
National Youth Music Theatre 6, 8–9, 10–12
National Youth Theatre 26, 77–8, 79–80
New York City 143–5
Newman, Nick 163
Newman, Rob 231
Nighthawks 102–3
Oasis 54–5

Oddie, Bill 288
O'Donnell, Rosie 238

Paddington 248
Paige, Elaine 252
Paramount Channel 156, 157
Peel, John 287
Perez, Rosie 279
Plowman, Jon 155, 170–1
Police, The 239
Pollard, Clive 28, 38
Pollard, Vicky (character) 163–4, 169–70, 220
Pompidou 279–80
Popper, Robert 133
Posner, Geoff 223, 224
Power, Samantha 161, 222, 231
Precious (character) 226
Prick Up Your Ears 273–4
Prince, Javone 252
prison 123–8
Proclaimers, The 208, 234, 240
prosopagnosia 205–6
prosthetics 222
Punchlines 29, 30–2
Punt, Steve 268–9
Putner, Paul 86, 158, 161, 231

Queen 208–9, 214–15

racism 225–7
Radio 4 159, 166
Rea, Chris 287–8
Reeves, Vic 34–5, 269, 302

and *Shooting Stars* 281–3, 284–5, 287, 292, 293–4, 295, 297
Rhys Jones, Griff 294
Richard, Sir Cliff 190–1
roast dinners 67–70
Rock Profile 158–9, 217
Roman Invasion of Ramsbottom, The 6–12
Root, Jane 155–6, 160, 166, 170–1
Rose, Florence (character) 221
Ross, Jonathan 232, 282
Ross, Leelo 49
Rossotti, Ian 6, 128, 129
Rowntree, Dave 55

Sams, Jeremy 229–30
satsumas 64–5
Saturday Kitchen 60
Savile, Jimmy 78
Schönberg, Claude-Michel 261–2
Schwimmer, David 238, 239
Sebastian (character) 165, 169
Secombe, Katy 262
Section 28 93
Self, Will 298, 300
Serafinowicz, Peter 232
Shakin' Stevens 90
Shearsmith, Reece 156
Shooting Stars 19, 55–6, 85, 193, 236, 281–3, 284–9, 292–301
Sir Bernard Chumley is Dead . . .

and Friends! 81–5
Sir Bernard Chumley's Gangshow 85
Sir Bernard's Grand Tour 85–7
Sir Bernard's Stately Homes 156–7
Small Apartments 278–9
Smell of Reeves and Mortimer, The 269–70, 282
spaghetti Bolognese 70
St George's Medical School 45–6
Sting 239

Taaj (character) 226–7
Taboo 258
Talalay, Rachel 273
Tate, Catherine 202, 220
Taylor, Jeremy James 7, 8–10
Taylor, Roger 214, 215
Temple, Juno 279
Thatcher, Margaret 93
Theakston, Jamie 158
theatre 189–90, 255–65
Thomas, Dafydd (character) 90, 161, 162–3
Thomas, Mark 43
Thompson, Dave 31–2, 33
Thornton, Kate 232
Ting Tong (character) 226
Top of the Pops 300–1
Troilus and Cressida 115, 246
Tucker, Ian 257
Tyler, David 133
UK Play 157, 158

Up the Creek 43–5

VD Clinic 29, 32–3, 34, 35–6
Vegas, Johnny 298, 300
vegetables 66, 68–9
Vic Reeves Big Night Out 34–5

Walliams, David 26, 29, 52, 53,
    55, 73, 307
  and BAFTAs 220–1
  and fame 193
  and *Little Britain* 90, 159–60,
    162, 164–5, 167–8, 170–1,
    217, 221–2
  and Lucas 81–4, 86–7, 250–1
  and NYT 77, 79–80
  and tour 231, 232, 233, 235–6
Ward, Don 33, 37
Wasikowska, Mia 275, 276
Waterman, Dennis 161, 168,
    232–3
Weald College 96–8

Weight Watchers 59
Wembley 211–12
Whitehouse, Paul 298
Wiig, Kristen 278
Williams, David *see* Walliams,
    David
Williams, Robbie 158, 232,
    294
Williams, Robin 47
Wilson, Rebel 278
Wilson, Richard 252
Wind in the Willows, The 272–3
Winehouse, Amy 113
Wing, Anna 198–9
Wright, Edgar 156
Wright, Steve 191

Yorkshire pudding 69–70
Young, Will 237

Zanuck, Richard 'Dick' 275